THE DIARY OF JACK THE RIPPER

The
DIARY
of
JACK
the
RIPPER

UPDATED NARRATIVE BY

SHIRLEY HARRISON

SMITH GRYPHON
PUBLISHERS

First published in paperback in Great Britain in 1994 by
SMITH GRYPHON LIMITED
Swallow House, 11–21 Northdown Street
London N1 9BN

First published in hardback in 1993 by Smith Gryphon Limited

Design: Hammond Hammond
Map artwork: Simon Roulstone

A CIP catalogue record for this book is available from
the British Library

ISBN 1 85685 074 9

Typeset by York House Typographic Ltd
Printed in Great Britain by
Cox & Wyman Ltd, Reading

Contents

FOREWORD

BY COLIN WILSON

In June 1993 I took part in a conference at the Tower Hotel in London where many old friends – including Paul Begg, Keith Skinner, Martin Fido and Don Rumbelow – were gathered with other Ripperologists (a word I had coined in the magazine *Books and Bookmen* in the 1970s) to discuss a startling new theory. I also met there author Shirley Harrison, who was in the throes of writing a controversial book about this theory, which was based on a diary that had recently been discovered in Liverpool. This claimed to be the confessions of Jack the Ripper. We were all there to take part in a video documentary about the diary and Shirley's book, which was being filmed by Paul Feldman for MIA Productions.

When, four months earlier, Paul Feldman had rung me out of the blue to tell me he had learned of the identity of Jack the Ripper, I had that familiar 'here we go again' feeling. Ever since 1960, when I wrote a series of articles for the London *Evening Standard* called 'My Search for Jack the Ripper', I have been a clearing-house for all the latest theories. Dan Farson told me, in confidence, that the Ripper was Montague John Druitt. I was the first to hear Dr Thomas Stowell's theory that the murderer was Queen Victoria's grandson, the Duke of Clarence, and the first to hear Michael Harrison's suggestion that Jack was Clarence's tutor, J.K. Stephen. Other candidates who have been brought to my attention have been Sir William Gull, Aleister Crowley, Joseph Barnett (husband of the final victim, Mary Jane Kelly), Frank Miles (a friend of Oscar Wilde), John Hewitt (a doctor who died insane in 1892) and even Lewis Carroll.

Not one of these has ever even begun to convince me. In *Jack the Ripper: Summing Up and Verdict*, which I wrote with Robin Odell for the centenary of the Ripper murders in 1988, I suggested that the likeliest candidate so far was the father of a man who wrote to Dan Farson from Melbourne, Australia, after a television programme in 1959. Signing himself G.W.B. 'Georgie' (he offered his first name only), he claimed that his father was a drunken manure collector who lived in the East End of London at the time of the murders. Around 1908, before 'Georgie' left for Australia, his father had confessed to him that he was Jack the Ripper and that when he became drunk he experienced sadistic rage towards any prostitute who accosted him. Georgie's father told him that he would make a public confession of guilt before his death; but when he died in 1912 he had failed to keep his promise. Many serial killers, as we now call them, have committed murders while under the influence of drink or drugs and it seemed to me that this unknown manure collector fitted the psychological profile of the Ripper far better than the Duke of Clarence or M. J. Druitt.

It was on the last day of February 1993 that Paul Feldman and the script writer of the video, Martin Howells, met me at the London flat of my friend Bill Hopkins and asked me to sign a confidentiality statement, before divulging the identity of the new candidate: James Maybrick, the Liverpool cotton merchant who died of arsenic poisoning in May 1889, the year after the Ripper murders.

They then told me how Mike Barrett, a former scrap-metal dealer from Liverpool, had been given the diary by an ailing friend and had taken it to London literary agent Doreen Montgomery of Rupert Crew Ltd. She, in turn, had sold the publishing and ancillary rights to Robert Smith of Smith Gryphon Limited. Montgomery and Smith were convinced the diary was genuine but Shirley Harrison was commissioned to investigate its authenticity, carry out extensive research and write the commentary for the book. Paul Feldman, too, had become so convinced that the diary was genuine that he bought the video rights and a film option from Smith Gryphon.

According to the evidence of the diary, Maybrick had committed the murders in a state of manic jealousy of his young wife Florence, who banished him from her bed – although she slept with other men. When Maybrick himself died, Florence was accused of poisoning him by arsenic and sentenced to death. I had always assumed that Florence was guilty – a maid had seen her soaking fly papers in her bedroom sink – but Paul insisted that this was out of the question and that Maybrick took so much arsenic, as a stimulant, that he was bound to die of arsenic poisoning sooner or later.

Now, it so happened that I had recently written about the Maybrick case and had had to consult books on toxicology to learn about the effects of arsenic. I had discovered, to my surprise, that arsenic – in small quantities – can be used as a powerful stimulant, and that Styrian peasants took it before climbing mountains because it creates tremendous stamina. As soon as I heard Paul Feldman's theory it seemed to me that arsenic was the key to the Ripper murders. After the murder of the second victim, Annie Chapman, the streets of Whitechapel were full of policemen and vigilantes; yet on September 30th 1988 the Ripper murdered two women in one night. Moreover, although he was interrupted while cutting the throat of Elizabeth Stride in a backyard off Commercial Street, he immediately walked half a mile or so and found himself another victim, Catharine Eddowes, whom he killed not far from a patrolling policeman. This demonstrates coolness of nerve and a manic sense of purpose that few criminals possess. It was the combination of the fact that Maybrick was an arsenic eater and that arsenic is such a powerful stimulant that convinced me he was the likeliest candidate so far.

Paul Feldman gave me a copy of the diary, which I read on the train travelling home to Cornwall. I found it a muddled and confusing affair, and was dubious about the handwriting, which did not strike me as particularly Victorian. My wife, who is something of an expert on old documents, raised the same objection. It *could*, I felt, be a forgery, although there was some interesting internal evidence to suggest it was not.

Yet the more I read of the Maybrick case, the more likely it seemed to me that this highly disturbed man, maddened by arsenic and his wife's infidelity, might kill prostitutes as an expression of inner torment. Florence was a flirt – Shirley Harrison notes how she liked to touch men – and soon gave Maybrick reason for jealousy. Suspecting her infidelity, he had outbreaks of rage, during which he left her covered in bruises, and then begged her forgiveness. Life with Florence must have been something of a roller-coaster. There was no doubt in my mind that Maybrick fitted the psychological profile of a sadistic killer. And when the evidence that his purchases of arsenic – hundreds of them – and his appointments with his Liverpool doctors in the autumn of 1888 never once coincided with the murders in London, I began to believe that *if* the diary were a forgery then the forger had had an unbelievable run of luck with the facts.

One thing did continue to worry me. For some odd reason, all known serial killers have been working class. This seems to be because a deprived background produces the kind of frustration that can explode into motiveless murder. Maybrick was not working class, although what we do know of his family suggests a fairly poor lower-middle-class childhood. There have been other serial killers who were living in reasonable affluence at the time of their murders – Ted Bundy, Richard Cottingham, Chris Wilder – but a study of their background reveals that they were from the working class. Yet Wilder (who went on a murder rampage across America) was, like Maybrick, a highly successful businessman. As I looked at other, similar cases I realized that the working-class argument is far from conclusive.

In April 1993 rumours of the diary's existence began to leak into the press, and when I went to the Tower Hotel for the videotaped conference, I was astonished to find that I was almost the only one present – apart from Shirley Harrison – who thought the diary might be genuine. The consensus was that it was a forgery, and that it dated from after 1987. The general attitude seemed to be that it would prove to be another hoax like the Hitler and Mussolini diaries. One of the Ripperologists predicted that as soon as the book appeared in print, someone would announce dramatically: 'This is a forgery and this is how I did it.'

Even so, I was sufficiently convinced to begin a *History of Serial Murder* with a chapter on Jack the Ripper, in which I argued that the diary is almost certainly authentic. I crossed my fingers that no hoaxer would make his appearance too soon after my book was published.

A few months later, when I was in Melbourne, it seemed as though my worst fears were about to be realized. Someone in the Savage Club told me that the diary had just been proved a fake, and that its American publisher had withdrawn. But when I saw the news item about the 'fake', I heaved a sigh of relief. It seemed that the diary had been examined by New York document expert Kenneth Rendell and scientist Rod McNeil, who stated that, on the basis of the ink, the diary was a forgery dating 'from about 1921 plus or minus 12 years'. As far as I could see, far from proving the diary to be a hoax, this meant that it had to be genuine and that McNeil's analysis was only very slightly inaccurate.

For a while my faith was shaken by the strange tale of the gold watch, which sounded even more suspicious than Mike Barrett's story of his acquisition of the diary. The watch was also 'found' in Liverpool, just before publication of the book. Inside the back cover were scratches that under a microscope revealed the signature of J. Maybrick and the words 'I am Jack'. Surely this had to be a forgery, part of some conspiracy to support the diary. Yet it seemed that an eminent metallurgist, Dr Stephen Turgoose, who had examined the scratches under an electron microscope, found brass particles in two of the scratches – particles that had come from the tool with which they were made: and the surface of these particles showed corrosion due to ageing of at least several decades, and possibly much longer.

The book *The Diary of Jack the Ripper* by Shirley Harrison was published on October 7th, 1993. It made a tremendous impact – but not at all in the way the publisher had intended. The *Sunday Times* printed a thoroughly biased and unconvincing piece of journalism, denouncing it as a fraud. Everyone waited impatiently for some further evidence to prove the case one way or the other.

On November 4th I attended the launch party of Paul Feldman's video, in a pub close to the murder sites. There I was allowed to look at the scratches on the watch, held at a distance by Richard Nicholas, the solicitor of Albert Johnson, who had taken the watch to Robert Smith's office in London in June 1993. I asked him if he was convinced of Albert Johnson's honesty and whether he was sure about the watch's provenance, and on both counts he assured me he was. Later, when Mr Nicholas went to talk with someone else, I sat down beside a quiet man who was holding the watch and asked him if I could examine it more closely. He handed it to me without hesitation, and when I asked his name, he told me – to my embarrassment – that he was Albert Johnson. After five minutes' conversation with him, I no longer entertained the slightest doubt of his honesty, or of the watch's genuineness. If Albert Johnson is a fraudster, then he is the most brilliant character actor I have ever met.

With the book and the video out, everybody waited impatiently for the next piece of evidence – either for the hoaxer to go public on how he or she had fooled the experts, or for something that might prove conclusive either way.

Some evidence has emerged, particularly a second electronic analysis of the watch, which supports its authenticity. What seems to me more interesting is that, with so many people determined to prove it a fraud, so far no one has produced any convincing evidence against it.

There is still plenty of scepticism. Quoting Dr Wild's report on the watch, which is described on pages 218 and 219 of this book, in the magazine *Ripperana*, that determined sceptic Nick Warren makes the most of Wild's admission that he has only acquired a 'limited amount of evidence' from his analysis, and that a far longer (and extremely expensive) period of testing would be needed to establish his findings beyond doubt. Of course, it is possible that the forger of the diary is also an expert in ageing scratches on gold and somehow managed to plant the watch on Albert Johnson. But this idea really beggars belief. Turgoose and Wild substantially undermine the hypothesis that the diary is a forgery.

To summarize, I am still not totally convinced by all of Mike Barrett's account of how he acquired the diary. His story about the late Tony Devereux seems a little too convenient, and it seems to me odd that if Tony Devereux owned the diary he never even mentioned it to his family. About the diary I have only minimal doubts and these tend to dissolve when I consider all the arguments against its being a fraud.

To my mind, Maybrick is far and away the most likely Ripper candidate so far.

Colin Wilson
Summer 1994

ACKNOWLEDGEMENTS

The opportunity to work on such an extraordinary project happens once in a lifetime. To take it through all the necessary stages before we could safely reveal it to readers worldwide, we have relied on the goodwill and freely given time of many people. As the material poured in, Sally Evemy, my partner in the Word Team, researched, checked and collated the facts that have formed the backbone of this book. In particular we are grateful to:

Doreen Montgomery of Rupert Crew Ltd, our agent, whose iron glove conceals a velvet hand and without whose vision the project would not have been born.

Robert Smith, our publisher. His enthusiasm and consumption of midnight oil was well beyond the call of a publisher's duty.

Paul Feldman of MIA Productions, whose insatiable appetite for research and indefatigable energy kept us all on our toes and yielded so many useful leads.

Keith Skinner, Martin Fido and Paul Begg, who have been our advisers and guided our first steps into the world of Jack the Ripper.

Richard Nicholas of Roberts Moore Nicholas & Jones of 51 New Chester Road, Liverpool L62 1AA, who has advised and supported Albert Johnson in all matters concerning the watch.

Our caring editor, Richard Dawes.

Roger Wilkes, whose generous loan of his entire personal collection of Maybrick notes launched our research.

Naomi Evett of Liverpool Library, whose patience kept us afloat.

Malcolm Peacock of Sutton, Surrey, who oils our PCW wheels, and the Disc Doctor service of Paddock Wood, Kent, which has rescued us from major disasters time and again and whose profits are donated to BACUP, the cancer support group.

Dr Nicholas Eastaugh; Dr David Forshaw; Sue Iremonger; Anna Koren; Melvyn Fairclough; Martin Howells; Dr A. Morton; Sidney Sabin; Nicholas Campion; John Astrop; Lawrence Warner; Dr Glyn Volans; Judge Richard Hamilton of Liverpool; Bill Waddell; Tony Miall; Richard and Mollie Whittington Egan; Paul Dodd of Battlecrease House; Brian Maybrick; Gerard Brierley; Mr Berkeley Chappelle-Gill; Derek Warman and John Matthews of the Isle of Wight; Dr W. Taylor of Fazakerley Hospital; Seddons Funeral Services, Southport; David Fletcher Rogers; Walkleys Clogs; The Special Hospitals Service; Andrew Brown of the Metropolitan Police Archives, New Scotland Yard; Colin Inman of the *Financial Times*; Nick Pinto of the Public Record Office; R. H. Leighton and Co., Southport; Colin Wilson; Donald Rumbelow; Peter O'Toole BEM and Lee Charles Allen of the Museum of the SAS Regt and the Artists Rifles; the staff of libraries and local history departments countrywide. In the USA: Dorothy MacRitchie of South Kent School and Peggy Haile of Norfolk Public Library.

We are grateful to the American Heritage Center, University of Wyoming, for permission to use excerpts from the recollections of Florence Aunspaugh in the Trevor Christie collection, and to HarperCollins Publishers for permission to use an extract from *Hunting the Devil* by Richard Lourie.

THE DIARY'S KEY SITES

SCALE
1 in = 50 mls
0.3 cm = 10 km

Sunderland
Durham ●
● Whitehaven
● Harrogate
Southport ● Rochdale
THE WIRRAL ● Manchester
Neston ● Liverpool
Birmingham ●   E N G L A N D
W A L E S
Aylesbury ●
London ●
Ascot ●
● Goodwood
Ryde
ISLE OF WIGHT
Truro

JAMES MAYBRICK'S LONDON

James Maybrick's brother, Michael lived in Regent's Park. Maybrick's mistress, Sarah Robertson, lived in New Cross, Sydenham and Tooting, as well as in Whitechapel.

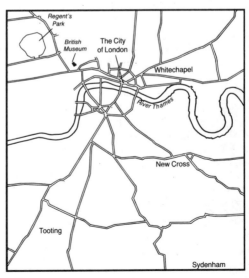

Regent's Park
British Museum
The City of London
Whitechapel
River Thames
New Cross
Tooting
Sydenham

THE FIVE WHITECHAPEL MURDER VICTIMS

Name	Date of murder in 1888	Time Discovered	Location	Mutilations
Mary Ann 'Polly' Nichols	Friday, 31 August	3.45 a.m.	Buck's Row, now Durward Street	Disembowelled
Annie Chapman	Saturday, 8 September	6.00 a.m.	29 Hanbury Street	Uterus missing
Elizabeth Stride	Sunday, 30 September	1.00 a.m.	Duffield's Yard, Berner Street, now Henriques Street	No mutilations
Catharine Eddowes	Sunday, 30 September	1.45 a.m.	Mitre Square	Uterus and left kidney missing, flap cut in each cheek
Mary Jane Kelly	Friday, 9 November	10.45 a.m.	13 Miller's Court, off Dorset Street	Gross mutilations, heart missing

The Whitechapel Murders

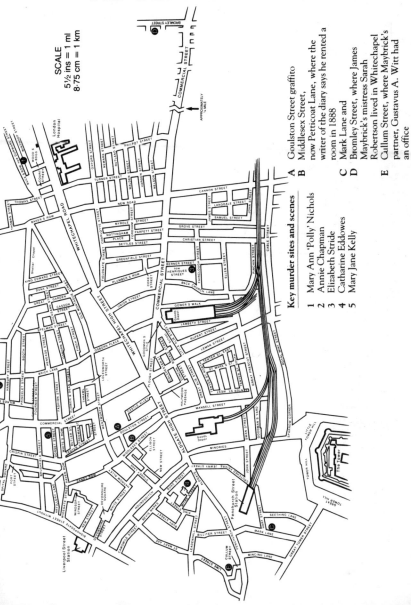

SCALE
5½ ins = 1 ml
8·75 cm = 1 km

Key murder sites and scenes

1 Mary Ann 'Polly' Nichols
2 Annie Chapman
3 Elizabeth Stride
4 Catharine Eddowes
5 Mary Jane Kelly

A Goulston Street graffito
B Middlesex Street,
  now Petticoat Lane, where the
  writer of the diary says he rented a
  room in 1888
C Mark Lane and
D Bromley Street, where James
  Maybrick's mistress Sarah
  Robertson lived in Whitechapel
E Cullum Street, where Maybrick's
  partner, Gustavus A. Witt had
  an office

James Maybrick's Liverpool, 1888

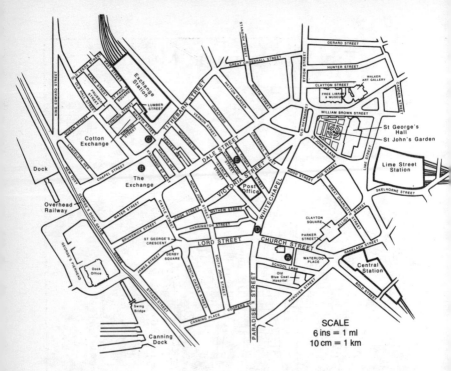

SCALE
6 ins = 1 ml
10 cm = 1 km

Key sites

A St Peter's Church and
   Church Alley
B The Exchange (The Flags)
C James Maybrick's office
D Whitechapel
E Cumberland Street
   (Poste House)

Enlargement of Liverpool City
Centre to show sites closely
associated with James Maybrick

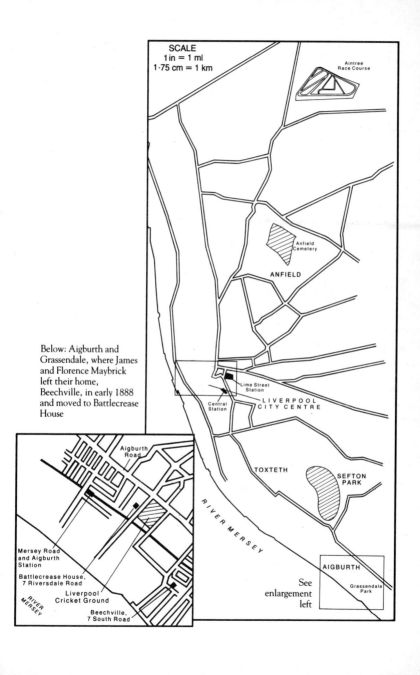

SCALE
1 in = 1 ml
1·75 cm = 1 km

Aintree
Race Course

Anfield
Cemetery

ANFIELD

Below: Aigburth and
Grassendale, where James
and Florence Maybrick
left their home,
Beechville, in early 1888
and moved to Battlecrease
House

Aigburth
Road

Lime Street
Station

Central
Station

LIVERPOOL
CITY CENTRE

TOXTETH

SEFTON
PARK

RIVER MERSEY

Mersey Road
and Aigburth
Station

Battlecrease House,
7 Riversdale Road

Liverpool
Cricket Ground

Beechville,
7 South Road

RIVER
MERSEY

AIGBURTH

See
enlargement
left

Grassendale
Park

ONE

'Perhaps in my tormented mind I wish for someone to read this and understand'

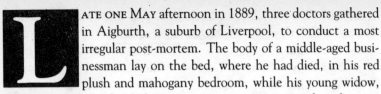

L ATE ONE MAY afternoon in 1889, three doctors gathered in Aigburth, a suburb of Liverpool, to conduct a most irregular post-mortem. The body of a middle-aged businessman lay on the bed, where he had died, in his red plush and mahogany bedroom, while his young widow, distraught and confused, lay in a mysterious swoon in the adjoining dressing room. Under the watchful eye of a police superintendent, two of the doctors dissected and inspected his internal organs while the third took notes.

The brain, heart and lungs seemed normal and were returned to his body. There was a slight inflammation of the alimentary canal, a small ulcer on the larynx and the upper edge of the epiglottis was eroded. The stomach, tied at each end, the intestines, the spleen and parts of the liver were put into jars and handed to the police officer.

About two weeks later the same three doctors drove to the cemetery where the body had by that time been buried. They arrived at 11 p.m. and, in the yellow light of naphtha lamps, stood by the fresh grave while four men dug up the coffin. Without lifting the body from its container, they removed the brain, heart, lungs, kidneys and tongue for further investigation. An eye-witness reported: 'There was scarcely anyone present who did not experience an involuntary shudder as the pale, worn features of the dead appeared in the flickering rays of a lamp, held over the grave by one of the medical men.

'What everyone remarked was that, although interred a fortnight, the corpse was wonderfully preserved. As the dissecting knife of Dr Barron pursued its rapid and skilful work there was, however, whenever the wind blew, a slight odour of corruption.'

Eventually the authorities concluded that the 50-year-old James Maybrick, a well-known Liverpool cotton merchant with business connections in London, had been the victim of 'irritant poisoning'. They could not specify what substance was to blame, but they were sure he had been murdered. And they had little doubt who did it.

That August, after a sensational trial that gripped Britain and America alike, Maybrick's 26-year-old widow, Florie, was convicted of his murder and condemned to death. She was the first American woman to be tried in a British court.

. . .

Six months before Maybrick's death, a shop assistant named Thomas Bowyer walked through Whitechapel, a squalid neighbourhood in London's East End. He was on his way to collect the overdue rent from Mary Jane Kelly, the tenant of 13 Miller's Court. It was about 10.45 a.m. on November 9th, and cheerful crowds were making their way to watch the passing of the gold coach amid the traditional celebrations that, even today, mark the annual inauguration of a Lord Mayor of London.

There was no response to Bowyer's knock. Reaching through the broken window, he pulled back the grubby, makeshift curtain and peered into the hovel that was Mary Jane Kelly's pathetic home. On the blood-drenched bed lay all that remained of a girl's body.

It was naked, apart from a skimpy shift. There had been a determined attempt to sever the head. The stomach was ripped wide open. The nose, breasts and ears were sliced off, and skin torn from the face and thighs was lying beside the raw body. The kidneys, liver and other organs were placed around the corpse, whose eyes were wide open, staring, terrified, from a mangled, featureless face.

Mary Jane Kelly was the latest victim of the fiend who had been butchering prostitutes since the end of August. The killings all took place around weekends and within the same sordid square mile of overcrowded streets that was, and is, one of London's most deprived areas. The women were strangled, slashed, and finally torn apart in progressively more brutal attacks.

Mary Ann ('Polly') Nichols, the first victim, was a locksmith's daughter in her early forties who moved from workhouse to workhouse. Then came Annie Chapman, 47, Elizabeth Stride, 44, and Catharine Eddowes, 46. Now there was Mary Jane Kelly, at about 25 the youngest of them all.

Hideous as these crimes were, they might have been forgotten or dismissed as an occupational hazard of prostitution had not the murderer taunted the police with notes and clues and, in one infamous mocking letter, given himself a nickname that sent shudders through London and far beyond: Jack the Ripper.

No-one in 1889 had reason to link the exhumation of James Maybrick in a windy Liverpool graveyard with that earlier blood-bath in a squalid London slum, 250 miles away. Neither the police nor the medical men in Liverpool guessed James Maybrick's dark secret. In those days no one could possibly have connected the doctor's macabre midnight dissection of a respectable middle-aged businessman and the gruesome disembowelling of a young Whitechapel prostitute. The link was finally made in 1992: a newly found diary exposed the possibility that James Maybrick was Jack the Ripper.

. . .

Mike Barrett has spent all his life in Liverpool, apart from a time sailing the world as a merchant seaman or working on the oil rigs. Later he worked as a chef and a scrap-metal dealer. He met his wife, Anne, at the city's Irish Centre in 1976 and within weeks they were married.

In recent years Mike was forced by illness to stop working. So instead he cared for the couple's daughter, Caroline, while Anne went off to work as a secretary. His great joy was the tiny, flower-filled garden overlooked by the kitchen. His big dream was to own a greenhouse.

Mike recalled that on his way to collect Caroline from school, he would often drop into the Saddle, a friendly Victorian pub looking today much as it did in James Maybrick's time. There, he usually enjoyed a pint and a chat with a pal, Tony Devereux. When Tony fractured his hip around Christmas 1990, Mike became his Good Samaritan, shopping for him and occasionally doing other chores. One day, a few months later, when he arrived at Tony's house there was a parcel wrapped in brown paper on the table.

'Take it. I want you to have it. Do something with it,' was all Tony said.

Mike took the parcel home, and opened it with Anne. That day the Barretts' life was turned upside down. Inside they saw what appeared to be a Victorian scrapbook, quarter-bound in black calf, untitled and with seven gold-leaf bands on the spine. The binding and paper were of high quality and well preserved. To judge by the evidence of glue stains and the oblong impressions left on the flyleaf, the book had served the common Victorian practice of holding postcards, photographs, reminiscences, autographs and other mementoes. The first 48 pages had been removed with a knife. Then followed 63 manuscript pages of the most sensational words Mike had ever read. The tone veered from maudlin to frenetic, with many lines furiously struck through.

Anne and Mike sat on the sofa by the fire in their living-room. She listened as he read. They were sickened by the story that unfolded in an erratic hand that reflected the violence of the words.

> I will take all next time and eat it will leave <u>nothing</u> not even the head. I will boil it and eat it with freshly picked carrots.

> The taste of blood was sweet, the pleasure was overwhelming.

Towards the end of the diary, the mood softened:

> Tonight I write of love.
> tis love that spurned me so,
> tis love that does destroy.

And then, on the last page, they read the words:

> Soon, I trust I shall be laid beside my dear mother and father. I shall seek their forgiveness when we are reunited. God I pray will allow me at least that privilege, although I know only too well I do not deserve it. My thoughts will remain in tact, for a reminder to all how love does destroy. I place this now in a place where it shall be found. I pray whoever should read this will find it in their heart to forgive me. Remind all, whoever you may be, that I was once a gentleman. May the good Lord have mercy on my soul, and forgive me for all I have done.
> I give my name that all know of me, so history
> do tell, what love can do to a gentle man born.
> Yours truly,
> Jack the Ripper
> Dated this third day of May 1889.

'I'll never forget Mike's face,' Anne recalled. 'It was that signature – it was like a knife going into me,' said Mike. 'But I didn't believe it. Who's going to believe that in a million years?' Her words were to prove tragically prophetic. For on that day, the Barretts' world was turned upside down. The diary, which should have secured their future and their family happiness, was to destroy their marriage and prove the final straw for Mike's already fragile health.

Later, over a period of intense checking and double-checking of his story, we became confident that Mike Barrett was incapable of forging the diary himself and also that there was no hidden mastermind behind the scenes. Mike signed an affidavit to that effect, which he lodged with his solicitor Richard Bark Jones of Morecroft Dawson and Garnetts of Liverpool. However, most of the British media and some 'Ripperologists' did not believe him. Mike eventually could no longer take the pressure of their hostility and intrusion or what he came to see as the violation of his family. His health finally cracked six months after publication of the hardback edition of this book. But on the day he sat with Anne and first read those terrible words in the diary, the future was still unknown – and exciting.

Mike phoned Tony straight away: 'Who are you kidding?' All Tony would say was: 'Ask me no questions.'

Could it really be that Mike Barrett had the solution to what is one of the world's greatest crime mysteries? He read the diary over and over again, trying to piece together the story.

The depraved writer, who did not sign his real name anywhere in the diary, boasted of hunting down his victims and then murdering and mutilating them. But just as Jack the Ripper tormented the police with cat-and-mouse games – either in the form of verbal clues left at the scene of the crime, or letters to the press – so the diary writer left clues to his identity throughout the diary. As early as the second page, for example, he says:

I may return to Battlecrease.

'I bought all the Jack the Ripper books I could find,' Mike recalled, 'and spent hours down at the library trying to research the Ripper story to see if the diary fitted. Then one day I read a book by Richard Whittington Egan called *Murder, Mayhem and Mystery*. It was about crime in Liverpool, and there was the name 'Battlecrease House' in an account of the Maybrick affair.'

In fact, 'Battlecrease' was a name known to the many Liverpudlians acquainted with the tragic tale of the ill-fated couple who made it their home. James and Florie Maybrick had moved to the mansion, in the agreeable suburb of Aigburth, in their last turbulent year together. Could it be, Mike wondered, that Maybrick, who was believed to have been killed by his wife, was himself one of history's most feared and despised murderers? Could the diary in Mike's hands link the stories of the outwardly respectable, loving father, the middle-aged merchant, broken by a lifetime of secret drug taking, with that of Jack the Ripper?

On the other hand, he asked himself, if the diary was a hoax, why had it surfaced now? Tony didn't want any money for it. Where had it been all this time? And how did Tony come to have it?

'The next day I went over to Tony's and asked what on earth he was playing at,' Mike remembers. 'But he would tell me nothing, and simply repeated: 'I know it is real. Do something with it.' He would not tell me where it came from, or how long he had had it. But I trusted him. He would not have let me down.'

Before Mike could prise out any answers to the riddle of the diary's origins, sadly Tony Devereux died of heart failure. By then Mike was a man obsessed. The Barretts' cosy front room was haunted by names from the diary, ghosts from a sinister Victorian past. There was 'Bunny', as Maybrick called his flirtatious wife; George, the loyal friend; Michael, the successful and treacherous brother; Edwin, the apparently loyal brother; Gladys and 'Bobo', the beloved children; and Lowry, the meddlesome clerk.

Mike bought a word processor and launched himself into extensive research, intending to write the story of the diary himself. He had had a brief flirtation with the writing world as a member of the local writers' circle and as a contributor of simple word puzzles to the children's magazine *Look In*. He spent hours sifting through microfilm newspaper reports in the library. Night after night he read and worked, while Anne more and more regretted the day the diary had appeared in their home. Mike recalls: 'I haven't had a proper night's sleep from that day to this. I've eaten and drunk the diary. It virtually destroyed my life and my marriage.'

· · ·

7

Mike was out of his depth, and he knew it. He wanted to keep his promise to Tony, but had no idea how to get the diary verified, much less published. He rang a paperback firm in London and invited the publisher to visit Liverpool and read the document. London publishers are not easily enthused, hearing with regularity from legions of would-be writers with earth-shattering discoveries.

'Find yourself a literary agent,' the publisher told Mike, and directed him to Doreen Montgomery of Rupert Crew Ltd in London. So it was that, on a spring day in 1992, Mike boarded the train at Liverpool's Lime Street station, just as James Maybrick had done over a century before. Doreen Montgomery, who has been my literary agent for nearly 20 years, asked me to meet Mike that same day. Doubtful about his incredible story, she wanted a second opinion.

Mike was wearing a smart new suit and clutching a case containing the diary, still in its brown paper wrapper. He placed the diary on her desk among piles of hopeful manuscripts and watched nervously as we turned the pages slowly. The three of us then discussed what we had read, trying to keep our feet firmly on the ground in the face of such horror.

Logic told us there were three possibilities:
1) it was a hoax – either carried out soon after the murders or in the intervening years;
2) it was the result of delusions in which James Maybrick thought he was Jack the Ripper; or
3) it was true: James Maybrick was Jack the Ripper.

Doreen and I were suspicious, and both thinking about one thing in particular: the notorious 'Hitler diaries', which had caused so much embarrassment. Only after publication in 1982 did forensic tests determine that the paper contained nylon fibres and a chemical used to increase whiteness. Neither substance had been used in paper before 1950.

On impulse, Mike and I took the diary to the British Museum, just around the corner from Doreen's office. I was confident that we would find no better expert advice. But, as we later discovered, authenticating the diary was not as easy as that.

■ ■ ■

The front entrance of the British Museum is monumental. Inside, the scale is no less massive: the silence of 3 million learned tomes carpeting the walls envelops the visitor. It was here that the diary faced its first test. Mike and I carried it, in a plastic bag, through the libraries to the maze of corridors that are the administrative arteries of the building. Mike clutched my hand as elderly manuscript historians peered through magnifying lenses at the dramatic words, reading the contents again and again.

'Fascinating,' said Robert Smith, the Museum's curator of 19th-century manuscripts. 'Quite extraordinary. It looks authentic. But you'll have to take it to a document examiner. We don't have forensic facilities here.'

In Jarndyce, the antiquarian bookshop opposite the museum, Brian Lake looked up from his first-edition Dickens and was also enthusiastic. Brian, the shop's owner, is a specialist in 19th-century literature and immediately recognized in our diary a sensational discovery. He agreed with Robert Smith across the street. 'It looks exciting,' he said. 'But find a forensic scientist to settle its precise date.'

So began my painstaking efforts to investigate the origins of the diary scientifically. I decided to consult as wide a range of specialists as I could find, in order to understand it from every major perspective. Not only was a leading scientific expert in the history and composition of ink and paper consulted, but I also enlisted the voluntary help of a forensic document examiner, a graphologist, a psychiatrist and medical consultants. The first step was to establish, as clearly as possible, that the diary was indeed Victorian and that the words had been written more than 100 years ago.

I was entering an unfamiliar and costly world, which I approached with considerable awe, only to discover that even experts are fallible.

I took the diary to Dr David Baxendale of Document Evidence Ltd, a former Home Office forensic scientist whose team in Birmingham has an excellent reputation. Dr Baxendale was asked, in particular, to tell us the age of the ink and, if possible, when it was applied to the paper. His brief report, in summary, said that he viewed the diary with suspicion. We asked for a fuller account of his reasoning. This, had it been scientifically correct, would have been a bombshell. The paragraph dealing with the ink said:

The ink of the diary was readily soluble in the extractant and only a small amount of insoluble black residue was left on the paper. The chromatogram showed only a partial separation: much of the ink remained on the baseline but there was a strip of partially resolved coloured components and a few colourless fluorescent spots. This pattern is characteristic of inks based on a synthetic dye called nigrosine, which is a complex mixture of substances but one which has been tested and used in many inks at least since the 1940s. There was nothing to suggest the presence of iron.

Our belief in Dr Baxendale's report was soon to be shattered. Iron was an ingredient of most Victorian inks – it is this that sometimes produces the brownish look of old handwriting. We were to learn from another scientific analyst, Dr Nicholas Eastaugh, that in the tests of several samples of the ink taken from the diary, iron is indeed present; and that the observation that the diary ink is 'freely soluble' is unsupported. Even worse, with the help of the Patent Office in London, it took very little time for us to establish that nigrosine was, in fact, patented in 1867 by Coupier and was in general use in writing inks by the 1870s.

One of the key reasons why Dr Baxendale dismissed the diary was, therefore, simply wrong.

The report was so fundamentally inaccurate that we lost confidence in its value. In writing, we agreed with Dr Baxendale's request that it would not be used in the hardback version of the book or 'for any purposes whatsoever.' (That restriction has now been removed, by mutual agreement.)

Dr Eastaugh, who now became our chief scientific expert on the ink, paper and binding of the diary, is primarily a specialist in identifying and dating materials used on Old Masters and manuscripts, and in conservation, with an international clientele. He has worked for the Museum of London, the National Gallery, the Tate Gallery and Christie's. He said straight away that documents as potentially important as the diary I had brought him were rare.

Dr Eastaugh examined the diary at his studio in Teddington, southwest London. The diary lay in distinguished company. On his desk was a 16th-century painting by Bruegel the Elder, whose provenance he was hoping to establish. He began by studying the ink to establish the diary's age and, if possible, when it was applied to the paper. Later he would attempt to date the paper itself. Dr Eastaugh would also investigate what was left of the missing pages, and examine some black powder that had been found deeply embedded in the 'gutter' between the pages of the diary.

The most crucial tests were carried out with a proton microprobe. This employs a 'non-destructive method of exciting atoms in a small target area on a page with an accelerated beam of protons, in order to detect, to the parts per million, what chemicals are present in inks, papers, parchments and pigments tested,' Dr Eastaugh told me. Minute samples of ink painstakingly lifted from the diary were prepared and mounted on slides before being taken into the Star Wars world of the laboratory. A similar device was used by the Crocker National Laboratory in California to determine how the Gutenberg Bible was printed, and to establish that the Vinland Map, which appeared to be medieval in origin, actually contained a chemical, titanium, not used in paper production before the early 20th century.

Details on the work of Dr Eastaugh and other experts enlisted to study the diary will be presented later. But Dr Eastaugh's preliminary conclusion was heartening: 'The results of various analyses of ink and paper in the diary performed so far have not given rise to any conflict with the date of 1888/9.'

As my confidence grew in the diary's pedigree, our attention turned to the kind of man who might have written it. Could it have been the work of someone trying to destroy James Maybrick? Or by Maybrick himself in a deluded state? Was it truly the tortured confession it purported to be? In an attempt to throw light on such questions, I telephoned Dr David Forshaw, then a specialist consultant in addiction at the Maudsley Psychiatric Hospital in London. (At the time of Jack the Ripper, the hospital was better known as the notorious Bedlam lunatic asylum.)

David Forshaw has completed three years of research into forensic psychiatry at the Institute of Psychiatry in London, holds a diploma in the history of medicine from the Society of Apothecaries and has published extensively on psychiatry and addiction. I did not ask him to prove that the author of the diary was Jack the Ripper. I asked him first to assess whether, in his view, the writer had genuinely committed the crimes described, or whether he could merely be a sick and cynical forger.

Dr Forshaw spent several months examining the diary, eventually producing a 15,000-word report, excerpts of which will also be presented later. His principal conclusion was encouraging: he said that for a forger to have faked this deceptively simple diary he would have needed to master a profound understanding of criminal psychology and the effects of drug addiction. Forshaw believes that whoever wrote the diary was writing from personal experience.

So now Mike and I had one expert who agreed the diary could be old, and another expert who believed the author was indeed writing from gruesome experience. And as I would eventually come to see, the most compelling evidence would be found on the battered pages of the diary itself. These are the uncontrived outpourings of a man writing from the heart, however black that heart may be. The natural spontaneity, even touching moments of weakness, convinced me too that this could not be the calculated work of a forger. It was on this material, I was sure from the start, the diary would stand or fall. The evidence surrounding the Ripper is itself controversial, and I was wary of building hypothesis upon hypothesis. I had in my possession a unique document. My task was to establish its authenticity, for if the diary is genuine, James Maybrick is not merely another suspect. He *is* Jack the Ripper and his confession would rewrite Ripper history. I was impressed by the way that the diary narrative, which relives James Maybrick's last months, perfectly overlayed the known facts surrounding the murderous life of Jack the Ripper.

I knew I must wade through bookshelves of Ripper legend and lore, for the mystery of the Whitechapel murders is fiercely debated. To guide me in my research and to play devil's advocate, three of Britain's leading authorities on Jack the Ripper – Martin Fido, Paul Begg and Keith Skinner – were consulted throughout the researching and writing of the book. They graciously offered me access to their own extensive records. Later they were joined by two other 'Ripperologists', Melvyn Fairclough and Martin Howells. All of them are unreservedly committed to advancing serious Ripper research, and became totally absorbed in the diary, despite their scepticism.

Since each had written books examining the evidence concerning different suspects, I was confident that between them they would pounce on any errors in the document. But they could find nothing to prove the diary a fake. Neither can any other Ripper expert who has since examined it.

It was at this stage that Paul Feldman burst on the scene. He had been researching material for a new, original view of the Ripper murders when news of the diary fired his imagination. From the outset he was convinced. He bought the video rights and an option on film rights in the book and began his own untiring quest for the truth behind the diary and its disappearance for 100 years.

So, while the experts were busy reconstructing the bones of the story, I went in search of its soul. I drove first to Liverpool, where it had all begun.

TWO

'My hands are cold, my heart I do believe is colder still'

IN LIVERPOOL I found a city in which neatly painted Victorian terraces march in orderly rows over the hill which drops down through acres of council houses to Albert Dock and the River Mersey. Windows are boarded up, shops and offices are derelict, and beer cans sprout on waste land. Yet the pubs are noisy and full behind their ornately patterned glass and shiny-tiled façades. Liverpool, once a prosperous city, is struggling to survive, its heart torn out by poverty and unemployment. The ships that once served the busiest port in Britain have long since gone.

The city is surrounded by a protective cloak of beautiful parks and fine suburbs. There, the ornate mansions of prosperous 19th-century Victorian merchants stand, proud mausoleums recalling an energetic past, occupied today by students and their landladies and the elderly residents of eventide homes. One such suburb, Aigburth, lies to the south of the city centre, on the banks of the Mersey. Battlecrease House is, as it was when the Maybricks lived there, half of an impressive mansion that recalls the days when horse-drawn carriages bumped along the unpaved lane. Now known simply as 7 Riversdale Road, Battle-crease House is a 20-room, mushroom-coloured house set well back from the road. It stands opposite the spacious grounds of the Liverpool Cricket Club, of which James Maybrick was an enthusiastic member. Riversdale Road runs from the Aigburth Road down to the Mersey. The views are uninterrupted still, sweeping down to the river and across to the distant mountains of Wales.

Maybrick was probably aware of rumours that a murder had taken place at the house many years before. Nevertheless, he moved in, with his young American wife and two children. In 1889, not much more than a year later, visitors gathered by the gate – they still do – pointing curiously at the upstairs windows of the room where Maybrick died. Some broke twigs from the shrubs by the gate as mementoes, unaware that the house could have another, even more shocking, claim to notoriety.

. . .

Jack the Ripper struck at a time when the newspapers were thirsting for sensation. Better education and an improvement in technology had led to a circulation war among Britain's nearly 200 dailies. The Ripper's gruesome crimes and taunts to the authorities – and their inability to stop him – were headline news.

Where did he come from? What drove him on to kill and kill again? Why did he mutilate his victims? What compulsion made him leave clues? It was the stuff of Victorian gothic horror, at a time when Robert Louis Stevenson's *Dr Jekyll and Mr Hyde* was scaring audiences at London's Lyceum Theatre.

While the murders had apparently stopped with Mary Jane Kelly's death, the terror persisted, for despite the greatest manhunt Britain had ever seen, the killer was never captured.

The Ripper was, and remained, an obsession, spawning penny dreadfuls and scholarly investigations, novels and music-hall verse. An entire literary and theatrical industry is based on his awful exploits.

In the years that followed the Whitechapel murders many of those involved in the Ripper investigations put pen to paper. Memoranda emerged and books were written; documents vanished and came to light again.

With each new 'discovery' came a flood of new theories. Among these, in 1959, journalist Daniel Farson discovered a memorandum from Sir Melville Macnaghten, who became Assistant Chief Constable CID at Scotland Yard in 1890. Two versions of the document exist, and a third has been described. In the version that Farson saw, owned by Macnaghten's daughter, Lady Aberconway, the Assistant Chief Constable named for the first time the three men who, he said, were suspected by the Yard in 1888. They were Montague John Druitt, Kosminski and Michael Ostrog.

Druitt, the son of a surgeon and himself also described, erroneously, as a doctor, was formerly a barrister but had become a schoolteacher by the time of the murders. He was found drowned in the Thames at Chiswick in December 1888, his pockets full of stones; the body had been in the water for about a month.

Macnaghten named Druitt as a suspect largely because his body was discovered soon after the Kelly murder, the assumption being that Druitt's mental state had collapsed just before his suicide. He also claimed that Druitt's own family believed him to be the killer – it was not known why – and that he had access to 'private information' and 'certain facts', which he never specified, suggesting that Druitt was 'sexually insane'.

By contrast, in 1903, Inspector Abberline of the Metropolitan Police, who had been in charge of detectives investigating the Whitechapel murders, said of Druitt: 'I know all about that story but what does it amount to? Simply this. Soon after the last murder in Whitechapel the body of a young doctor was found in the Thames but there is absolutely nothing beyond the fact that he was found at that time to incriminate him.'

Of Kosminski, Sir Robert Anderson (Assistant Commissioner of the Metropolitan Police CID at the time of the Whitechapel murders) stated that his guilt 'was a definitely ascertained fact'. Kosminski was a woman-hater with homicidal tendencies who had become insane from years of indulgence in 'solitary vices'. He was sent to Stepney Workhouse and then, in 1891, to Colney Hatch lunatic asylum. However, in the police evidence against him dates, names and places are wrongly listed.

The remaining police suspect was the Russian sneak thief and confidence trickster Michael Ostrog. Little is known about him beyond his being habitually cruel to women. It is probable that suspicion fell on him largely because he carried surgical knives and instruments in his pockets when he roamed the streets of Whitechapel. The police could never prove he was in that area at the time of the crimes, and despite the implication in Macnaghten's report that Ostrog was put in an asylum after the murders, between 1889 and 1893, research has failed to find records confirming this.

Macnaghten also stated with apparent authority that the Whitechapel murderer had claimed five victims and five victims only, contradicting the belief of public and many fellow policemen alike that there were at least two more.

In the 1970s several writers produced a sensational new candidate, Prince Albert Victor, Duke of Clarence, grandson of Queen Victoria. The fact that his inclusion as a suspect is remembered by many people is perhaps because the public loves a royal scandal.

This story arose from an article in *The Criminologist* by Dr Thomas Stowell in November 1970. He based his arguments on alleged private papers of Sir William Gull, physician to Queen Victoria, who treated the prince for syphilis and said that he died of softening of the brain. These papers have never been expertly examined and are now missing. However, it is known from diaries and Court circulars of the time that Prince Albert Victor was in Scotland and the royal retreat of Sandringham, in Norfolk, at the time of the murders.

About 1980 there came to light some pencil notes by Chief Inspector Donald Swanson, who had also played a leading role in the investigation of the Whitechapel murders. These were comments, written in about 1910, in the margins and on the endpapers of his own personal copy of the memoirs of Sir Robert Anderson. Published in the *Daily Telegraph* in 1987, Swanson's marginalia named Anderson's own suspect: Kosminski. However, they contained inaccuracies that only served to fuel, rather than end, the debate.

That same year a large brown envelope was sent anonymously to Scotland Yard, which contained, among other documents, a letter signed 'Jack the Ripper' that had vanished years earlier. Then, in 1993, investigations were afoot to examine the credentials of a letter, contemporary with the murders. It is said to name the writer of the Jack the Ripper letter and of the postcard from 'Saucy Jacky' that followed it within 24 hours.

Most of the early theories about the Ripper's identity were easily discredited. Typical of these was that propounded by the first full-length book to identify a suspect named as American-born Alios Szemeredy, a self-styled surgeon later described as a sausage-maker, who committed suicide in Vienna in 1892. This colourful account was based on a wild rumour overheard in Vienna.

. . .

Now Mike Barrett had entered the arena with a new name, James Maybrick, never previously connected with the case. Like Mike, I found myself drawn to retrace the steps of the man who had confessed to terrorizing London and shocking the world. I walked along the narrow alley at the side of the former grounds of Battlecrease House which leads to the tiny railway station where Maybrick boarded the train into town.

The gravel crunched as I walked up the driveway to the front door.

I knocked at the letterbox once used by the Maybricks and found myself talking to Paul Dodd, a primary-school teacher who grew up in Battle-crease House. As I walked with him around the still splendid rooms, it was easy to imagine the whispered gossip of servants below stairs, to conjure up the immaculate figure of James Maybrick, with his sandy hair and moustache, striding down the drive, and coquettish Florie, the sun lighting her golden hair, reading romances in the conservatory.

The house has suffered structurally over the years. It was the only building in the road to escape the bombs of World War II, but was damaged by a land-mine and then by an earth tremor in 1984. A falling tree destroyed the conservatory. Even so, little imagination is needed to reawaken the past.

Through the reception hall and the dining-room, with its stained-glass windows picturing water birds, is the ballroom that opens on to the garden. Intact are the beautiful, ornate ceiling mouldings and the Italian marble fireplace, with its exquisite carved grapes and large mirror above.

Up the splendid oak staircase are rooms for guests and staff, a nursery for the children and, overlooking the cricket pitch, the rather sombre bedroom where Maybrick died.

Later that day I paced the 'Flags', the vast open forum in the centre of Liverpool that was once the hub of Britain's cotton industry, and visited the grave where Maybrick is buried. The large cross that once capped the headstone is today mysteriously missing. That evening I sat in the snug bar of the Poste House, where the idea of murder first took root in Maybrick's mind.

. . .

At the time of James Maybrick's birth, there had been Maybricks in Liverpool for 70 years. They had come originally from the West Country, and one branch settled in the Stepney and Whitechapel area, the heart of London's East End. Later, when unemployment became bad, some moved on to the more prosperous port of Liverpool.

The parish church of St Peter, in the centre of Liverpool, had been a focus for James's well-respected family. There had been Maybricks at the organ, Maybricks on the parish council and, when James was born, on October 24th 1838, his grandfather was parish clerk.

The christening, on November 12th, must have been a particularly happy affair for the parents, William, an engraver, and Susannah, who had already lost a four-month-old son the year before. They decided to follow the Victorian custom and name the new baby after his dead brother. James's older brother, William, was then aged three.

By the time James was six, his grandfather was dead and his father had succeeded him as parish clerk. Yet despite their childhood involvement with St Peter's and respect for Victorian convention, none of the brothers remained churchgoers as they grew up.

The family was living at 8 Church Alley, a narrow lane in the shadow of St Peter's that ran into busy Church Street. It was only a few seconds' walk from the road whose name was later to play so large a part in Maybrick's life – Whitechapel. This Whitechapel, in contrast to its seedy London namesake, was then a fashionable shopping street. Just around the corner was the Blue Coat Hospital, a school for poor boys and girls. In Church Street itself James could linger at the Civet Cat, a knick-knack shop that sold exciting foreign toys. Or he could dream of faraway places while peering in the window of Mr Marcus the tobacconist, who ran flag-bedecked train excursions from Liverpool to London.

The Maybricks' house was cramped, and conditions became worse with the arrival of three younger brothers, Michael (born 1841), Thomas (1846) and Edwin (1851). (Another son, Alfred, had died at the age of four in 1848.) After the birth of Edwin, the family moved to a more spacious house around the corner: 77 Mount Pleasant.

The family led a simple life, with no staff until after Maybrick had left home, when the 1861 census credits them with a house-servant named Mary Smith. Nothing is known about the parents' influence and personality, and little about the boys' childhood or schooling. James probably attended Liverpool College, like Michael, but records were lost during World War II. We do know that the boys threw themselves into sport, especially cricket.

From an early age, according to a later profile in *The New Penny Magazine*, Michael was the shining star, with the musical gift of 'harmonious invention'. At 14, one of his compositions was even played at the Covent Garden Opera in London, and he was awarded a Book of Sacred Music for his performance in the choir of St George's Church.

The dedication reads: 'Presented to Master Michael Maybrick as a token of regard for his musical perception'. William and Susannah encouraged Michael to study in Leipzig. From there he went to the Milan Conservatoire, where he discovered that he possessed a fine baritone voice. He went on to join the Carl Rosa Opera Company, before entering the Victorian equivalent of the pop scene, touring concert halls in Britain and in America.

Michael gave himself the stage name Stephen Adams, and formed a partnership with the librettist Frederick Weatherly. Together they wrote hundreds of songs such as 'Nancy Lee' and 'A Warrior Bold'. By 1888 Stephen Adams was Britain's best-loved composer of popular songs. Indeed, in 1892 his 'The Holy City', was published, an extremely successful song still selling today. This was followed, ironically, by a lively nautical ditty called 'We All Love Jack'.

For his siblings, Michael was a hard act to follow. William became a carver and gilder's apprentice, but eventually, the story goes, ran away to sea and became the black sheep of the family. Thomas and Edwin went into commerce. By 1860 James Maybrick had gone to work in the capital, perhaps to learn the cotton trade. That period of his life has been a blank page, until now.

. . .

In 1891, two years after Florie's trial, Alexander William MacDougall, a respected Scottish lawyer, published a 606-page *Treatise on the Maybrick Case*, in which he asserted: 'There is a woman who calls herself Mrs Maybrick and who claims to have been James Maybrick's real wife. She was staying on a visit at a somewhat out of the way place, 8 Dundas Street, Monkwearmouth, Sunderland, during the trial; her usual and present address is 265 Queens Road, New Cross, London, S.E.'

. . .

Who was the mysterious Mrs Maybrick? Census records, street directories and certificates of birth, death and marriage can resurrect the skeleton of any life long after it is over. But it is a long, slow process, fraught with problems, since Victorian form-filling was not always precise.

Census records for 1891 were not released until January 2nd 1992, according to British custom. Only then could the truth of MacDougall's assertion be established. Only then was it possible to fill in some of the details of Maybrick's secret life in London. I found those records and for the first time established the names of the inhabitants of 265 Queens Road: they were Christiana Conconi, a 69-year-old widow of independent means from Durham; her surprisingly young daughter, Gertrude, aged 18; and a 14-year-old visitor. There was one other person in the household: Christiana's niece, Sarah Robertson, single, aged 44.

Sarah had been born in Durham. Her aunt Christiana had married a watchmaker named Charles James Case in 1847 and went to live at 40 Mark Lane, near the Tower of London. It seems likely that young Sarah joined them there later, to work as a jeweller's assistant in the shop.

Was this when fate took Maybrick, as a young man on his first foray into London's East End, where his ancestors had lived, in pursuit of Sarah? Across the road from Mark Lane is Whitechapel itself. When in 1888 he embarked on the campaign of killing chronicled in the diary, he would certainly have been familiar with its wretched, teeming streets. Serial killers often work on their own patch, as our psychiatric consultant, Dr Forshaw, confirmed. Maybrick may not have wanted to kill in Liverpool, but his return to Whitechapel many years later as a murderer was indeed a return to the familiar haunts of his youth.

Charles Case died in 1863 and three years later Christiana remarried. Her new bridegroom was a paymaster in the Royal Navy named Thomas David Conconi. One of the witnesses at their wedding signed her name 'Sarah Ann Maybrick'.

In 1868, Thomas Conconi added a codicil to his will: 'In case my said wife shall die during my life time then I give and bequeath all my household goods furniture plate linen and china to my dear friend Sarah Ann Maybrick, wife of James Maybrick of Old Hall Street Liverpool now residing at 55 Bromley Street Commercial Road London.'

Bromley Street is where the Conconis lived at that time. According to MacDougall, all Sarah's family thought they were married, but no marriage certificate from that period has been found for James or Sarah Ann.

The street is still there, its small, two-storey houses, restored in 199ℴ, framed by shiny black railings. Number 55 was demolished for redevelopment after World War II. Turn right at the end of the street onto Commercial Road and it is but a brisk ten-minute walk west to Whitechapel, the scene of Jack the Ripper's murders.

According to the 1871 census, Sarah Ann, listed as a 'merchant's clerk wife' (sic), continued to live with the Conconis in Bromley Street, but the census also showed that Maybrick was no longer in residence there. When Thomas died in 1876, Sarah appeared again, this time listed as 'S. A. Maybrick, niece' on the death certificate, with the address for all three given as Kent House Road, Sydenham, in South London. By 1891 Christiana's niece is listed in the census as Sarah Ann Robertson, by which time she was, as MacDougall stated, living in Queen's Road, New Cross. But when Christiana died in March 1895, the 'informant' on the death certificate was, curiously, once again 'Sarah A. Maybrick'. However, at the time of her own death on January 17th, 1927, the records listed her as 'Sarah Ann Maybrick, otherwise Robertson, spinster of independent means of 24 Cottesbrook Street, New Cross'.

Where was James Maybrick? By 1871 he was back in Liverpool after the death of his father. According to the census he is living with his 54-year-old mother, Susannah, at 77 Mount Pleasant. He is unmarried. His occupation is described simply as 'commercial clerk', whereas brother Thomas is a 'cotton salesman' and Edwin is a 'cotton merchant/dealer'. He was in business with Gustavus A. Witt, Commissioning Agent, in Knowsley Buildings, Tithebarn Street, off Old Hall Street. Two years later, he was still working with Witt from the same overcrowded premises, where some 30 cotton merchants and brokers were crammed into one building. Maybrick established Maybrick and Company, Cotton Merchants, around this time, and Edwin eventually joined him as a junior partner. The building was finally demolished in the late 1960s to make way for an imposing modern development, Silk House Court.

It was a rough world, vigorously characterized in 1870 in the April 30th edition of the local magazine *Porcupine*. An article headed 'Cotton Gambling' described the ever-more unscrupulous world that had attracted the young Maybrick. A once-prestigious trade changed almost overnight after the cotton famine that followed the American Civil War; it became a business open to 'anyone, with no capital whatever, anyone with a shadow of credit', reported the magazine.

In 1868 a system of 'bear' sales was introduced, which was similar to that of the Stock Exchange. This involved 'selling cotton you have not got in the hope you may cover the sale by buying at a lower price at a later period'. It brought to the market an element of pure gambling. 'It is to be regretted,' noted *Porcupine*, 'that the Cotton Brokers' Association should have given their sanction to this system of trade and thus lower the tone and character of the market.'

Maybrick was an opportunist who thrived in this world of ruthless competition. In 1874, when he was 36, he went off to start a branch office in the newly booming cotton port of Norfolk, Virginia. Like many others, he divided his time between Britain and America, working in Virginia during the picking season from September to April, then returning home to Liverpool in the spring.

Norfolk had been ruined by the Civil War, but its recovery had been energetic. Ten square miles of the town's 37 square miles were water-logged, especially around the mosquito-infested Dismal Creek Swamp.

To encourage foreign investment, a piped supply of fresh water was needed. So the water system was modernized, and the improved conditions coincided with the opening of the railway connecting Norfolk with the cotton-growing states of the Deep South. The town was transformed into a successful international port, nearly half of whose ships plied between Liverpool and America.

In the year that Maybrick arrived in Norfolk, the town's Cotton Exchange was set up, giving rise to a tidal wave of commerce back and forth across the Atlantic. Three years later, while Maybrick was living in York Street with Nicholas Bateson and a Negro servant named Thomas Stansell, he caught malaria. When the first prescription, for quinine, did no good, a second, for arsenic and strychnine, was dispensed by Santo's, the chemist on Main Street.

'He was very nervous about his health,' recalled Bateson when he testified for the defence at Florie's trial. 'He rubbed the backs of his hands and complained of numbness in his limbs. He was afraid of paralysis. The last year I lived with him he became worse. He became more addicted to taking medicines.'

When it was his turn to give evidence, Stansell remembered running errands for Maybrick. 'When I brought him the arsenic, he told me to go and make him some beef tea . . . . He asked me to give him a spoon . . . he opened the package and took a small bit out. This he put in the tea and stirred it up.'

Stansell was surprised at the quantity of pills and potions in Maybrick's office. 'I am,' the prosperous cotton merchant once told him, 'a victim of free living.'

Maybrick's constant companion during this time was Mary Howard (also known as Hogwood), who kept one of the most frequented whorehouses in Norfolk. Years later, after Florie had been condemned to death, Mary pulled the rug from under Maybrick's reputation. Persuaded by Florie's supporters in America to describe her association with him, she gave a deposition to the State Department in Washington in which she said: 'I knew the late James Maybrick for several years, and that up to the time of his marriage he called at my house, when in Norfolk, at least two or three times a week, and that I saw him frequently in his different moods and fancies. It was a common thing for him to take arsenic two or three times during an evening. He would always say, before taking it, 'Well, I am going to take my evening dose.' He would pull from his pocket a small vial in which he carried his arsenic and, putting a small quantity on his tongue, he would wash it down with a sip of wine. In fact, so often did he repeat this that I became afraid that he would die suddenly in my house, and then some of us would be suspected of his murder. When drunk Mr James Maybrick would pour the powder into the palm of his hand and lick it up with his tongue. I often cautioned him, but he answered: 'Oh, I am used to it. It will not harm me.' '

The chemical element arsenic is found widely in nature, usually associated with metal ores. It has claimed uncounted victims, including, it is believed, Napoleon Bonaparte, who was possibly fatally poisoned by the arsenic-backed wallpaper of his prison sitting-room on St Helena. But it has also had a variety of medicinal and other uses throughout the ages. For example, in the 16th century Queen Elizabeth I used arsenic as a cosmetic, applying it to her face to make it matte-white, just as Florie Maybrick used an arsenic preparation for her complexion. In 1786, Dr T. Fowler reported on the medical benefits of arsenic in cases of fever and sporadic headaches. Fowler's Medicine was a popular tonic in Maybrick's time.

The Greek word for arsenic – *arsenikon* – means potent. Maybrick, like many men of his day, believed that arsenic increased his virility, which is why he began to take it. Because it was addictive, he became hooked.

. . .

The year 1880 was crucial for Maybrick, for at the age of 41 he fell in love. He was booked to return to Liverpool aboard the SS *Baltic* that spring, as usual. The *Baltic* was one of the White Star Line's powerful screw-driven trans-Atlantic steamers, designed 'to afford the very best accommodation to all classes of passengers'. The six-day voyage cost 27 guineas.

On March 12th, the *Baltic*, in the command of Captain Henry Parsell, steamed from New York. Among the 220 first-class passengers was the impulsive, cosmopolitan Belle of the South, Florence Chandler, known as Florie. Only 18, she was in the care of her mother, the formidable Baroness Caroline von Roques, and they were on their way to Paris. Also on board was the ladies' friend General J. G. Hazard, from Liverpool, who introduced them to Maybrick in the elegant bar.

Maybrick learned that the lively, five foot three strawberry blonde hailed from America's high society. She had been born on September 3rd 1862, during the Civil War, in the sophisticated city of Mobile, Alabama, into a way of life entirely dominated by cotton. Florie's much-travelled mother and her first husband (and Florie's father), William Chandler, were cousins to almost everyone who mattered in Southern society. Florie and her older brother, Holbrook St John, were children of wealth and privilege.

In 1863, when Florie's father died in his thirties, his side of the family was convinced, on no evidence at all, that his wife had given him poison. Prosecution was threatened, but was dropped with the understanding that Mrs Chandler, as she then was, would leave Mobile. Within six months she was married to a distinguished soldier, Captain Franklin du Barry. A year later, he, too, died, while on a steamer headed for Scotland. Inevitably, tongues began wagging again.

So Florie grew up without a father, leading a lonely life, living in institutions or with relatives while her mother travelled in Europe. Ten years after du Barry's death her mother married a Prussian cavalry officer, the Baron Adolph von Roques, who was to prove unfaithful, beat her and squander her money.

James Maybrick must have appeared to Florie the perfect mix: at once the mature father-figure she longed for and a worldly and self-assured man with a taste for living dangerously. And she, he must have imagined, was to be his entrée into a class and way of life that were not his by birth but to which he nevertheless aspired. She would bring him cachet among the socially-conscious worthies of Liverpool and, perhaps, a fortune.

With breathtaking speed Maybrick swept young Florie off her feet, and by the end of the voyage he had proposed. When they disembarked in Liverpool, plans were already made for a stylish wedding the next summer. Then, with typical delusions of grandeur, the cotton merchant arranged for the wedding to take place at the suitably named St James's Church, Piccadilly, one of the most fashionable settings in London. At the ceremony, which was conducted on July 27th 1881 by the Reverend J. Dyer Tovey, the bride wore pleated ivory satin and lace, and her bouquet was of white columbines with lilies of the valley. The bridegroom, 24 years her senior, wore a white satin waistcoat embroidered with roses and lilies of the valley and a cutaway coat lined with elaborately quilted satin.

Florie's brother, Holbrook St John, came from Paris to give her away. Although Maybrick's brothers Edwin, Thomas and Michael were there, he must have been disappointed that there was no great enthusiasm for the match. Michael, who dominated the trio, was sceptical. Guests reported, with some justification, that he did not believe the Baroness's tales of estates to be inherited, but saw in her scheming a crafty plot to secure for herself a settled British home in her old age. (After Florie's trial, however, she wrote to the Home Secretary, Henry Matthews, of her daughter: 'She had no pecuniary temptation to murder, as I assisted the family for years.')

At the time of the wedding, Maybrick had taken out an insurance policy, with Florie as beneficiary, for £2,000, which he later increased to £2,500. He also set up a trust fund of £10,000, a sum equal today to 40 times this amount, but never paid in a penny. Florie had a small income of £125 a year from her grandmother's house in New York, and there was occasional income from her late father's lands near Mobile. There was hardly enough money, however, to finance the kind of façade the Maybricks wished to present.

From the outset the match was founded on deception: even the marriage certificate reveals Maybrick in his true colours. His profession he listed pretentiously as 'esquire', his father's as 'gentleman', and his address as London's exclusive St James's.

Little more than a child, why should Florie suspect his life was based on hypocrisy, villainy and deceit? Nevertheless she would soon discover the awful truth that there was already a Mrs Maybrick living in London.

Worse still, Florie had no idea the man she loved would soon become one of the most terrifying figures of modern times.

THREE

'A dark shadow lays over the house, it is evil'

EIGHT MONTHS AFTER the wedding, James Chandler, affectionately known as 'Bobo', was born to the Maybricks. He was a sickly, premature baby, and Florie had a difficult birth.

In the spring of 1882, Maybrick returned with the family to America. For the next two years they spent half their time in Liverpool, half in Norfolk, Virginia, living in a rented house in Freemason Street.

At 8 o'clock every morning Maybrick left home and walked to work. Rather than go directly to his office in Main Street, near Boston Quay, he would stop at C. F. Greenwood's, a chemist in Freemason Street, to buy his daily supply of arsenic.

It was during this time that John Fleming, a merchant sailor from Halifax, Nova Scotia, spotted him adding the greyish powder to hominy grits, an American form of porridge. In a later affidavit he recalled Maybrick telling him: 'You would he horrified, I daresay, if you knew what this is. It is arsenic. We all take some poison more or less. For instance, I am now taking arsenic enough to kill you. I take this arsenic once in a while because I find it strengthens me.'

From the chemist's Maybrick would go on to the Cotton Exchange, where exporters, brokers and buyers mingled. Lunch was at one, and the rest of the day was spent on letters and paperwork before calling at one of Norfolk's many clubs. The minutes of the Cotton Exchange record his regular and enthusiastic attendance as a committee member.

Florie later wrote in a letter that it was during this time that her husband started rubbing the backs of his hands. What she did not know was that dry, itchy skin is one of the long-term symptoms of arsenic abuse. Maybrick was hardly alone in his indulgence. Use of arsenic, along with strychnine, which had similar effects, was a rapidly growing fashion among professional men in both Britain and America. Indeed the *Liverpool Citizen* commented at the time of Florie's trial: 'We are all perfectly aware that men-about-town are much in the habit of taking these dangerous drugs, strychnine and arsenic and what-not, as they are of drinking champagne and smoking tobacco. Why, we are told there is enough taken on the Exchange Flags alone to poison all Castle Street.

'When once they contract the habit of arsenic eating they remain slaves for life . . . . Once they enter on the downward path, there is no looking back, as it is asserted by toxicologists that if they are ever prevented obtaining their daily dose they may say, with truth, 'the pains of Hell got hold of me' and they experience all the dreadful horrors of slow arsenic poisoning.'

．　．　．

Coal began to replace cotton as Norfolk's prime export, so in March 1884 James decided to take his wife and young Bobo home to Liverpool for good. On August 22nd 1884 James posted his letter of resignation from the Norfolk Cotton Exchange. By now, they were renting a brand-new detached house called Beechville, in South Road, in the exclusive suburb of Grassendale. He and Florie went for drives in a horse and carriage, played whist and above all shared a love of horse-racing. They were constant visitors to Aintree, near Liverpool, home of the world-famous Grand National.

The Maybricks were accepted at Liverpool's social centre, the Wellington Rooms in Mount Pleasant, where carpet was laid over the pavement for the five annual balls, and ladies emerged from carriages 'dressed with such gorgeousness as befits the wives and daughters of the wealthiest men in Britain's greatest seaport'. Maybrick also belonged to the fashionable Palatine Club; in his diary he refers to dining at his club with his friend George (Davidson). But socially, the couple did not quite qualify for what was known as the 'currant jelly set'. Like many status-seeking Victorians, Maybrick became a Freeman of the City, although he was not mentioned among the worthies in up-market journals. Nor did his marriage and the move back to Liverpool contain a drug habit that was becoming more pernicious all the time. He had ready access to drugs through his cousin, William, who worked for a wholesale chemist, John Thompson, at 58 Hanover Street. When William was dismissed in 1886, Maybrick even asked Thompson to reinstate him, but the move failed. (Cousin William died in October 1888 in the Liverpool Workhouse.)

No matter, for Maybrick already had another source for his 'medicine': a dispensing chemist named Edwin Garnett Heaton, in Exchange Street East. Heaton served him for about ten years in total, over which time the dose he prescribed increased from four to seven drops. (Arsenic was commonly dispensed by the drop as well as in powder form.) Maybrick went regularly to the shop, sometimes five times a day, for what the chemist described as his 'pick-me-up' to 'excite passion'. Seven drops five times a day would be nearly equal to one-third of a grain of arsenic, and one grain is enough to kill. When Maybrick went on business trips, Heaton would make up eight or sixteen doses, according to the size of the bottle.

The drug was clearly having an impact on Maybrick. Florie's brother, Holbrook St John Chandler, who was by now a doctor in Paris, became concerned about his brother-in-law's behaviour, and wrote: 'I don't pretend to know his tricks, but he has forbidden Florie telling us a word of his affairs and has completely thrown dust in her eyes. We, unfortunately, cannot write to her or hear from her except through him, and he dictates her letters. I greatly regret this most unexpected attitude of Maybrick's, turning out to be such a bully and a brute, but such being the fact we have to protect ourselves as far as practicable.'

About this time Maybrick contacted a Pauline Cranstoun, in London, who had advertised that she cast horoscopes and so was able to diagnose obscure diseases. Her story is mentioned by J. H. Levy in his book on the Maybrick case, *The Necessity for Criminal Appeal* (1899). 'He wrote me,' she said, 'a strange account of his various ailments and told me he was in the habit of taking large quantities of arsenic, and put it in his food as he found that the best and safest way of taking it. He said it aided his digestion and calmed his nerves.'

In an interview with the *New York Herald* after Florie's trial, Pauline Cranstoun said: 'I wrote to him that he should stop using arsenic or it would certainly result in his fatal illness sometime. I received no reply from him to that.'

Sadly, all that correspondence was destroyed.

During 1884 there was a brief economic downturn in Britain. Friends said that Maybrick became as worried about his money as he was about his health. Florie herself had never been taught to budget. She was extravagant in her passion for pretty clothes, which she bought in quantity from Woollright's. The fashionable department store in Bold Street was a snare for any clothes-conscious woman, with its glossy image and immense stock of furs, jewellery and exotic fabrics.

It was hardly surprising that family tempers were becoming frayed.

As the Baroness wrote to her lawyer in New York: 'My poor little girl is completely in the power of her husband and he does not prove a son to me.'

In December of that year Florie's brother fell ill with consumption and died four months later. Maybrick went alone to his funeral in Paris as it was not the custom for women to attend.

Florie had few close friends. To the ladies of Liverpool she was an outsider. Two exceptions were Matilda Briggs, a former admirer of Maybrick's, and her sister, Louisa Hughes, who called regularly. After her brother's death, Florie asked Mrs Briggs for a loan of £100 to quieten creditors, which she repaid in instalments.

On July 20th of the following year, a daughter, Gladys Evelyn, was born. In attendance was the dapper, sharp-featured Dr Arthur Hopper from Rodney Street, who had cared for the Maybricks since their marriage.

Gladys's birth did nothing to restore marital bliss. In 1887 a distraught Florie discovered what others already knew: there was someone else in her husband's life. The diary, too, makes it clear that there was a woman living in Liverpool with whom he was having an affair. She is there for him whenever he feels the need.

Tonight I shall see mine.

Who was the woman referred to several times in the diary as 'mine'? Could she have been Sarah Ann Robertson? She vanished from the records between 1876 and 1891, and there is no evidence of her whereabouts in 1887. It is possible that she followed Maybrick to Liverpool.

More likely, though, is that Maybrick had abandoned her in London. If so, who was his other woman? Florie's friend, John Baillie Knight, said in a later affidavit that Florie had told him she knew Maybrick had a woman in Liverpool. The local papers at the time of Florie's trial also reported that a woman was living in Liverpool who had been his mistress for twenty years. When visited by Michael and by Edwin she was found to possess jewellery and clothes belonging to Florie which she said had been given her by James in part payment for money lent. Moreover, William Stead, the editor of the Victorian weekly magazine *Review of Reviews*, and Bernard Ryan, in his 1977 book *The Poisoned Life of Mrs Maybrick*, both maintain that 1887 was when, at Florie's insistence, the couple moved into separate beds.

In addition to suspecting adultery, Florie was by now worried that her husband was overdosing himself on his 'medicines'. And friends who saw Maybrick occasionally when they came on business trips from America remarked at his broken and rapidly ageing condition, despite the fact that he was only 48.

The growing coolness between the couple meant that Florie now spent more time on her own. When, in the spring of 1887, a scarlatina epidemic swept the country and five-year-old Bobo became ill, Florie stayed to look after him while Maybrick took nine-month-old Gladys out of harm's way to Wales for six weeks.

When he returned, Maybrick cut Florie's allowance for food, servants' wages and other household expenses. In October that year she wrote to 'my darling Mammy' that Maybrick had made only £125 profit in the previous five years, and that his assets were reduced to £1,500. She claimed that they had been using capital to furnish their home, and complained: 'I am utterly worn out and in such a state of overstrained nervousness I am hardly fit for anything. Whenever the doorbell rings I feel ready to faint for fear it is someone coming to have an account paid and when Jim comes home at night it is with fear and trembling that I look into his face to see whether anyone has been to the office about my bills . . . . my life is a continual state of fear of something or somebody. There is no way of stemming the current. Is life worth living? I would gladly give up the house and move elsewhere but Jim says it would ruin him outright. For one must keep up appearances until he has more capital to fall back on to meet his liabilities, since the least suspicion aroused, all claims would pour in at once and how could Jim settle with what he has now?'

Maybrick was far from consistent – and not always honest – in his handling of their finances. When he died he left over £5,000, the equivalent of about £200,000 today. He was not as impoverished as Florie believed. In addition to all the financial worries, Florie was also concerned about the well-being of little Gladys. In the same letter she adds: 'Nurse is quite changed since baby's birth. Poor little mite, it gets neither petting nor coaxing when I am not with it and yet it is such a loving little thing and ready with a smile for every cross word that nurse says to her. I cannot understand why she does not take to the child. I am afraid she is getting too old for a young baby and has not the . . . patience to look after Gladys which she had for Bobo. With him it was a labour of love, with poor little Gladys it is a labour of duty only.'

So it was that nurse Alice Yapp, described by the *Liverpool Echo* as a 'somewhat pre-possessing young woman', joined the family. She lived with her employers, Mr and Mrs David Gibson, in Birkdale, Southport. Maybrick flouted convention by going alone to engage her. There were hints in the newspapers later that relations between Alice and Maybrick might not be all that they should have been.

The strain on Florie became even more intense. She knew what no one else realized – that her life was out of control. She was in debt, and worried about her husband's drug habit, his health and his infidelity. Such was Florie's state of mind when she first met the personable Alfred Brierley.

.   .   .

In the winter of 1887 the Maybricks gave a dinner party. Among the guests was a cotton broker named Alfred Brierley, whose company, Brierley, Wood and Partners, was in Old Hall Street, just round the corner from Maybrick's office.

Brierley was born in Rochdale, Lancashire, in 1851, and grew up with ten brothers and sisters. The Brierleys were pillars of the community, having risen within the security of the Church of England and the Tory Party to a position of considerable affluence and influence, thanks to the cotton trade. Streets were named after them. At the age of 36, Brierley was unmarried, attractive and susceptible. Later, he would always insist, unconvincingly, that he met Florie only in company throughout the next year and that they were no more than 'distant acquaintances'.

Troubled as she was by her husband's affairs, Florie was herself a flirt, an animated woman who loved the attention of men. Moreover, as she explained to her mother, 'He was kind to me.'

In Liverpool in those censorious times it would have taken very little for a high-spirited girl from America's Deep South to step out of line. And this was someone who, according to an American friend, had grown up in a 'swift place where the women were much swifter'. There an unchaperoned girl might join a group of male and female friends on a Saturday night on a chartered river boat and dance and drink all night before returning home to sleep all day. Such behaviour would never have been tolerated in Victorian England.

Whatever the truth about Florie's feelings for Brierley, or whether she had begun to indulge them as early as 1887, it is clear from his diary that James Maybrick nursed a growing paranoia about her suspected infidelities.

. . .

Probably early in March 1888 the Maybricks moved from Grassendale to Aigburth, less than a mile away, into the far more imposing and better situated Battlecrease House, on which they took a five-year lease. They were accompanied by Nurse Yapp, gardener James Grant, who had just married the former housemaid, Alice, and the maid, Mary Cadwallader. Elizabeth Humphreys rejoined them later in the year as their cook.

The quality of the Maybricks' female staff was remarkable. A reporter described the girls' appearance later, at the time of Florie's arrest:

> One thing struck me with interest and wonder, not unmingled with admiration, was the smart appearance of the female servants and nurses . . . they were all dressed "a la mode", and the cook, especially [Elizabeth Humphreys], looked very fascinating, not to say coquettish.

Alice Yapp grew up with a brother and four sisters in the Nag's Head, Ludlow, Shropshire, where her parents were innkeepers. The girls were always extremely well dressed.

Mary Cadwallader, known as 'Gentle Mary', grew up on a 160-acre farm, also in Shropshire, and was privately educated. Why Mary – the eldest of 14 children – went into service is a mystery. She was tiny, with deep auburn hair, and was generally described as 'a lady'. She shared with the Maybricks a passion for horses, rode well and every week asked a man friend to put sixpence on a horse for her, since women were not allowed to bet.

The couple's neighbours in Riversdale Road were professional people and businessmen, although cows wandered up and down the muddy lane and made the going heavy for carriages. Florie wasted no time in furnishing the house in style. Every room had velvet carpets, and curtains in dark red plush, lined with pale blue satin, hung at the windows. The gold-painted furniture was upholstered in dark red with blue.

Maybrick's den, which was always locked, had deep, comfortable leather chairs. It was there that he kept the wine, cigars, tobacco, cards and poker chips he used while entertaining men friends. Upstairs, his dressing room, which was reached through the main bedroom, was forbidden territory to everyone.

That summer there would be a guest at Battlecrease House from whom would come recollections of an increasingly strange domestic scene. 'Little Miss' was Maybrick's pet name for the young Florence Aunspaugh, a boisterous eight-year-old American who stayed with the family while her father, John, head of Inman Swann and Co. of Atlanta, Georgia, was in Europe.

Florence told her story when she was an old lady to the author Trevor Christie. Most of the notes made by Christie did not appear in his book about the Maybrick case, *Etched in Arsenic*. Along with these notes, the unused material has only recently come to light. Stored in the archives at the University of Wyoming, Laramie, it figures prominently among the many Maybrick archives and memorabilia that have proved invaluable in the present reconstruction of the couple's life and times.

'Battlecrease was a palatial home,' Florence told Christie, 'typical of the style of an English estate. The grounds must have consisted of five or six acres, and were given most excellent care. There were large trees, luxuriant shrubbery and flowerbeds. Dotted around the grounds were little rock nooks or summer houses, with seats, covered with old English ivy and other running vines. A conservatory was near the house and a pair of peacocks roamed the grounds . . . running through the grounds was a small natural stream of water, part of which had been broadened and deepened to form a small lake . . . this pool was stocked with fish and swans and ducks were swimming on the surface. I think I remember this pool better than anything else as I fell in it twice and was pulled out by the yard man.

'Mr Maybrick was very fond of hunting and had quite a few dogs . . . I saw six horses, a pair of handsome looking blacks which were always hitched to the carriage, a pair of greys which were hitched to what they called the trap, and two bay saddle horses: one Mr Maybrick used, the other Mrs Maybrick.'

To young Florence, Florie was a beguiling figure. 'The crowning glory of her person was her hair. It was a blonde, but not the dead, faded out type of yellow, had just enough of a tinge of red in it to make a glossy, rich golden.

'Mrs Maybrick's eyes were the most beautiful blue I have ever seen. They were a large round eye of such a very deep blue that at times they were violet; but the expression was most peculiar . . . . You would focus your eyes on hers with a steady gaze and they would appear entirely without life or expression as though you were gazing into the eyes of a corpse. Utterly void of animation or expression. As you continued your gaze her eyes seemed to change and have the look of a frightened animal.

'At no time was there any expression of intellectuality, either in eyes or face, yet there was a magnetic charm about her countenance that . . . seemed irresistible.

'She was extremely conscious of her beauty and attractiveness and courted admiration, especially from the male sex. She seemed to be very fond of being very close to them and putting her hands on them. I have seen her pat a man on the top of his head, put her arm on another's arm, and rest her hand on another's knee. She acted that way before Mr Maybrick. Since I have reached the years of maturity I have wondered that he tolerated it, but he did.'

The James Maybrick of young Florence's memory was stern and formidable, but with brief flashes of tenderness to his children.

'After breakfast Mr Maybrick would take his little boy and myself, one on each knee, and talk to us. He would tease me to see what kind of pert answer I would give him . . .

'One day Mr Maybrick instructed Nurse Yapp to have the little boy and myself dressed unusually well, as he wished to have us in the parlour a while before dinner was announced . . . I don't think I ever looked better in my life . . . we were taken down the beautiful stairway in the front hall by the upstairs housemaid. Mr Maybrick met us at the door of the hall leading to the front parlour. Taking me by the hand and walking to the arch between the parlours he said: 'Ladies and gentlemen, I want to introduce you to this charming little miss from the USA.'

'While you would not term him a handsome man . . . he had a fine forehead, very pleasant intellectual face and an open, honest countenance. He had light sandy coloured hair, grey eyes and a florid complexion. He had none of that blunt abrupt manner, so characteristic of the English but was exceedingly cultured, polished and refined in his manners and was a superb host.

'But there were two unfortunate features in his make-up. That was his morose, gloomy disposition and extremely high temper. He also imagined he was afflicted with every ailment to which 'the flesh was heir.'

'Yes, Mr Maybrick was an arsenic addict. He craved it like a narcotic fiend. He used it right in our home. He was always after the doctor to prescribe it and the druggist to make him up a tonic with arsenic in it. He said once to my mother, 'They only give me enough to aggravate and worry me and make me always craving for more.'

'He was always taking strychnine tablets and was great on beef broth and arsenic. My father once said, 'Maybrick has got a dozen drug stores in his stomach.'

'I have seen him angered on several occasions,' Florence wrote, 'and twice he was furious. I was the cause of his second outburst . . . . His baby [Gladys] had a little bed with high railings all round . . . . One morning the baby cried and I ran to the bed to try and get her out. I was tugging to get her over the railings but I became so exhausted I could not hold on to her any longer and let her go . . . . If I had gotten her outside and she had fallen on the floor it might have broken her back . . .

'The nurse came in and was mad. She seized me by the back of the neck, jerked me around and said: 'If you do it again I will slap your jaws black and blue.'

'As this scene was being enacted Mr Maybrick passed by the door . . . Mr Maybrick was furious . . . he said: 'I saw you grab that child by the back of the neck – you might have broken her neck. This child is far from her father and mother, in my house under my protection and if I ever hear you talking to her in that way again I will kick you down the steps and break every God damn bone in you.'

Though only a girl, Florence sensed the strangeness of Battlecrease House. 'A current of mystery seemed to circulate all round which gave you an uncanny feeling, a feeling that something was going on that you could not understand. In the yard you would see the servants conversing in low suppressed tones. If anyone came up they would stop abruptly and disperse.'

The cast of characters at Battlecrease House included Mrs Briggs, who, Florence recalled, was 'a woman near Mr Maybrick's age, and my father was told she had been madly in love with him and had made a desperate effort to marry him. It is very evident he did not reciprocate'.

There was Nurse Yapp, who was 'a very efficient, capable woman' but also 'a most deceitful and treacherous one'.

'Both Mrs Briggs and Nurse Yapp despised and hated Mrs Maybrick and the most pathetic part about it was that Mrs Maybrick did not have the brain to realise their attitude towards her . . .

'Mrs Briggs took all kind of authority around the place and with the servants. She would address Mr Maybrick as 'James'. At the table I have heard her say things like this: 'James, don't you think a roof on the porch by the side of your den would be much better . . . James, I suggest you wear your heavy coat . . . James, a pork roast would be nice for dinner today?' Not one time did she ever address Mrs Maybrick.

'When Mr and Mrs Maybrick were gone she would go into every room in the house. Mr Maybrick's bedroom and Mrs Maybrick's bedroom. Only one room escaped her – that was Mr Maybrick's den. He had a Yale lock on the door and it was never opened, only when he was there. It was never cleaned up. Only when he was there.'

. . .

Among the regular callers and overnight visitors to Battlecrease House were Maybrick's brothers, Thomas, Edwin and, less frequently, Michael, who lived in London. William, the eldest brother, although resident in Liverpool, apparently never visited the house.

Michael was thought to be the brains of the family. According to Florence Aunspaugh, 'he had a very pretentious estate which far surpassed James's in every way'. He was unmarried in 1888 and was looked after by a housekeeper.

For a man who had already achieved something of star status, both as a singer and a composer, Michael is an enigma. Surprisingly little is known of his professional or private life; he is hardly ever mentioned in the diaries or reminiscences of his many famous contemporaries, with whom his relationships appear to have been on a superficial level.

Apart from his appearances at the London Ballad concerts and on the concert stage, he was a member of the Constitutional Club and could be seen sporting the uniform of the Artists Rifles Volunteers, where his training would have included bayonet practice. He had enrolled in 1886 at the age of 45. According to the muster roll, the rest of the recruits that year were in their twenties. So Michael obviously docked five years and signed on as 'age 40'. His chest measurement is given as '41"' and his height '6' 0½"'.

He had also by this time achieved considerable status as a Freemason, where he was a member of the Athenaeum and St. Andrew's Lodges and founder and first Principal of the Orpheus Lodge for Musicians. He rose to the coveted level of 30 degrees rite. By 1889 he had reached the even greater position of organist to the Grand Lodge.

Musical historian Tony Miall says of Michael Maybrick: 'He is one of the less attractive musical figures of the period. His endless pursuit of respectability and money is at variance with the image of an artist concerned with his art. One seeks in vain for any sympathetic bone in his body. His relations with his family and friends were more formal than warm. One suspects deeply that his relationship with his wife was similar – all in all, a cold fish.'

The youngest brother, Edwin, was, according to the impressionable Florence, one 'of the handsomest men I have ever seen'. He was of medium height, fair, with a well-proportioned and finely formed figure. He had a beautiful singing voice – even better than Michael's – but had had no opportunity to make the most of it. At the age of 37 he too was unmarried.

Maybrick's relationship with Michael and Edwin was in large part shaped by the power that Michael seems to have wielded over the other two. In his diary Maybrick refers repeatedly to his jealousy of Michael, whom he called 'the sensible brother'.

And Edwin's daughter, Amy, acknowledged years later that her father 'would not do up his shoes without consulting Michael'.

But Maybrick was close to Edwin, with whom he worked. He missed him greatly when he was away. Florie may have done so too. Rumours about Florie's feelings for her brother-in-law had been circulating for some time at the Cotton Exchange. There was even suspicion of an affair. The chit-chat among the servants after Maybrick's death was that letters had been found from Edwin to Florie. John Aunspaugh told his daughter, Florence, that Michael had destroyed those letters. However, she recalled an incident, told her by her father, that justifies the suspicion. 'The first indication my father had of anything being amiss was the night of the formal dining. There were twenty couples which, of course, made a long table. The conversation was in groups. Mr Edwin was near Mrs James Maybrick and they were laughing and talking. My father glanced at Mr James and as he did he heard Mrs Maybrick say to Edwin with a laugh: 'If I had met you first things might have been different."

It could have been a harmless joke. But Maybrick took it at face value.

'He dropped his knife,' Florence went on, 'clenched his fist and his face flushed the colour of fire. In a second he had recovered, picked up his knife and everything passed off smoothly.'

As Florence Aunspaugh and the Maybrick children played by the pond and raced around the flowerbeds, a storm was about to break that would overwhelm them all.

Thus far is fact. What happened next are facts, interpreted now, through the pages of the diary.

. . .

FOUR

'There are times when I feel an overwhelming compulsion to place my thoughts to paper'

THE POSTE HOUSE, in Cumberland Street, near Liverpool's docks, has hardly changed since 1888, when its lunchtime hotpot was famous far and wide. Customers still crowd elbow-to-elbow into the tiny, dimly lit bar, with a green ceiling and deep red walls closed in by the heavy drape of curtains.

Prince Louis Napoleon drank here. So, too, did James Maybrick. Not far from the Poste House is the once-fashionable shopping street known as Whitechapel. In those days it was a far cry from its more squalid namesake in London. Yet it is here that the bloody trail of Jack the Ripper began. It was in this street, early in 1888, that Maybrick first records in his diary that he thought he had seen Florie with the man he believed to be her lover.

Florie's lover is never mentioned in the diary by name, perhaps because Maybrick could not bear to write or read it. Instead, he is called 'the whoremaster', and when Maybrick thought of Florie with her lover she was no longer his 'darling Bunny' but 'the bitch' or 'the whore'.

Of that day he wrote:

> I took refreshment at the Poste House it was there I finally decided London it shall be. And why not, is it not an ideal location? Indeed do I not frequently visit the Capital and indeed do I not have legitimate reason for doing so. All who sell their dirty wares shall pay, of that I have no doubt. But shall I pay? I think not. I am too clever for that . . .
>
> The bitch and her whoring master will rue the day I first saw them together.

So, undermined by his own failing health, his drug addiction and banishment from Florie's bed, Maybrick was insanely jealous. He was angered by Florie's tactless coquetries. But it was without doubt her developing friendship with Brierley that sowed the seed for murder.

Maybrick had the motive. He now needed the location.

> I said Whitechapel it will be and Whitechapel it shall . . . Whitechapel Liverpool Whitechapel London, Ha Ha. No one could possibly place it together. And indeed for there is no reason

---

for anyone to do so.

There is a reference in the diary, probably entered in March, to a communication from brother Thomas requesting Maybrick to meet him in Manchester, where Thomas lived in the suburb of Moss Side and was the manager of the Manchester Packing Company. Maybrick agreed, although his mind was already preoccupied with matters other than business.

> Tomorrow I travel to Manchester. Will take some of my medicine and think hard on the matter . . . I will force myself not to think of the children . . .
> Time is passing much too slowly. I still have to work up the courage to begin my campaign. I have thought long and hard over the matter and still I cannot come to a decision to when I should begin. Opportunity is there, of that fact, I am certain . . . . My medicine is doing me good, in fact, I am sure I can take more than any other person alive.

Just as Maybrick used Michael as his cover in London, so Thomas provided a reason for a business trip to Manchester. The train from Liverpool ran direct from Mersey Road and Aigburth Station to Manchester, a journey of just over an hour, and it was there that Maybrick claims he committed his first murder. He later recorded the experience, which had clearly not given him the satisfaction he craved.

> My dear God my mind is in a fog. The whore is now with her maker and he is welcome to her. There was no pleasure as I squeezed. I felt nothing. Do not know if I have the courage to go back to my original idea. Manchester was cold and damp very much like this hell hole. Next time I will throw acid over them.

Fantasies of this kind are common among serial killers, according to Dr David Forshaw. Studies on a number of psychopathic patients have shown them to be preoccupied with sadistic sexual fantasies. 'Over time,' he explains, 'the fantasies became more extreme and they started to act out parts of the fantasy . . . For example following potential victims. Memories of these behavioural 'try-outs' would then be incorporated into the fantasies and lead to further elaboration . . . inexorably the movement was towards a full try-out. During this process patients became less and less able to distinguish between reality and a fantasy world . . . where there was total control. Inflicting suffering was the route to control . . . the striving to control was an attempt to compensate for feelings of inadequacy.'

Police records are incomplete, coroners' records have been destroyed and research has so far found no murder in Manchester in February or March of 1888. But the disappearance of a provincial prostitute could have easily passed unrecorded.

Henry Mayhew, in his classic *London Labour and the London Poor*, first published in 1851, estimated that there were approximately 80,000 prostitutes working in London alone, and a suspected strangulation of one in Manchester would not have merited more than a simply routine investigation.

Even the vicious murder of Emma Smith, who was savagely mutilated in London in April 1888, was not widely reported in the press, although the story did appear in the *Manchester Guardian*. It was barely noticed, however, until it was linked with the Ripper killings later that year.

There was no reason for Maybrick to invent such a murder for his diary. His account seems to be an accurate description of a death that, unlike the Ripper's subsequent killings, simply never made headlines. He strangled his first victim, as he did all the others. But there was no 'ripping', and he did not enjoy it.

From the beginning, Maybrick felt compelled to record his thoughts and deeds on paper. According to David Forshaw, his language is that of a man playing games, perversely giving himself confidence by pretending to be less educated than he is. There is a morbid delight in distorting grammar, in solecisms and in word play.

'It is not uncommon for intelligent, but insecure people to adopt a less educated personality on paper,' he says. In addition to the obvious word play there are many errors of spelling, grammar and punctuation which appear to play no part in the diary's verbal games. While these may well be part of the 'less educated' persona Maybrick adopted, they could result from a genuinely modest schooling, for Maybrick was a self-made man with no pretensions to learning.

The whole undertaking was dangerous, of course. It was easier for Maybrick to write in the privacy of his office, away from the prying eyes of his family and servants. After several entries he speaks of 'returning', presumably to Battlecrease House, and there is nothing to contradict the idea that the entire diary was written in his office, perhaps in the early evenings when the staff had gone home. However, even there he had to exercise extreme caution to protect his secret from accidental discovery by employees such as the book-keeper, George Smith, and the young clerk, Thomas Lowry.

> If Smith should find this then I am done before my campaign begins.

> I am beginning to believe it is unwise to continue writing. If I am to down a whore then nothing shall lead the persuers back to me and yet there are times when I feel an overwhelming compulsion to place my thoughts to paper . . . . However, the pleasure of writing off all that lays ahead of me . . . thrills me so. And oh what deeds I shall comit. For how could one suspect that I could be capable of such things, for am I not, as all believe, a mild man, who, it has been said would never hurt a fly.

Thomas Lowry, the 19-year-old son of a Liverpool clog-maker who was Maybrick's clerk, played no part in his boss's life, at least on the face of it. Yet for a brief moment he plays a major role in the diary.

> If I could have killed the bastard Lowry with my bare hands there and then I would have done so. How dare he question me on any matter, it is I that should question him. Damn him damn him damn him. should I replace the missing items? No that would be too much of a risk. Should I destroy this? My God I will kill him. Give him no reason and order him poste haste to drop the matter, that I believe is the only course of action I can take. I will force myself to think of something more pleasant.

The next day Maybrick, disorientated by drugs, could hardly remember what had happened.

> . . . I have taken too much my thoughts are not where they should be. I recall little of the events of yesterday. Thank God I stopped myself in time. I will show my wrath towards the bastard in such a manner that he will wish he had never brought up the subject. No one, not even God himself will [take] away the pleasure of writing my thoughts . . . My head aches. God has no right to do this to me the devil take him.

Whatever the interfering young Lowry had said or done, had placed him in more danger than he realized. He knew far more than was good for him, but what did he know? We can only guess that Lowry had asked Maybrick about some missing office materials, perhaps connected with the diary. If so, then Maybrick is over-reacting dramatically, but he is feeling threatened at a very sensitive stage – it is June 1888 and he is excited by the planning of his first Whitechapel ripping.

Whatever the 'missing items' were, and whatever 'the matter' was, Lowry's uncontrived appearance in the diary is completely convincing. For a second, the office door to Maybrick and Company is ajar and we catch a fleeting glimpse of a dark corner of Maybrick's personality. It is the same Maybrick that young Florence Aunspaugh saw threatening Nurse Yapp.

· · ·

Maybrick often went to London. There was a regular train service from Liverpool and the express took about five hours. His former Liverpool partner, Gustavus A. Witt, ran a London office in Cullum Street, a mere 400 yards from Mitre Square, where later in the year Maybrick would kill for the fifth time. Even closer than Mitre Square was Mark Lane, where as a young man he had probably first paid court to Sarah Robertson.

When in London, Maybrick usually stayed with brother Michael, who was living in Wellington Mansions, in fashionable Regent's Park. His neighbours were largely of the shipowner class. There was also an editor, an artist, a fine-art publisher, three comedians and Arthur Wing

Pinero, the dramatist.

Maybrick was not relaxed in the company of his arrogant, self-satisfied younger brother, but the Regent's Park chambers were comfortable – and convenient.

> I will visit Michael this coming June. June is such a pleasant month, the flowers are in full bud, the air is sweeter and life is almost certainly much rosier. I look forward to its coming with pleasure. A great deal of pleasure.

June, to which he looked forward so much, started disappointingly unsettled and wet, but by the end of the month a heat wave brought water rationing to Liverpool. Commerce was fair – 'steady but idle' was how the newspapers put it.

According to the diary, Maybrick went to see Michael with the idea of starting his 'campaign'. But something went wrong. He was not ready to kill; he had not laid his plans carefully enough, although the urge to strike was almost too much for him to control. Indeed, he was forced to resort to using Michael as his jailer.

> How I succeeded in controlling myself I do not know. I have not allowed for the red stuff, gallons of it in my estimation. Some of it is bound to spill onto me. I cannot allow my clothes to be blood drenched, this I could not explain to anyone, least of all Michael. Why did I not think of this before? I curse myself. The struggle to stop myself was overwhelming and if I had not asked Michael to lock me in my bedroom for fear of sleepwalking, to which I had said I had been prone to do recently, was that not clever? I would have done my dirty deeds that very night.

We know from the diary and from medical evidence at Florie's trial that Maybrick was in a state of panic about his health that June. His usual hypochondria fuelled a craving for medical attention and a downward spiral of drug abuse.

Between late June and September he paid around 20 visits to Dr Hopper, the family physician. He complained of violent headaches that had begun in June, around the time of the Royal Ascot race meeting, along with a numbness in his feet and legs.

Had the advantages of modern science been available to Dr Hopper, he would have realized that his patient's health was in a dangerous condition because of the volume and variety of drugs being consumed.

The doctor was sceptical and unsympathetic about Maybrick's hypochondria, as well as irritated that his patient was dosing himself between visits with remedies recommended by friends. One of these medicines, Fellows' Syrup, was a brew containing arsenic, strychnine, quinine, iron and hypophosphites. Maybrick also doubled the dose of Dr Hopper's prescriptions when he felt they were having no effect. The doctor warned him that he would 'do himself a great injury'.

Strychnine pills were formerly sold widely for a variety of medical purposes, especially as a tonic or an aphrodisiac. Their long-term effects have not been studied, say doctors at the Poisons Unit at Guy's Hospital, London.

Pills containing strychnine are no longer marketed and are considered ineffective and dangerous. However, the substance is sometimes used to 'cut', or increase the volume of, street drugs such as amphetamines. Its presence in the body can result in excessive neuron activity, although under strict medical supervision it has a participatory role in the treatment of impotence, among other complaints.

Maybrick used strychnine pills recklessly, like sweets.

Once Maybrick gave Dr Hopper some prescriptions written for him by a Dr Seguin in New York, which he had often passed through on business. They were for strychnine and nux vomica, a strychnine-based medicine popular with Victorians that was also used as an aphrodisiac. Dr Hopper destroyed them. 'I thought he was seriously hipped,' he said at Florie's trial, explaining that he meant Maybrick 'attached too much importance to trifling symptoms'.

At Easter there was a family holiday in Wales, and in July, at the doctor's suggestion, Maybrick went off to take the waters at Harrogate Spa, Yorkshire. He booked into the Queen Hotel, a modest establishment, and his name was duly recorded in the Visitors' Register, a regular feature in the local newspaper, the *Harrogate Advertiser*. He stayed there alone for four days.

Goodwood Races at the beginning of August were a social must for the Maybricks. They journeyed together down to the gloriously situated racecourse in Sussex, where they met John Baillie Knight, Florie's childhood friend, and his aunts. Afterwards they all dined together at the Italian Exhibition in London.

The Misses Baillie had first become acquainted with the Baroness von Roques and her daughter at a pension in Switzerland. Florie had stayed with them several times as a girl and they visited Liverpool after her marriage. They later told their nephew that they had noticed all was not well between the Maybricks. John and Florie did not meet again until 1889, but she wrote to him several times and confided to him her distress over her husband's infidelities.

Maybrick did not describe these events in his diary, which focused only on the relentless progress of his campaign of terror. Thoughts of murder, and little else, drove him to use it solely as a confessional.

. . .

On August Bank Holiday Monday a prostitute, Martha Tabram, was murdered in Whitechapel, London. She had been out drinking and looking for men in the evening. At 4.50 the next morning she was found in a pool of blood on the first-floor landing of George Yard Building. She had suffered 39 stab wounds, mainly to her breasts, stomach and genitals.

Martha was almost certainly killed by an unidentified soldier – a Guards private was her last client. But the press and the police decided that she and Emma Smith, who had been murdered and mutilated on April Bank Holiday Monday, were victims of the same man. When the terror began in earnest that autumn, they linked Martha Tabram and Emma Smith with the Whitechapel killings of Jack the Ripper. At the time, the public believed that they were all committed by the same criminal.

The diary does not refer to the murders of Emma Smith and Martha Tabram. Had it been the work of a contemporary forger these killings would have been included. Conversely, we know from doctors' appointments and social events that each time the Ripper struck Maybrick could have been in London.

. . .

Some time during August, several weeks after his last stay with Michael, Maybrick went down to London again, but this time he rented a room in Whitechapel.

He was almost ready.

FIVE

'Tomorrow I will purchase the finest knife money can buy, nothing shall be too good for my whores'

I have taken a small room in Middlesex Street, that in itself is a joke. I have paid well and I believe no questions will be asked. It is indeed an ideal location. I have walked the streets and have become more than familiar with them . . . I have no doubts, my confidence is most high. I am thrilled writing this, life is sweet, and my disappointment has vanished. Next time for sure.

MIDDLESEX STREET IS better known as Petticoat Lane, site of the famous Sunday street market. After the first two of the Ripper's murders, the police concluded that the killer must have had a hide-away somewhere in Whitechapel – but no one has yet discovered where. The diary's identification of Middlesex Street is invaluable. It explains the Ripper's ability to move freely about the squalid neighbourhood, which would have been an easy place in which a stranger could have gone to earth.

Nearby, according to the street directory of 1888, lived Mrs Polly Nathan, who ran the fish and chip shop; Solran Berlinski, a rag merchant; George Bolam, cowkeeper; Isaac Woolf, a dealer in playing cards, and Samuel Barnett, who ran the coffee rooms. Since the local vicar was the Rev Samuel Barnett, it seems probable that he and his wife Henrietta had opened the coffee rooms as a meeting-place for the poor.

Why Middlesex Street was a joke we can only guess. Perhaps Maybrick found irony in its titillating nickname, Petticoat Lane, which dates back to at least Tudor times. Or perhaps it was because Middlesex Street was a commercial centre for London's Jewish community and therefore the focus of anti-Semitic unrest. Maybrick made it clear in early entries in the diary that he was no friend of the Jews.

Why not let the Jews suffer? I have never taken to them, far too many of them on the Exchange for my liking.

Towards the end of his life, however, he felt remorse over this prejudice. After meeting a former colleague on the Exchange floor, he wrote:

I felt regret for was he not Jewish. I had forgotten how many Jewish friends I have. My revenge is on whores not Jews.

There are several other possible explanations for Maybrick's choice of

Middlesex Street as his hide-out. The boundary between the rival Metropolitan Police and City Police lay down the centre of Middlesex Street, and so he could profit from a conflict of interests and tease the police by border-hopping from side to side while on his rampage. Middlesex Street was also conveniently close to the office of his colleague, Gustavus A. Witt. Ironically, at the end of Middlesex Street is Liverpool Street station.

Before the 19th century, Whitechapel was an area of respectable merchants and quiet prosperity. But by 1888 the neighbourhood had declined. The dingy back yards and stinking, rubbish-littered alleys surrounding Middlesex Street were over-populated and violent. There were hundreds of lodging houses where, for threepence a night, a bed could be bought in a fetid, unheated room. Those with no money slept in gutters or in stairwells. Families squeezed seven to a tiny room, with one bed and broken, rag-plugged windows. There was a choking stench of urine, mildew and rotting fruit, vegetables and fish.

And there were at least 1,200 'unfortunates' – prostitutes – working the area. Like so many Victorian working-class women, they were mostly old before their time, worn out by inhuman conditions, poverty, beatings and drink. Murder was not unheard of.

On August 18th, less than two weeks before Maybrick first struck in Whitechapel, his brother, Edwin, left for America aboard the SS *Adriatic*. Dr Forshaw believes this was significant. Emotionally, the absence of his devoted younger brother left Maybrick free of restraint. Effectively, there was no one looking over his shoulder when he said that he was off to London on business.

And so the scene was set.

. . .

At 12.30 a.m. on Friday August 31st, Mary Ann Nichols, known as Polly, left the Frying Pan public house in Brick Lane, Whitechapel, and walked into history. Polly Nichols had been refused lodgings at 18 Thrawl Street but, undeterred, was overheard saying: 'I'll soon get my doss [rent] money.' She went off, wearing 'a jolly new bonnet', to earn her bed for the night. She looked young for a woman in her early forties and was described by Dr Rees Ralph Llewellyn, who would later examine her body, as 'very clean'. But she was an alcoholic, and drink and lodgings had to be paid for.

Polly Nichols was seen by at least three people wandering the murky streets, looking for a customer in need of a 'fourpenny knee trembler'. The clock of the parish church of St Mary Matfellon struck 2.30 a.m. as she staggered off for a mile along Whitechapel Road. There she must have met Maybrick. By 3.40 that morning she was dead.

They had walked away from the main road into Buck's Row, a cobbled street which was, according to the *Evening News*, 'not overburdened with gas lamps'. A terrace of new workers' cottages ran along one side. On the other were tall warehouses. There, Maybrick held Polly Nichols by her jaw against a stable yard gate and strangled her. He pushed her to the ground and with his new, shiny knife slashed her throat through to the vertebrae.

Maybrick's fantasy and obsession with decapitation is a consistent theme in all his accounts of the Whitechapel murders – and the official medical reports at the time do confirm that on each occasion there were deep cuts around the neck.

I have shown all that I mean business, the pleasure was far better than I imagined. The whore was only too willing to do her business. I recall all and it thrills me. There was no scream when I cut. I was more than vexed when the head would not come off. I believe I will need more strength next time. I struck deep into her. I regret I never had the cane, it would have been a delight to have rammed it hard into her. The bitch opened like a ripe peach. I have decided next time I will rip all out. My medicine will give me strength and the thought of the whore and her whoring master will spur me on no end.

Frustrated by his failure to remove his victim's head, the Ripper then tore at her skirt and wildly ripped and slashed her stomach.

Afterwards he walked silently away. None of the residents or night-watchmen heard a thing.

. . .

Charles Cross, a carter, was on his way to work down shabby, cobbled

Buck's Row when he saw what he thought was a useful tarpaulin bundled against the gates to some stables. It was Polly Nichols. Because she was dead before her throat was cut, there had been no mess – only a wineglassful of blood in the gutter. The body was still warm where Maybrick had left her, with her prized black velvet-lined bonnet lying nearby.

A few hours later, two workhouse paupers at the mortuary were told to clean the body. Only then was it discovered that she had been mutilated.

Maybrick had smelt blood. The hunt had begun.

The inquest, in the packed Whitechapel Working Lads Institute (next to the present Whitechapel Underground station), was conducted by the stylish coroner Wynne Edwin Baxter, who turned up, fresh from a Scandinavian tour, in black and white checked trousers, white waistcoat and crimson scarf.

Dr Llewellyn was called from his surgery in Whitechapel Road to examine the body. He reported a jagged wound running for two or three inches on the left side of the abdomen. It was very deep and the tissues had been cut through. There were several other incisions across the abdomen and three or four cuts running down the right side, all of which had been caused by a knife.

From this report arose the belief that the killer stood in front of his victim, steadied her jaw with his right hand and cut her throat from left to right with the knife in his left hand. But such a technique would have required a contortionist.

By contrast, the authors of *The Jack the Ripper A-Z* suggest that 'he stood in front of his victims in the normal position for standing intercourse; that he seized them round the throat with both hands, thus instantly silencing them and rapidly inducing unconsciousness; that he pushed them to the ground with their heads to his left, and cut their throats dragging the knife towards him. The initial arterial bloodflow would thus be away from him and he would avoid heavy bloodstaining. Also, this suggests the probability that he was right handed.'

On Saturday September 1st the *Liverpool Echo* reported, under the heading 'Who is Jim?':

There is another point of some importance on which the police rely. It is the statement of John Morgan, a coffee stall keeper, who says that a woman whose description answers that given him of the victim, called at his stall three minutes walk from Bucks Row, early yesterday morning. She was accompanied by a man who she addressed as 'Jim'.

It has to be admitted, sadly, that the description of Jim given by Mr Morgan does not fit James Maybrick. All we can safely note is that a man called Jim was at the murder site within minutes of the murder.

• • •

Back home in Liverpool Maybrick eagerly scanned the newspapers for reports of his second killing. He was not disappointed.

The wait to read about my triumph seemed long, although it was not . . . They have all written well. The next time they will have a great deal more to write, of that fact I have no doubt . . . . I will remain calm and show no interest in my deed, if anyone should mention it so, but I will laugh inside, oh how I will laugh.

A reporter for the *Star*, probably either Lincoln Springfield or Harry Dam, combed the local pubs and doss houses, seeking a description of the killer. He claimed to have interviewed about 50 women in three hours, each of whom had given identical details of a man the locals called 'Leather Apron'. This claim may well have been true, if the reporter plied the women with beer first, then asked them to rubber-stamp his own suspicions.

So Leather Apron made his appearance in the *Star*. He was described as about 40 years old, short, and Semitic-looking, with an exceptionally thick neck and a black moustache. His movements were 'silent and sinister', his eyes gleamed and he had a 'repulsive smile'.

In fact, the Polish Jew they called Leather Apron – a boot finisher whose real name was John Pizer – was innocent, although he had been charged with a couple of minor assaults in the past. But on the night of Polly Nichols's murder, he was in Seven Sisters Road, Holloway, in North London, watching the glow in the sky from two huge fires at the docks, and he was seen not only by a lodging-house keeper but also by a policeman. So, despite the eagerness of a detective, Sergeant William Thick, to arrest him, he could not be linked to the murder and even received some small compensation from the newspapers for libel.

This sort of sensationalism was a Victorian novelty, and the case provided ideal material for an unwholesome trend. Readers were confronted with words never before printed in their newspapers and full-frontal anatomical illustrations of shockingly mutilated bodies. The repressed Victorian audience lapped up every appalling, depraved detail.

Even the American press revelled in the case, likening it to Edgar Allen Poe's story 'The Murders in the Rue Morgue'. American newspapers wrote of a small man with wicked black eyes moving silently with a 'queer run'. One over-imaginative reporter for the *New York Times* described how Polly Nichols had run from the scene of her attack and was found several streets away, with her head almost severed.

The capital was in the thick of the first London County Council elections, in which the radicals sought control of the East End. The banner headlines referring to the Ripper's crimes also threw light on unemployment and the appalling living conditions of London's underclass. His terrible deeds were in part responsible for later social reforms as well as improvements in police procedures. The five women he murdered in the East End of London thus became martyrs to a cause.

It was coincidence, of course, that Robert Louis Stevenson's *Dr Jekyll and Mr Hyde* was thrilling London theatre audiences at the time. Though the play was not about sexual repression, it was nearer the truth than anyone imagined. It tells of the elderly, respectable Dr Jekyll, who discovered a potion which freed the hidden side of his personality – 'comparative youth, the light step, leaping pulse, and secret pleasures' – but which also awakened in him 'the spirit of Hell' and sent him forth to kill in the streets of London.

Such a divided spirit was James Maybrick. Within a week of slaughtering Polly Nichols, he was plotting his next murder.

SIX

'I look forward to tomorrow nights work, it will do me good, a great deal of good'

MAYBRICK WAS ENJOYING his notoriety. He had not been able to resist the thrill of discussing the murder of Polly Nichols with his closest friend, George Davidson, although taking care not to suggest his own involvement. The two had talked about the excellent local police and agreed that events such as the Whitechapel killing could not happen in Liverpool, where women could walk the streets in safety.

Maybrick would write about the conversation afterwards.

Indeed they can for I will not play my funny little games on my own doorstep. ha ha

He was exhilarated and immediately planned to repeat the thrill.

I will not allow too much time to pass before my next. Indeed I need to repeat my pleasure as soon as possible. The whoring master can have her with pleasure and I shall have my pleasure with my thoughts and deeds. I will be clever. I will not call on Michael on my next visit. My brothers would be horrified if they knew, particularly Edwin, after all did he not say I was one of the most gentlest of men he had ever encountered. I hope he is enjoying the fruits of America. Unlike I for do I not have a sour fruit . . .

The gentle man with gentle thoughts will strike again soon. I have never felt better, in fact, I am taking more than ever and I can feel the strength building up within me. The head will come off next time, also the whores hands. Shall I leave them in various places about Whitechapel? Hunt the head and hands instead of the thimble. ha ha. Maybe I will take some part away with me to see if it does taste like fresh fried bacon.

The next weekend he was off to London once more. None of the passengers on the train that Friday, September 7th, a week after Polly Nichols's death, could have suspected that they were travelling in the company of the most wanted man in Britain.

Maybrick made the journey to London's Euston station in the comfort of an upholstered maroon and gold carriage of the London and North Western Railway. In such luxury, he tells us in his diary, he jotted down some clumsy attempts at verse.

> One dirty whore was looking for some gain
> Another dirty whore was looking for the same.

With just these two lines Maybrick recalls his encounter with Polly Nichols. He is so pleased with the result that after all the subsequent murders he writes verses packed with puzzling references to items of significance to him. The rhymes become an obsession, with much scratching out and rewriting. They are an important way for Maybrick to convince himself of his intellectual superiority, especially over his younger brother. Repeatedly in the diary, he expresses both awe and jealousy of him.

> If Michael can succeed in rhyming verse then I can do
> better, a great deal better he shall not outdo me. Think
> you fool, think. I curse Michael for being so clever, I
> shall outdo him, I will see to that. A funny little
> rhyme <u>shall</u> come forth.

In fact Maybrick significantly showed little real interest in Michael's career and seems unaware that his brother wrote the music, but not the words, that had become so popular. In 1888 Michael was billed in the *Pall Mall Gazette*, appearing amid 'an army of talent' in the newly inaugurated Ballad Concerts that were taking place in London.

What matters is Maybrick's deep feeling of inferiority. His terrible deeds and the need to write about them are all part of his desperate attempt to prove to himself and to the world his immense intellectual and physical prowess. Throughout the diary he has to reassure himself that he is indeed 'clever'. The word appears no fewer than 25 times.

• • •

The Ripper's second Whitechapel victim was 47-year-old Annie Chapman. The daughter of a Lifeguardsman, she had abandoned her husband and her two children to live by selling flowers – and occasionally herself.

At the time of her death she was already terminally ill with a disease of the lungs and the brain, but was forced to continue earning a bed for the night. She was short and stout but well proportioned. Friends described her as a steady woman who drank only on Saturday nights.

At about 11.30 p.m. on September 7th, Timothy Donovan, caretaker of Crossingham's Lodging House, let Annie Chapman into the kitchen, where she took from her pocket a box containing two pills. The box broke and she wrapped the pills in a torn envelope she found on the floor. She then said she was off to earn some money.

Annie Chapman was last seen by Mrs Elizabeth Darrell on the pavement outside 29 Hanbury Street. The exact time is uncertain, but it was between 5 and 5.30 a.m. She was talking to a 'shabby genteel' man who was overheard by Mrs Darrell to say, 'Will you?'

'Yes,' she replied. The man was undoubtedly Maybrick. He and the prostitute disappeared together along the narrow alley leading down two steps into the small yard at the back of 29, a ramshackle house providing lodging for 17 people. There, Maybrick grabbed her by the throat and strangled her. Slashing from left to right, he again failed to sever the head.

I wish to God I could have taken the head.

He ripped open her stomach and flung her intestines across her left shoulder, then tore out her uterus and part of her abdomen.

Mrs Amelia Richardson, a packing-case maker; Mrs Hardyman, a cat's meat woman; Mr Walker and his simpleminded son, carman Thompson; Mr and Mrs Copsey, who were cigar makers; and the elderly John Davis, his wife and their three sons – all slept undisturbed a few feet away.

At about 5.30 a.m., Albert Cadosch, a carpenter from the house next door, heard someone talking in the yard. He thought he heard a voice say 'No', then a thud against the fence. But he took no notice and walked off to work down Hanbury Street. There was not a soul about.

When John Davis woke up at 5.45, he went down to the yard and was horrified to see the mangled, bloody corpse of Annie Chapman.

'What was lying beside her I can't describe,' he said. 'It was part of her body.'

It did not take long for an excited crowd to gather. What they all later remembered was the grotesque spectacle of Annie Chapman's striped woollen stockings protruding from beneath her dishevelled skirt. It was a tale to terrify friends and relations.

The murdered woman was covered with a sack and removed, leaving all her worldly goods where Maybrick had abandoned them. There was a scrap of muslin and two combs. 'In the dress of the dead woman were two farthings, so brightly polished as to lead to a belief that they were intended to be passed as half sovereigns,' said the *Evening News* of September 8th. These coins were not referred to at the inquest and were never mentioned again.

A torn envelope lay separated from the rest of the woman's belongings. In all other books, and in previous reports since that day, it has been stated that Inspector Chandler, who was on duty in the Commercial Street Police Station that night, noticed an 'M' on one side of the envelope in what he took to be a man's writing, along with the post office stamp 'London, August 28th 1888'. On the back was the seal of the Sussex Regiment.

So we were all amazed when sifting through the private collection of the late Stephen Knight (author of *The Final Solution*) that Paul Feldman had unearthed. There we found an original document written by Inspector Chandler after he had visited the depot of the 1st Battalion of the Sussex Regiment at North Camp, Farnborough, on September 1st. It said:

> Enquiries were made amongst the men but none could be found who corresponded with anyone living in Spitalfields, or with any person whose address commencing [sic] with 'J'. The pay books were examined and no signature resembled *the initials* on the envelope.

For the first time there was talk of more than one initial. We knew about the 'M'; now, it seems, there was also a 'J'. Was this the first of the clues James Maybrick was to leave at each murder site?

Three days after Annie Chapman's murder, while the East End was being turned inside out by the police, Maybrick sat in Liverpool, alone with his thoughts.

At home, one of his great delights was to tease. Earlier in the year, little Florence Aunspaugh had remembered him reducing Florie to tears over a hole in her stockings. Now, he was beginning to enjoy playing games with the police. Jokes and riddles are scattered throughout the diary, especially in the doggerel, and at the scenes of his crimes. The entry Maybrick would write three days after the murder of Annie Chapman is full of such clues.

> The pills are the answer
> end with pills. Indeed do I always not oh what a joke.

The discovery of his latest victim's pills clearly amused Maybrick. After all, he did not know she was already dying, and it may be assumed that he thought they shared an addiction. His poetic response was a rambling, incoherent rhyme around the pills whose meaning is unclear.

> Left two*
> No pill, left but two

> Am I not indeed a clever fellow? It makes me laugh
> they will never understand why I did so.

(Here and throughout the rest of this book an asterisk (*) indicates that a line in the diary has been struck through.)

Did the murderer take Annie Chapman's pills from the envelope and exchange them for two of his?

Referring to the envelope with the letters 'J.M.' on the front, Maybrick writes:

> Letter M it's true
> Along with M ha ha
> Will catch clever Jim

It was the torn envelope which appears to have given Maybrick the idea that he would leave his surname's initial at the scene of his crimes.

Mystery also surrounds the brass rings that Annie had, according to friends, been wearing. Maybrick tells us that he wrenched them off because they reminded him of his wife's wedding ring.

> Begin with the rings,
> One ring, two rings
> bitch, it took me a while before I could wrench them off. Should
> have stuffed them down the whores throat. I wish to God I could
> have taken the head. Hated her for wearing them, reminds me too
> much of the whore.
> One ring. Two rings
> One ring, two rings . . .

Inspector Abberline notes: 'The deceased was in the habit of wearing two brass rings (a wedding and keepers); these were missing when the body was found and the fingers bore the marks of their having been removed by force.'

A journalist, Oswald Allen, wrote in the *Pall Mall Gazette*: 'A curious feature of this crime is that the murderer had pulled off some brass rings, with some trumpery articles which had been taken from her pockets and were placed carefully at her feet.'

This story was changed in the telling and became 'a pile of rings and coins'. There was no pile of rings; they were missing because Maybrick had taken them.

Another distinctive aspect of the second Whitechapel killing was the actual 'ripping' of the victim's body. Dr George Bagster Phillips, a police surgeon who conducted or attended post-mortems on four of the victims, believed that the murderer must be a doctor. Since then, the medical prowess of the killer has been debated. But most doctors now agree that although the lower end of Annie Chapman's uterus and her cervix had been detached with a single clean slash through the vaginal canal, the rest of the 'operation' was extremely inept.

The coroner, Wynne Baxter, put forward an ingenious theory, prompted by a press report, that an American doctor had been visiting London hospitals with a plan to export preserved uteri, for which he was prepared to pay high prices. Such a macabre trade could, the coroner argued, suggest a motive for the crime. But the medical press refuted this idea promptly. On October 1st the Curator of the Pathological Museum had given the current market price for whole and partial corpses:

<pre>
For one corpse complete..............£3.5s.0d.

For one thorax........................... 5s.0d.

For one arm, one leg, one head and
neck and abdomen net..................15s.0d.
</pre>

It is therefore nonsense, the Curator said, to claim that as much as £20 was being offered for complete bodies. His message was clear: there was not enough profit in such a trade to offer a motive to the Whitechapel killer.

Little was understood at the time about the psychology of the serial killer. His need to remove the female organs as a means of control would have been unknown. The cannibalization of these organs was an additional and perverted power game. In fact, in a fit of fury when he realized he had forgotten the chalk with which he planned to write a clue, Maybrick turned back and took a second helping.

> I took some of it away with me. It is in front of me. I intend to fry it and eat it later <u>ha ha</u>. The very thought works up my appetite.

Few people have tasted human flesh and fewer still would admit it. Whether the uterus, vagina or bladder are edible is a matter of dispute. These organs are largely muscle and would be difficult to eat.

Maybrick's self-confessed pleasure in cannibalism was echoed during the trial of the Russian Ripper, Andrei Chikatilo, in 1992. 'I like to nibble on a uterus,' he testified. 'They are so pink and springy, but after nibbling them I throw them away.'

. . .

After Annie Chapman's murder 16 East End businessmen formed themselves into the Whitechapel Vigilance Committee. Under the presidency of builder George Lusk they demanded brighter street lights and better policing of the area. On September 14th a telling letter signed 'JFS' was printed in the *Pall Mall Gazette*:

> Yesterday, at 11 a.m. a gentleman was seized and robbed of everything in Hanbury Street. At 5 p.m. an old man of 70 was

attacked and served in the same manner in Chicksand Street. At 10 p.m. today a man ran into a baker's shop at the corner of Hanbury Street and King Edward Street and ran off with the till and its contents. All these occurred within 100 yards of each other and midway between the scenes of the last two horrible murders.

If all this can happen now, when there is supposed to be a double police patrol in the area and where plain clothes policemen are said, literally, to jostle one another in the streets, the ease with which the murderer conducted his dissection and made his escape ceases to be at all wonderful.

Soon afterwards *The Times* suggested yet another theory: that the killer might not, after all, be a member of the working class and was lodging somewhere quite respectable in the area.

There was also a popular feeling, no doubt based on bigotry more than evidence, that only a foreigner could possibly commit such crimes. In Whitechapel, foreign meant Jewish, and so the police were, with reason, worried about a growing anti-Semitism.

I have read all of my deeds they have done me proud. I had to laugh, they have me down as left handed, a Doctor, a slaughterman and a Jew. Very well, if they are to insist that I am a Jew then a Jew I shall be. Why not let the Jews suffer? I have never taken to them.

On September 22nd the magazine *Punch* published a cartoon that amused Maybrick, with his love of word games. It showed a policeman blindfolded and confused by four villains. The caption: 'Turn round three times, and catch whom you may!'

I could not stop laughing when I read Punch. there for all to see was the first three letters of my surname. They are blind as they say.

I can not stop laughing it amuses me so I shall write them a clue.

May comes and goes
In the dark of the night
he kisses the whores

BLIND-MAN'S BUFF.

(As played by the Police.)

"TURN ROUND THREE TIMES,
AND CATCH WHOM YOU MAY!"

> The jews and the doctors
> Will get all the blame
> but its only May
> playing his dirty game.

It is apparent from the verse that Maybrick has conceived a plan to use anti-Semitism as a major diversionary tactic in throwing the police off the scent when he commits his next murder. Then, as so often in the diary, he suddenly switches mood.

> I am fighting a battle within me. My disire for revenge is overwhelming. The whore has destroyed my life. I try whenever possible to keep all sense of respectability . . . I miss the thrill . . . of cutting them up. I do believe I have lost my mind.

After the second gruesome murder in Whitechapel, and the resulting outcry, Maybrick's megalomania was clearly overwhelming him. Only a few months earlier, during her holiday at Battlecrease, little Florence Aunspaugh had heard Nurse Yapp referring to her master as Sir James. The title obviously tickled him, though it was not the name that finally earned him a place in history.

He refers to himself in the diary as 'Sir Jim', and occasionally as 'Sir Jack'. Jack is a long-established familiar form of James. We can imagine the delight of the man who enjoyed word-games when he noticed that the first two letters of James and the last two letters of Maybrick formed 'Jack'. Only twice in the diary (once where he signs off) does he use the infamous pseudonym 'Jack the Ripper', which the public and press first picked up from letters signed with that name and sent from September 1888 onwards. Most of them were from practical jokers, but not all.

> Before I am finished all of England will know the name I have given myself. It is indeed a name to remember . . . It shall be, before long, on every persons lips within the land. Perhaps her gracious Majesty will become acquainted with it. I wonder if she will honour me with a knighthood. ha. ha.

It is at this point that Inspector Abberline is first mentioned in the diary.

> Abberline says, he was never amazed
> I did my work with such honour

For Maybrick, Abberline represents the forces opposed to him, the police, referred to throughout the diary as 'headless chickens'. He greatly enjoys making fun of their fruitless efforts to capture him, but later in the diary Abberline becomes the 'persuer' and the 'hangman', who haunts his nightmares.

Despite his cruel taunts and grotesque images, Maybrick could be surprisingly vulnerable. These glimpses of completely natural weakness ring true. Such secret moments belong to Maybrick and his diary alone.

> I visited my mother and father's grave. I long to be reunited with them. I believe they know the torture the whore is putting me through.

He appeared tender and loving with his children and yet he was frightened that as the drugs increasingly dominated his actions, even they were in danger.

> I am beginning to think less of the children, part of me hates me for doing so.

But for Florie there was no compassion. He gave her every opportunity to meet her 'whoremaster' and revelled in the thoughts of what they might be doing.

> The whore seen her master today it did not bother me. I imagined I was with them, the very thought thrills me. I wonder if the whore has ever had such thoughts?

That September Maybrick took out the first and larger of two more insurance policies. It was for £3,000 of life insurance for himself with the Mutual Reserve Fund Life Association of New York. Presumably he had fooled the company, since friends had noticed a dramatic deterioration in his physique. He was ageing rapidly, and John Aunspaugh even doubted that he would see out the year. Maybrick's fear of illness and death was becoming a reality.

So far as Maybrick's campaign, as he called it, was concerned, all was going according to plan. He was basking in publicity. Speculation that he might be Jewish appealed to his sense of irony, while the idea of being a doctor flattered his drug-abused ego. He was encouraged, ready now to carry on his work.

Next time he would take the chalk.

SEVEN

'To my astonishment I cannot believe I have not been caught'

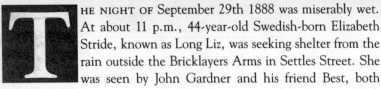

THE NIGHT OF September 29th 1888 was miserably wet. At about 11 p.m., 44-year-old Swedish-born Elizabeth Stride, known as Long Liz, was seeking shelter from the rain outside the Bricklayers Arms in Settles Street. She was seen by John Gardner and his friend Best, both labourers, being fondled by a respectably dressed man in a black morning suit and overcoat. A little later old Matthew Packer claimed that a man accompanying Elizabeth Stride bought some grapes from his shop in Berner Street.

The Jewish-run International Workingmen's Educational Club had already disgorged its 150 or so radical members from a lively meeting on the first floor of 40 Berner Street. A few members had stayed behind and the sound of Russian folk music could be heard on the night air.

Constable William Smith thought he saw Elizabeth Stride at about 12.30 a.m. while on his beat. She was with a well-dressed man, wearing a black coat, hard felt hat and white collar and tie. He also noticed a red flower pinned to her jacket.

After Mrs Fanny Mortimer of 36 Berner Street heard 'the heavy stamp' of Constable Smith passing her house, she went to her front door and stood there listening to the music from the club.

Beside the club building, through a wicket door between a pair of wooden gateposts, was a dark passage leading to an unlit yard used by van and cart builder Arthur Dutfield. Mrs Mortimer said that during the time she was at her door she saw no one enter or leave the yard.

Five minutes later, Israel Schwartz walked past the gateway to Dutfield's Yard. He did not testify at the inquest and his account was reported only in the *Star* and the *Evening Post* – although the police believed it. Indeed it remained virtually unnoticed in Home Office files until Stephen Knight's *Jack the Ripper: The Final Solution* appeared in 1976.

Schwartz claimed he had seen a man on the far side of the street accost a woman who was standing by the wicket gate to the yard. The man threw her to the ground and pushed her into the alley. Schwartz said that: 'She screamed three times but not very loudly.' He described the man as about 30 years old, with a small brown moustache and a black peaked cap.

This description fitted Kosminski, the Polish Jew, and could

Left: James Maybrick during the 1880s. An eyewitness who claimed to have seen Mary Jane Kelly talking to Jack the Ripper described the man as wearing a thick gold watch chain. (Richard Whittington Egan)

Below: A recently discovered gold watch, hallmarked in 1846, and made by Henry Verity of Lancaster. Scratched on the inside cover which closes over the works are: the signature of J. Maybrick; the words, 'I am Jack'; and the initials of the five Whitechapel victims, MK, ES, CE, MN and AC. (Albert Johnson)

Left: The teenage Florence Chandler, before her marriage to James Maybrick in July 1881. (Richard Whittington Egan)

Below: Florence's spirited mother, Baroness Caroline von Roques. (Richard Whittington Egan)

Bottom: The White Star transatlantic liner, SS *Baltic*, on board which James Maybrick first met Florence Chandler. (Stewart Evans)

Left: The grounds of Liverpool Cricket Club, opposite Battlecrease House. Maybrick was a member. (Smith Gryphon)
Far left: Maybrick walked each day to Aigburth station to catch a train to Liverpool. (Smith Gryphon)

Above: The imposing Battlecrease House, 7 Riversdale Road, Aigburth, to where the Maybricks moved at the start of 1888. (Smith Gryphon)
Right: The former night nursery of the Maybrick children. (Smith Gryphon)

Above: Members of the Cotton Association, 1887–8, on the 'Flags' of the Liverpool Exchange. (Liverpool Record Office)
Left: Lord Street, Liverpool, led to Whitechapel where Maybrick said he saw his wife with Alfred Brierley, a cotton broker. (Smith Gryphon)

Right: A contemporary drawing of Alfred Brierley, whose affair with Florence Maybrick provoked violent rages in her husband. (Richard Whittington Egan)

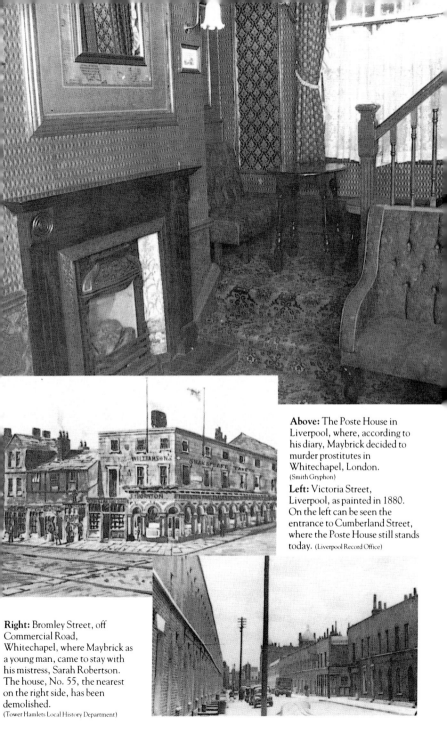

Above: The Poste House in Liverpool, where, according to his diary, Maybrick decided to murder prostitutes in Whitechapel, London. (Smith Gryphon)

Left: Victoria Street, Liverpool, as painted in 1880. On the left can be seen the entrance to Cumberland Street, where the Poste House still stands today. (Liverpool Record Office)

Right: Bromley Street, off Commercial Road, Whitechapel, where Maybrick as a young man, came to stay with his mistress, Sarah Robertson. The house, No. 55, the nearest on the right side, has been demolished. (Tower Hamlets Local History Department)

Above: Mary Kelly, the last Whitechapel prostitute to be murdered by the Ripper. On the wall, immediately above her body, are two letters, FM, the initials of Florence Maybrick. The second picture, reproduced here for the first time, was taken from the opposite direction, looking towards her table, piled with the flesh from her abdomen and thighs. (Public Record Office, Kew)

Top: An enlargment of the same photograph, which shows the initials FM (ringed) more clearly. (Public Record Office, Kew)

WHITECHAPEL VICTIMS

Above: The early morning Victorian crowd in the Middlesex Street market, now known as Petticoat Lane. It was here that Maybrick rented a room in the autumn of 1888.
(Tower Hamlets Local History Department)

WHITECHAPEL VICTIMS

Mary Ann Nicholls
Bucks Row
31. 8. 88.

Annie Chapman
Hanbury Street
8. 9. 88.

MITRE SQUARE.
30. 9. '88

Elizabeth Stride
Berner Street
30. 9. 88.

THE LONDON HOSPITAL GAZETTE

Above: The first four victims, Mary (Polly) Nicholls, Annie Chapman, Catharine Eddowes and Elizabeth Stride.
(Public Record Office, Kew)

Right: A drawing made at the time of Catharine Eddowes' murder shows a triangular flap cut on each cheek. When the two inverted Vs are put together, they form an M, the mark of Maybrick. (London Hospital)

Right: Mike Barrett, the owner of the diary, with his wife Anne and daughter Caroline.
(Smith Gryphon)

Below: The diary of Jack the Ripper, with black covers and seven gold-leaf bands on its quarter-bound leather spine. Its normal use in Victorian times would have been as a family scrapbook.
(Duocrave)

Left: Knowsley Buildings, near the junction of Tithebarn Street and Old Hall Street. Maybrick & Co.'s offices were in these buildings, which survived until their demolition in 1970.
(Richard Whittington Egan)

account for his inclusion as a Ripper suspect. Sir Robert Anderson, Assistant Commissioner of the Metropolitan Police CID, who was in charge of Ripper investigation from October 1888 to 1892, was convinced of Kosminski's guilt. Anderson based this view on evidence provided by an unnamed witness, who, he claimed, was 'the only man ever to have a good look at the murderer'.

At about the same time, said Schwartz in his interview with the *Star* on October 10th, a second man came out of the ale house on the corner of Fairclough Street and stood, silently, in the shadows. The attacker, spying Schwartz, suddenly shouted 'Lipski'. It was a term of abuse, since Lipski was a Jew who had been convicted of murder the year before. Even taking the darkness of the wet night and the unreliability of any visual identification into account, Schwartz's description of this second man tallies with that of the man seen outside the pub and the man who bought the grapes. Schwartz thought he was about 35 years old, 5 feet 11 inches tall, with light brown hair and moustache. He was dressed in a dark overcoat with a hard, wide-brimmed felt hat, and was carrying a knife.

However, Inspector Abberline reported to the Home Office on November 1st that Schwartz, who spoke no English and needed an interpreter, had described the second man as lighting a pipe and not carrying a knife.

This confusion demonstrates the risk in attaching too great an importance to contemporary records. Whether he was carrying a knife or a pipe, I believe the second man could have been Maybrick.

The first attacker ran off and Schwartz fled in the opposite direction, not wanting to be involved with the man or the assault – and giving Maybrick the opportunity he needed. Maybrick could have followed for a moment to be sure Schwartz had gone, then perhaps with the pretence he was helping her, led Elizabeth Stride into Dutfield's Yard. The enclosed space would have appealed to a gambling man with a taste for danger, such as Maybrick. There was only one exit, so that if anyone else arrived he might be caught. On the other hand, he had the advantage of cover.

There was no time to waste. Frenetically grabbing Elizabeth Stride by the scarf around her neck, he pulled back her head, throttling her before she had time to cry out. Then he slashed her throat.

In her hand she still clutched a small packet of the cachous that smokers chewed to conceal the habit. Maybrick himself is known to have used them. In the midst of the carnage, it was their smell he remembered.

I could still smell her sweet scented breath

The woman was dead, but there had been no chance to mutilate her body. Louis Diemshutz, a seller of cheap jewellery, described in the *Star* on October 1st how he had arrived in Dutfield's Yard at 1 a.m. with his pony and cart. He interrupted the murderous attack and, although he was too late to save Elizabeth Stride's life, his appearance prevented any further butchery.

As he drove into the yard the pony veered towards the left wall to avoid an obstruction in their path. Diemshutz leant down and poked the sodden bundle with his whip. It was the body of Elizabeth Stride.

Maybrick was lurking in the shadows, out of view. The terrified Diemshutz did not see him. His panic saved the Ripper's life.

To my astonishment I cannot believe I have not been caught. My heart felt as if it had left my body. Within my fright I imagined my heart bounding along the street with I in desperation following it. I would have dearly loved to have cut the head of the damned horse off and stuff it as far as it would go down the whore's throat. I had no time to rip the bitch wide, I curse my bad luck. I believe the thrill of being caught thrilled me more than cutting the whore herself. As I write I find it impossible to believe he did not see me, in my estimation I was less than a few feet from him. The fool panicked, it is what saved me. My satisfaction was far from complete, damn the bastard, I cursed him and cursed him, but I was clever, they could not out do me. No one ever will.

Within minutes several police officers and bystanders gathered in the yard, which was still so dark that a match was needed to light the gruesome scene. Elizabeth Stride was lying on her back behind the gate. Her killer was gone.

∎ ∎ ∎

Perhaps Maybrick should not have been surprised that he had not been caught. Psychiatry was a new discipline in 1888, and forensic science hardly existed. Senior police officials understood something of the sexual basis of the Whitechapel killings, but they did not discuss the subject with their juniors. Even experienced crime reporters were not yet familiar with the concept of the psychopathic serial killer.

All the Whitechapel murders except one came within the jurisdiction of the Metropolitan Police. Founded in 1829, the department was responsible for all of London except the square mile of the City. The Met's area was then organized in divisions, H-Division being Whitechapel. As a result, the newspapers compared the Met unfavourably with the City Police – though, of course, neither force came close to catching the Ripper.

The Met officials were answerable to the Home Office, whose civil servants had considerable power and made many of the decisions for which the public blamed the police. For example, these bureaucrats forbade the offer of a government reward for anyone providing information that would lead to an arrest. The Home Secretary, Henry Matthews, was a witty man with a fine legal mind who, nevertheless, became unpopular because of the case. He managed to provoke the resignation of two Metropolitan Police commissioners during his tenure. (Less than a year after the murders, incidentally, Matthews was to find himself facing challenging decisions over the alleged murder of James Maybrick.)

One of those police commissioners was Sir Charles Warren. An Evangelical Christian and former soldier, he ruled with military precision and was still being pilloried by the press for his heavy-handed treatment of a mass demonstration against unemployment the year before. The *Star* wrote on September 10th: 'To add to the list of clumsy follies, Sir Charles Warren, whose name stinks in the nostrils of the people of London, has lately transferred the whole of the East End detectives to the West and transferred the West End team to the East.' This was an action that was to guarantee that the men on the ground had no knowledge or understanding of their new patches.

Inspector Frederick George Abberline was the best-known name on the case, probably because he had a well-developed sense of his own importance. But because he knew the area and its villains well, he was in charge of day-to-day investigations. It was Abberline whom Maybrick selected as the butt of his sarcasm.

Oh Mr Abberline, he is a clever little man

At the same time that Maybrick was escaping from Dutfield's Yard, Catharine Eddowes, the 46-year-old daughter of a Wolverhampton tin worker, was being released from Bishopsgate police station in the City of London. Earlier in the day she had pawned a pair of boots to pay for a cup of tea. But by 8.30 p.m. she was drunk and in custody for causing a disturbance by pretending to be a fire engine.

She left the police station at 1 a.m., when it was 'too late for you to get any more drink', said PC George Hutt.

'Good night, old cock,' she replied, and then turned left, in the direction of Houndsditch. About eight minutes later she must have been by the entrance to Duke Street, at the bottom of which was a covered alley called Church Passage, which led into Mitre Square.

Maybrick had probably left Berner Street, turned left into Commercial Road and left again along Whitechapel High Street in the direction of Middlesex Street. He did not go to his room, however, but continued into Aldgate, cleverly crossing the boundary dividing the jurisdictions of the Metropolitan Police and the City Police.

Desperate with frustration, he went at a fair pace, though not fast enough to attract attention. In today's heavy traffic the walk takes about 25 minutes, but then it probably took him a quarter of an hour.

At Church Passage, near the Minories, Maybrick's path crossed that of Catharine Eddowes, and at 1.35 they were seen talking together by Joseph Lawende. A Jewish cigarette salesman, Lawende was among those who identified Eddowes by her clothing at the mortuary. Lawende also described to investigators the man he had seen and a report appeared in *The Times* on October 2nd. It said that he was about 30 years old, 5 feet 7 inches, with a fair moustache and a cloth cap.

Once again Maybrick had apparently lured his prey into a corner. This time his frenzy was uninterrupted. He pushed Catharine Eddowes to the ground, strangled her and cut her throat. Then, with uncontrolled fury, he slashed and mutilated her face, cutting the eyelids, jaws and upper lips. The tip of the nose and parts of the ears were sliced away.

With depraved relish he ripped her stomach, tearing at internal organs, severing the intestines and separating the colon in a pile at her side. With a final flourish he carved two inverted Vs, one below each eye. At the time reports referred to triangular flaps. No one spotted that together they formed an 'M' – the 'M' that was by now his calling card, the 'M' of Maybrick.

First it had been found on Annie Chapman's envelope. Now he carved it in the flesh of his victim. He had had no time to leave his mark on or near Elizabeth Stride.

The 'M' is clearly visible in a drawing that was discovered in the basement of the London Hospital and eventually published for the first time in its magazine, the *London Hospital Gazette*, in 1966. It accompanied an article by pathologist Professor Francis Camps and a sketch made at the time of Catharine Eddowes's mutilated face. There, most clearly, is the 'M'.

Maybrick, too, is unambiguous.

> Her nose annoyed me so I cut it off, had a go
> at her eyes, left my mark, could not get
> the bitches head off.

Rummaging in his victim's deep skirt pockets, Maybrick found a comb and some small tins, which he opened. The red leather cigarette case left beside the body could well have been his. It was an unlikely item for an impoverished prostitute to carry.

Finding nothing of interest, he replaced it all and fled, taking Catharine Eddowes's uterus and one kidney. The body lay crumpled in the corner, where it was found by Police Constable Edward Watkins at 1.45 a.m. The police surgeon, Dr F. Gordon Brown, arrived on the scene at just after 2 o'clock.

The somewhat forlorn police list of Catharine Eddowes's clothing and few tawdry possessions reads like an entry in the diary itself. But in comparing the list and the diary, there are vital clues that were not available to the public at the time.

> One whore no good
> decided Sir Jim strike another

I showed no fright and indeed no light
damn it, the tin box was empty . . .
Sweet sugar and tea
could have paid my small fee
But instead I did flee
and by way showed my glee
By eating cold kidney for supper
bastard
Abberline
bonnett
hides all
clue
clever
will tell you more . . .
Sir Jim trip over
fear
have it near
redeem it near
case
poste haste
He believes I will trip over
but I have no fear
i cannot redeem it here * . . .
Am I not a clever fellow

The police list of Catharine Eddowes's possessions includes:

'a very old green alpaca skirt
very old ragged blue skirt
man's white vest
no drawers or stays
pair of men's lace up boots
1 Tin Box containing tea
1 Tin Box containing sugar
1 small Tooth Comb
1 Red Leather Cigarette Case with metal fittings
1 piece of old White Apron

1 mustard tin containing pawn tickets
1 Tin Match Box, empty'

Only three newspapers reported that a strand of cotton was found in one of the boxes. This was not included on the police list.

Could it have been the cotton merchant's idea of a 'very good clue'?

And then there was the 'one tin match box, empty'. This apparently insignificant item was the clue that most dramatically impressed the Ripperology team. It was a fact not mentioned at all in any newspapers at the time. It was only referred to in the official police list, not opened to the public until 1984 and which is now with the City of London Archives.

The first published account of the list appeared in books by Donald Rumbelow and Martin Fido, both published in 1987. On October 6th 1888 *The Times* had reported on page 6:

> There was also found upon her a piece of string, a common white handkerchief with a red border, a match box with cotton in it, a white linen pocket containing a white bone handle table knife, very blunt (with no blood upon it), two short clay pipes, a red cigarette case with white metal fittings, a printed handbill with the name 'Frank Cater, 405 Bethnal Green Road' upon it, a check pocket containing five pieces of soap, a small tin box containing tea and sugar, a portion of a pair of spectacles, a three cornered check handkerchief and a large white linen pocket containing a small comb, a red button and a bag of worsted.

No mention of the 'tin matchbox, empty'. We have scoured the papers – as any forger would have had to do to pick up this throwaway item from the Coroner's report.

In statements at different times after Florie's trial, her mother and Maybrick's friend, George Bancroft, referred to the container in which he kept his drugs. The Baroness wrote to Lord Asquith of James using a 'tin box'; Bancroft says he saw him take powders from a cigarette case.

Either way, the explosive diary comment 'damn it, the tin box was empty' and his reference to the case mean that both these items found near the body of Catharine Eddowes had personal significance for James Maybrick.

．　．　．

From Mitre Square, where Catharine Eddowes was found, to Middlesex Street is but a short walk. But Maybrick could not take the direct route. Middlesex Street would soon be busy with stallholders setting up for the day.

Noted the *Morning Advertiser*: 'Many people would be about the immediate neighbourhood even at this early hour, making preparations for the market which takes place every Sunday in Middlesex Street, and the adjoining thoroughfares.'

It would have been safer for Maybrick to take the roundabout route into Goulston Street and double back. He headed down Stoney Lane, across the main road and into a parallel side street almost opposite it. This led into Goulston Street.

Perhaps a sudden need to hide forced Maybrick into the arched doorway of number 108-19. (PC Alfred Long had passed that way at 2.20 a.m. and saw nothing.) The unlit common stairs led up to a landing out of sight. There, in the gloom, he wiped his bloodstained knife and faeces-stained hands on a scrap of material torn from Catharine Eddowes's apron. It was then that he used the chalk. The message he wrote on the wall in that doorway was to become one of the most elusive and baffling of all the Ripper's clues, a focus of argument for more than a century.

Goulston Street was in Metropolitan Police territory, and Mitre Square, where Catharine Eddowes was killed, was under City Police control. So there was, the police admitted, catastrophic confusion following this second killing of the evening. In the uproar Maybrick escaped again.

At 2.55 a.m. PC Long returned and noticed the crumpled rag lying at the foot of the stair. He then saw the smudged graffito on the wall and realized that the Ripper must have been there. He copied what he saw, though he admitted at the inquest that he could have made a mistake when spelling the word 'Jews'. His note read:

The Juwes are the men who will not be blamed for nothing.

The City Police recorded a different message:

The Juwes are not the men who will be blamed for nothing.

The City CID instructed that the message be photographed immediately and then obliterated. After all, it was their murder. But Superintendent Thomas Arnold, who was in charge of the Goulston Street area, was terrified that, because of its anti-Semitic nature, the message might cause trouble among residents.

When the Metropolitan Police Commissioner, Sir Charles Warren, arrived on the scene at 5 a.m., he agreed with Arnold and personally rubbed out the offending words.

Crime writers have devoted a great deal of energy to the so far thankless task of solving the riddle on the Goulston Street wall. The diary suggests a different possibility.

I had to laugh they have me down as left handed a doctor, a slaughter man and a Jew. Very well, if they are to insist I am a Jew then a Jew I shall be.

So a Jew he became. Significantly, too, the phrasing recalls his earlier, *Punch*-inspired verse:

The jews and the doctors
Will get all the blame

In a report to the Home Office of November 6th 1888, Metropolitan Police Commissioner Sir Charles Warren enclosed a copy of the writing on the wall. The form and layout of the words has been exactly reproduced, so it is reasonable to assume that it is a good copy. The bizarre spelling of 'Juwes', with its five letters, significant 'e' and inverted 'm', strongly suggests that Maybrick was willing to risk writing 'James' on the wall, in a form that would be read as 'Juwes'. From the several anti-Semitic remarks in the diary, it can be safely assumed that Maybrick would have been more than happy to fuel the growing public speculation that a Jew was to blame for the murders in Whitechapel. Could this be 'my funny jewish joke'?

These taunting games were but a prelude. For the next day – Monday, October 1st – was the day the world would first hear the name Jack the Ripper.

EIGHT

'Before I am finished all England will know the name I have given myself'

THE LETTER, WHICH was dated September 25th, was published in the first edition of the *Daily News* on October 1st. It was to become perhaps the most infamous letter in the history of crime.

Had it not been for that letter, written in red ink, the Whitechapel murders might have been relegated in time to a place alongside the many equally horrific crimes in police Black Museums or Madame Tussaud's Chamber of Horrors. But Maybrick's new – and inspired – name gave him the fame he craved. He would never be forgotten.

> Dear Boss,
>
> I keep on hearing the police have caught me but they wont fix me just yet. I have laughed when they look so clever and talk about being on the <u>right</u> track. That joke about Leather Apron gave me real fits. I am down on whores and I shant quit ripping them till I do get buckled. Grand work the last job was. I gave the lady no time to squeal. How can they catch me now. I love my work and want to start again. You will soon hear of me with my funny litle games. I saved some of the proper <u>red</u> stuff in a ginger beer bottle over the last job to write with but it went thick like glue and I cant use it. Red ink is fit enough I hope <u>ha. ha.</u> The next job I do I shall clip the ladys ears off and send to the police officers just for jolly wouldn't you. Keep this letter back till I do a bit more work, then give it out straight. My knife's so nice and sharp I want to get to work right away if I get a chance. Good luck.
>
> > Yours truly
> > Jack the Ripper
>
> Dont mind me giving the trade name.

A second postscript ran down the side of the letter and read:

> Wasnt good enough to post this before I got all the red ink off my hands curse it No luck yet. They say I'm a doctor now. <u>ha ha</u>

The letter was forwarded to police headquarters at Scotland Yard on Saturday, September 29th. A covering letter from the editor to Chief

Constable Adolphus Williamson said: 'The Editor presents his compliments to Mr Williamson and begs to inform him the enclosed was sent to the Central News [Agency] two days ago and was treated as a joke.'

The text of the letter was published in the 2 a.m. edition of the *Liverpool Daily Post* and in the 5 a.m. edition of the *Daily News* in London on Monday October 1st.

That same Monday morning, the Central News Agency received a postcard written in red crayon and postmarked October 1st. Posted in the East End of London, it referred to the two murders that had occurred within less than an hour in Whitechapel early on September 30th, and said:

> I was not codding dear old Boss when I gave you the tip, you'll hear about Saucy Jacky's work tomorrow double event this time number one squealed a bit couldn't finish straight off. had not the time to get ears for police. thanks for keeping last letter back till I got to work again.
>
> Jack the Ripper

The text of the card was printed in the *Star* in the 1 p.m. edition on October 1st.

The fact that one of the ears of the Mitre Square victim was partially severed was known to very few people during the Sunday immediately following the crime and was only publicized when the story made the newspapers on Monday. Because the references to ear-ripping – as well as the same mannerisms and chilling signature – figured in both, it was assumed at the time that the letter and card must have been written by the same person.

The idea has taken root in the minds of most recent writers on the Ripper that the card was written by a copy-cat and that in those days of frequent and excellent postal services it would have been possible for a hoaxer to read the 5 a.m. newspaper account of the crime and send a prank card to make the midday edition. They have missed the conclusive evidence proving that the writer of the card could not have copied the handwriting style and signature of the 'Dear Boss' letter. At that stage the letter had only appeared in type. A facsimile of the handwriting was not published by any newspaper until two days later.

At 12.45 on the morning after Elizabeth Stride and Catharine Eddowes died, a short, one-inch-wide, round-ended knife was found outside Mr Christmas's shop in Whitechapel Road. Police surgeon Dr George Bagster Phillips claimed this knife might have been the murder weapon and could have belonged to Elizabeth Stride: many prostitutes carried knives for self-protection. Until now researchers mistakenly dated the discovery of the knife to two days before the murders. Dramatically, the diarist gets it right again. Most modern authorities agree that the knife that killed Elizabeth Stride was not the long, narrow, sharp-pointed weapon that mutilated the other four Whitechapel prostitutes, but a knife very similar to the one found in Whitechapel Road. It was in this very postal district where the 'Saucy Jack' card was posted later the same morning.

Maybrick makes a startling reference which confirms he used a second knife belonging to Elizabeth Stride. In two lines, deleted because they apparently displeased him, Maybrick says:

My shiny knife *
the whore's knife *

Together the letter and the card provoked a flood of about 2,000 copy-cat communications, which have never been fully investigated.

But at the time and for many years afterwards many of the police in charge were convinced of their authenticity; so much so that they issued a facsimile poster of the card and the letter, printed in red, which was circulated to every police station in the country on October 3rd.

Chief Inspector Henry Moore was probably the link between Abberline in Whitechapel and Chief Inspector Swanson at Scotland Yard. In 1896 he wrote a report which implies that, at the time, those involved with the case took the letters seriously and believed that the writer of the 'Dear Boss' letter and postcard was Jack the Ripper.

More than 20 years later, Sir Robert Anderson was to stir up a hornets' nest over the matter. He wrote in his autobiography, serialized in *Blackwood's Magazine* in 1910: 'The Jack the Ripper letter which is preserved in the Police Museum in Scotland Yard is the work of an enterprising London journalist.' However, he may not have been referring to the 'Dear Boss' letter. This letter was so closely linked with the 'Saucy Jacky' postcard, and it is unlikely that Anderson would have omitted to mention the card in his comment. We do not know which of the many Jack the Ripper letters was preserved at that time in the Police Museum. In a footnote Anderson wrote: 'I should be almost tempted to disclose the identity . . . of the pressman who wrote the letter', adding, as though to protect his uncertainty, 'provided that the publishers would accept all responsibility in view of a possible libel action.' Clearly the publishers did not believe they could offer the classic defence in libel cases: that the accusation was true.

Another two decades after this, a former *Star* journalist named Best, then 70 years old, told a colleague that he had written all the letters 'to keep the business alive'. He claimed he had done it with a provincial newspaper journalist and that they had used a flattened Waverley nib to give the appearance of semi-literacy. According to Sue Iremonger, our forensic document examiner, the 'Dear Boss' letter was definitely not written with a flattened Waverley nib.

In 1993 a letter came to light that was written in 1913 by Detective Inspector John Littlechild, who was head of Special Branch in the year of the murders. It is understood that he names journalists who were believed to have written the Jack the Ripper letters, including the 'Dear Boss' letter and the 'Saucy Jacky' postcard of October 1st. Research on the letter is currently in progress. But, however impeccable their reputations, the police at that time were indulging in a great deal of speculation on very little hard information.

The *Daily Telegraph* wrote on October 4th 1888: 'The post card appears to have been scribbled hastily and the hand is not so firm as that of the letter but there is very little doubt both came from the same pen.'

Commenting on the handwriting styles, David Forshaw considers that the handwriting of the diary reflects the true inner feelings of Maybrick, who was not a natural letter writer, whereas the style of the letter and postcard – which he believes could be by the same hand – is contrived to impress. It is also self-evident that if these and other communications intended for police scrutiny and public consumption were written by the murderer he would have made every effort to disguise his natural style.

The use of language in the letter repeatedly echoes that of the diary. 'Down on whores', 'the red stuff' and the 'funny little games' is

Maybrick talking. The hollow, sinister, underlined 'ha ha' of the diary and the letters is Maybrick mocking.

Sir Arthur Conan Doyle, when asked how Sherlock Holmes would solve the Ripper mystery, replied that he would look for a killer with connections in America. The reason, again, was the language. The Americanisms 'Dear Boss', 'fix me' and 'shan't quit' would all have been familiar expressions to Maybrick, not only from his days in Norfolk but from his American wife.

Finally there is this diary entry claiming authorship of two communications and various verses sent to the press.

Before my next will send Central another to remember me by.

Even more dramatic than the 'Dear Boss' letter was an undated letter posted in Liverpool that has, sadly, disappeared from Scotland Yard files. (In 1966 Professor Francis Camps said in an article in the *London Hospital Gazette* that the Liverpool letter was received before publication of the 'Dear Boss' letter.) It was first publicized in 1927, in J. Hall Richardson's book *From City to Fleet Street*. It apparently forecasts the killings about to happen in London.

Beware I shall be at work on the 1st and 2nd inst. in the Minories at 12 midnight and I give the authorities a good chance but there is never a policeman near when I am at work. Yours Jack the Ripper.

The expression 'inst' was used in commerce to mean 'of this month'. When used in September it cannot refer to a date in October. To the self-made businessman Maybrick, the use of officialese might well have been a badge of pride. He simply got it wrong.

Catharine Eddowes was indeed found murdered near the Minories on September 30th. The predicted dates of October 1st and 2nd were a day out. The assumption need not be that the letter was therefore a hoax, but perhaps that, in the style of terrorist warnings today, Maybrick wanted the police to know that the message was genuine, without giving enough away for the crime to be averted or the killer caught.

The second part of the 'Liverpool letter' was equally important.

What fools the police are. I even give them the name of the street where I am living. Prince William Street.

Prince William Street is in one of Liverpool's poorest areas, Toxteth. In 1888 it was lined with tenement lodgings used by ladies described as 'our disillusioned sisters of the pavement'.

Maybrick knew Prince William Street well. It was yards off the main road between Aigburth and his office.

The police response to the double murder was massive. Some 80,000 handbills were distributed requesting information, 2,000 lodgers were questioned in a house-to-house enquiry and plainclothes officers mingled with the customers of the East End's pubs and lodging houses.

On October 2nd the *Evening News* was very near the mark when it reported: 'A belief is gaining ground that the murderer is not a frequenter of common lodging houses, but that he occupies a single room or perhaps finds refuge in an empty warehouse. He is supposed to make his home somewhere between Middlesex Street and Brick Lane.'

Four days later the *Liverpool Echo* reported anxiously beneath the headline, 'The Whitechapel Murders': 'There can be no doubt that the police are coming to the conclusion that the Whitechapel murderer is not in that district and did not live there at the time of the murders.'

The *Liverpool Daily Post* carried a story on October 11th with the headline, 'Alleged Liverpool Clue'. It read: 'A certain detective of the Criminal Investigation Department has recently journeyed to Liverpool and there traced the movements of a man, which have been proved of a somewhat mysterious kind. The height of this person and his description are fully ascertained and amongst other things he was in possession of a black leather bag. This person suddenly left Liverpool for London and for some time occupied apartments in a well known first class hotel in the West End.' The story claimed that the man was in the habit of visiting the poorest parts of the East End and that he left behind in the hotel his black leather bag containing certain items of clothing, documents and 'prints of an obscene description'. 'It has been suggested that the mysterious person referred to landed in Liverpool from America,' it said.

According to the custom of the day, the hotel – the Charing Cross – had advertised in *The Times*, appealing for owners of lost property to claim their belongings. Paul Feldman traced that advertisement to June 14th 1888. There, among the list of names, was one S. E. Mibrac. This highly unusual name was almost certainly yet another of James Maybrick's name-juggling games, the primary purpose of which would have been to disguise his true identity.

Meanwhile the Metropolitan Police kept Israel Schwartz, the prime witness to the assault on Elizabeth Stride, out of harm's way, just as the City Police were keeping an eye on Joseph Lawende, who had described a man like Maybrick talking to Catharine Eddowes.

On October 6th a badly spelt, threatening letter was posted in 'London NW'. It was in a well-formed hand, similar in style to the first 'Dear Boss' letter.

6 October 1888
You though your-self very clever I reckon when you informed the police. But you made a mistake if you though I dident see you. Now I know you know me and I see your little game, and I mean to finish you and send your ears to your wife if you show this to the police or help them if you do I will finish you. It no use your trying to get out of my way. Because I have you when you dont expect it and I keep my word as you soon see and rip you up. Yours truly Jack the Ripper.

This letter remained undisturbed in Home Office files at the Public Record Office until it was uncovered by my publisher, Robert Smith, in the course of the present investigation. The 'Dear Boss' letter, the 'Saucy Jacky' postcard and this letter are all reproduced in the second plate section of this book. We can speculate that the letter was intended for either Schwartz or Lawende, who had given descriptions generally believed by the police to be of Jack the Ripper. It was sent from the postal district of Michael Maybrick's chambers in Regent's Park, where Maybrick often stayed. Anna Koren and Sue Iremonger agree that this letter is in the same hand as the 'Dear Boss' letter. The language of this letter is marked by the same vindictive fury that Maybrick shows later in the diary towards a suspected witness.

Damn it damn it damn it the bastard almost caught

me, curse him to hell I will cut him up next time, so
help me. A few minutes and I would have done, <u>bastard</u>.
I will seek him out, teach him a lesson.

On that same day, October 6th, the *Daily Telegraph* had published an artist's impression and description of the man the police were seeking in connection with the Whitechapel murders. It also appeared in the *Liverpool Echo* two days later. There is undeniably a resemblance to Maybrick. This image is reproduced in the second plate section. According to the newspaper description, the man was of education and means, probably about 40 years of age, with dark clothes and a dark silk handkerchief round his neck. 'His hat is probably a dark 'stiff' bowler and his appearance entirely respectable. His manner is quiet and composed and there is nothing to betray the monomaniac, except a certain mingled restlessness and cunning in the expression of the eyes.'

October 6th was a Saturday, the day of the week which appears to be pivotal to all five Whitechapel murders. Did Maybrick return to stay with Michael the weekend after the double murder, was shocked by what he read in the morning papers and feel prompted to write to Joseph Lawende, Israel Schwartz or another equally worrying witness? Lawende had seen Maybrick with Catharine Eddowes. The City Police regarded him as a key witness and gave him protection from the press prior to the inquest held on October 4th and 11th. The City Solicitor requested: 'Unless the jury want it, I have a special reason for not giving details as to the appearance of the man.' The coroner agreed and Lawende described only the suspect's clothes. If Lawende could identify the Ripper, as the police believed, and Maybrick had seen the picture in the press, he would have had every reason to fear and threaten him.

. . .

Back home with his family after the double murder on September 30th, Maybrick watched and waited. As always, the thoughts of Florie and her lover both titillated and enraged him. A lonely man, sick in mind and body, he turned once more for solace to his best friend, George Davidson.

Tonight I will celebrate by wining and dining George. I am in a good mood, believe I will allow the whore the pleasure of her whore master, will remark an evening in the city will do her good, will suggest a concert. I have no doubt the carriage will take the bitch straight to him. I will go to sleep thinking about all they are doing. I cannot wait for the thrill.

On October 12th the *Manchester Guardian* carried a disturbing story about an event that had taken place in Liverpool. 'On Wednesday evening, a young woman was walking along Sheil Road, Liverpool, not far from Sheil Park. She was stopped by an elderly woman, aged about 60, who in an agitated and excited manner urged her most earnestly not to go into the park. She explained that a few minutes earlier she had been resting on one of the seats in the park when she was accosted by a respectable-looking gentleman in a black coat, light trousers and a soft felt hat, who enquired if she knew any loose women in the neighbourhood and immediately afterwards produced a knife with a long, thin blade and stated he intended to kill as many women in Liverpool as in London, adding that he would send the ears of the first victim to the editor of a Liverpool paper. The old woman, who was trembling violently as she related this story, stated that she was so terribly frightened, she hardly knew how she got away from this man.'

She never knew that she might have been face to face with Jack the Ripper himself.

. . .

On October 15th, newspapers in Leeds reported that Jack the Ripper had been seen in Chorley, a small town a few miles north of Liverpool. The following day, George Lusk, president of the Whitechapel Vigilance Committee, found a three-inch-square cardboard box in his mail. Inside was half a human kidney preserved in spirits of wine, along with a barely intelligible letter that has since disappeared.

From hell.
Mr Lusk,
Sor
I send you half the Kidne I took from one woman and prasarved it

for you tother piece I fried and ate it was very nise. I may send you
the bloody knif that took it out if you only wate a whil longer

signed

Catch me when you can Mishter Lusk.

The medical experts disagreed. The City pathologist, Dr Sedgwick
Saunders, said at the time that the kidney did not belong to Catharine
Eddowes and that it was probably a hospital specimen, while Dr
Openshaw, Curator of the Pathology Museum at the London Hospital,
declared it to be the 'ginny' kidney of a 45-year-old woman with Bright's
disease. Although the Lusk incident was reported in the *Star* on October
19th, it is not mentioned in the diary. There was no need. The kidney
was not there because Maybrick tells us he had eaten it.

> Sweet sugar and tea
> Could have paid my small fee
> But instead I did flee and by way showed my glee
> By eating cold kidney for supper.

David Forshaw believes that Maybrick may, like other serial killers,
have cannibalized parts of his victims to assert absolute power over
them. It is possible that the Ripper believed, like some primitive
cannibal tribes, that eating human remains was a magical way of gaining
power, perhaps some sort of life-force from the dead person. Later in the
diary, as his behaviour grew less controllable, Maybrick had nightmares
and wrote of cooking Florie and serving her up to the children.

During the summer, Florie had been to see Dr Hopper. She
expressed her deep anxiety that her husband was taking some 'very
strong medicine which had a bad effect on him' and that he always
seemed worse after each dose. She begged the doctor to speak to him
and stop him. Her concern eventually produced a backlash in October,
the month of Maybrick's 50th birthday.

> The whore has informed the bumbling buffoon I am in the habit of
> taking strong medicine. I was furious when the bitch told me. So
> furious I hit her. ha. The whore begged me not to do so again. It
> was a pleasure a great deal of pleasure. If it was not for my work, I
> would have cut the bitch up there and then. . . . It has been far too

long since my last, I have been unwell. The whole of my body has pained. . . . Will visit the city of whores soon, very soon. I wonder if I could do three?

Maybrick was a man given to explosion under stress and if this was, as he indicated, the first time he had hit Florie, it was not to be the last.

Michael was now also concerned about his dissolute brother's health and, according to the diary, wrote several letters during October enquiring, in particular, about Maybrick's 'sleepwalking' problems. It is possible that Michael already had his suspicions about his brother and that sleepwalking was a euphemism masking his awareness of something far more sinister.

October was not a good month for Maybrick. His supply of drugs was intermittent; nor was he deriving from them the strength they usually gave him, which he needed to commit murder. He had temporarily lost control. There were no murders that month, and so there was no reason to write in his diary. He put aside his pen for three or four weeks. At the end of the month he writes again:

It has been far too long since my last, I have been unwell.

The age of 50 is for many people, especially men, a traumatic watershed. For a man like James Maybrick, the reality of his declining health and sexual prowess must have been a nightmare. On October 24th James Maybrick reached that watershed – he was 50. His morale was crumbling. During the second week in November, he went to London and stayed at Michael's home in Regent's Park. He had planned to go over to Whitechapel, but something went very wrong. Despite all efforts, Maybrick's ordeal must have been heard all over the apartment that night.

I was forced to stop myself from indulging in my pleasure by taking the largest dose I have ever done. The pain that night has burnt into my mind. I vaguely recall putting a handkerchief in my mouth to stop my cries. I believe I vomited several times. The pain was intolerable, as I think I shudder. No more.

I am convinced God placed me here to kill all whores, for he must have done so, am I still not here. Nothing will stop me now. The more I take the more stronger I become. Michael was under the impression that once I had finished my business I was to return to Liverpool that very day. And indeed I did one day later. <u>ha ha</u> . . .

So it was that on Friday, November 9th, all England was sickened by the unbelievable bestiality of one of the most depraved murders ever committed.

NINE

'God placed me here to kill all whores'

MARY JANE KELLY was only about 25, almost the same age as Florie Maybrick. Like Florie, and unlike the other victims of the Ripper, she was pretty. Indeed, with her reddish hair, the resemblance to his wife must have been overwhelming when Maybrick spotted her walking down Commercial Street past Thrawl Street in what the local vicar the Reverend Samuel Barnett called 'the wicked quarter mile'. Florie was almost certainly the person Maybrick had in his mind when he attacked Kelly with a ferocity unprecedented even by his demented standards.

Mary Jane Kelly had spent the afternoon and early evening of Thursday, November 8th, with friends, but her home was 13 Miller's Court. She rented a tiny partitioned ground-floor back room with Joe Barnett, an unemployed porter.

That evening, a neighbour, Lizzie Albrook, who also lived in Miller's Court, had dropped in for a chat. As she left, Kelly's poignant, parting words to the younger girl were: 'Whatever you do, don't you do wrong and turn out as I have.'

Mary Jane Kelly was in a musical mood that night, disturbing the neighbours by singing loudly in her room. The tune they remembered was a typically sentimental Victorian ballad: 'Only A Violet I Plucked From My Mother's Grave.'

In the small hours of the morning, George Hutchinson of the Victoria Home in Commercial Street was returning from Romford, in Essex. He saw a man approach Kelly, who was looking for trade. Hutchinson was probably a former client so knew her well: he sometimes gave her money, but this time he had none left. Hutchinson later told the Commercial Street police: 'About 2 a.m. 9th (November) just before I got to Flower and Dean Street, I met the murdered woman Kelly . . . a man coming in the opposite direction to Kelly, tapped her on the shoulder and said something to her they both burst out laughing. I heard her say alright to him and the man said you will be alright for what I have told you: he then placed his right hand around her shoulders. He also had a kind of small parcel in his left hand, with a kind of strap round it. I stood against the lamp of the Queen's Head Public House, and watched him.'

Hutchinson's description of the man is suspiciously detailed. Had they met before? He was, Hutchinson told the police officers questioning him, of a dark, 'foreign' appearance, wearing a long, dark coat with astrakhan collar and cuffs; a dark jacket and trousers; dark felt hat 'turned down in the middle'; light, button-over boots with dark spats; a linen collar; and a black tie with a horseshoe pin. A massive gold chain was displayed over his waistcoat, and his watch chain had a large seal with a red stone hanging from it. He carried a pair of kid gloves and a small package. He was 34 or 35 years old, 5 feet 7 inches tall, with a pale complexion and a slight moustache.

Horseshoe tie pins and thick gold chains were popular at the time. There are also magazine pictures of Michael Maybrick wearing a horseshoe pin. The first photograph in the first plate section in this book appears to show that Maybrick not only wore a thick gold chain but also sported a tie pin with a horseshoe or similar design.

At any rate, when he left Michael for work on Thursday, Maybrick was respectably dressed in business clothes.

'They both then came past me and the man hung down his head, with his hat over his eyes,' Hutchinson said. 'I stooped down and looked him in the face. He looked at me stern. She said alright my dear come along you *will* be comfortable. They both went into Dorset Street. I followed them. They both stood at the corner of the court for about three minutes. He said something to her. He then placed his arm on her shoulder and gave her a kiss. She said she had lost her handkerchief. He then pulled his handkerchief, a red one and gave it to her. They both then went up Miller's Court together. I then went up the Court to see if I could see them but I could not. I stood there for about three-quarters of an hour, to see if they came out. They did not, so at 3.a.m. I went away.'

Mary Jane Kelly led the way through the arch and down the passage. It was too narrow to walk side by side. Her room was just 12 feet square, and there was scarcely space to open the door, since the bed and small table occupied most of what meagre space there was. The window by the door was broken.

There is no way of knowing exactly what happened in those dreadful hours before the body of Mary Jane Kelly was found. Neighbours thought they heard a cry of 'murder' at around 4 a.m. They did nothing, for such cries were frequent in that violent neighbourhood and were commonly ignored.

The feeble light of the single candle was not enough to see by, so

Maybrick used a hat and some clothes to make a fire. For a short while they burned brightly enough in the grate. By the time he had finished, there was virtually nothing recognizable left of the young woman he had met two hours earlier. Someone was heard leaving the room at about 5.45 a.m.

It is almost impossible to imagine the butchery that took place that night in the cramped hovel, and Maybrick was haunted by nightmares to the end of his life. Mary Jane Kelly's injuries were so appalling that no one could be certain if there had been a struggle. Nick Warren, editor of *Ripperana*, has observed that cuts on her hands indicate that she had in fact tried to fend off her attacker. The police surgeon, Dr Thomas Bond, reported at the inquest: 'The corner sheet to the right of the woman's head was much cut and saturated with blood, indicating that the face may have been covered with a sheet at the time of the attack.'

Dr Bond also speculated that 'the murderer is quite likely to be a quiet, inoffensive looking man, probably middle-aged and neatly dressed'.

At 10.45 a.m. that Friday, Thomas Bowyer called to collect Mary Jane Kelly's rent. He could not believe what he saw through the broken window and ran for help. He returned with John McCarthy, who was Kelly's landlord and owned the local grocery. The two peered in nervously. 'It looked more like the work of a devil than of man,' said McCarthy.

Not until 1.30 p.m. did the police finally break open the door with a pick-axe handle. In the grate was the remains of the fire in which Maybrick had burned the clothing, including a bonnet. On the bed was an unrecognizable body; everywhere was blood.

The appalling mutilation of Mary Jane Kelly is detailed in an unemotional report by Dr Bond which disappeared around 1911 and was only rediscovered in 1987. 'The whole surface of the abdomen and thighs was removed and the abdominal cavity emptied of its viscera. The breasts were cut off, the arms mutilated by several jagged wounds and the face hacked beyond recognition of the features. The tissues of the neck were severed all round to the bone.

'The viscera were found in various parts viz; the uterus and kidneys with one breast under the head, the other breast by the rt foot, the liver between the feet, the intestines by the right side and the spleen by the left side of the body. The flaps removed from the abdomen and thighs were on a table.'

In the post-mortem account the police surgeon adds: 'The face was gashed in all directions, the nose, cheeks, eyebrows and ears being partly removed.'

After the greatest frenzy of his murderous career, Maybrick's recollection of events was accurate in all essentials, but not surprisingly, given the orgy of mutilation he had indulged in, he was confused over one of the details – where he had left her breasts.

> I left nothing of the bitch, nothing. I placed it all over the room, time was on my hands, like the other whore I cut off the bitches nose all of it this time. I left nothing of her face to remember her by . . . I thought it a joke when I cut her breasts off, kissed them for awhile. The taste of blood was sweet, the pleasure was overwhelming, will have to do it again. It thrilled me so. Left them on the table with some of the other stuff. Thought they belonged there. They wanted a slaughterman so I stripped what I could, laughed while I was doing so. like the other bitches she ripped like a ripe peach.

This placing of the breasts appears to tally with incorrect press accounts. The *Pall Mall Gazette* of November 10th 1888 reported under the headline: 'The Seventh Murder in Whitechapel. Story of unparalleled atrocity':

> The breasts had also been cleanly cut off and placed on the table which was by the side of the bed . . . the kidneys and heart had also been removed from the body and placed by the side of the breasts.

Other, similar reports appeared: in *The Times* of November 10th, the *Star* of November 10th and the *Pall Mall Budget* of November 15th.

The diary entry for this murder has been the focus of much discussion for it appears to repeat the mistakes made in the press by referring to the breasts on the table. Critics claim that this proves the diarist was gathering his material from newspaper sources, that he was a fraud because, had he been in Mary Jane Kelly's room that night, he would have remembered where he placed the breasts.

But would he? Maybrick says in the diary: 'I have read about my latest.' We know he was eagerly scouring the press for details of his deeds. Dr David Forshaw's view is that the ecstasy of what he was experiencing left the murderer unable to remember his frenzied movements accurately. When the newspapers later said he had placed the breasts on the table, then that was what he would have assumed to be the truth.

However, what really convinces me that this apparent error of fact is only a trick of the Ripper's mind, is that, within a few days of the murder, when the frenzy has subsided, he does begin to recall in his diary what he did with the breasts. In one of his rhymes, in which he speaks of kissing the severed breasts, he writes: 'I thought of leaving them by the whore's feet.' He now begins to accord with Dr Bond's recently discovered autopsy report, where we learn that the Ripper did indeed place one breast 'by the rt foot'.

Maybrick's account of Mary Kelly's murder continues with his disappointment at having failed, as in the previous mutilations, to decapitate his victim despite a strenuous attempt.

One of these days I <u>will</u> take the head away with me, I will boil it and serve it up for my supper.

This in turn is followed by an entry that, on first sight, appears to be a disconnected, even poetic flow of thought. In fact, this should be read not from left to right but top to bottom, so that the verse becomes a game of word association.

key	rip
flee	initial
hat	
handkerchief	whore master
whim	look to the whore
mother	light
father	fire

with the key I did flee*

> I had the key
> the clothes I burnt*
> along with the hat*
> the hat I did burn
> for light I did yearn
> for the sake of the whoring mother*
> and I thought of the whoring mother . . .
> a handkerchief red
> led to the bed
> and I thought of the whoring mother

At this point the diary poses a question. The police had to break into Mary Jane Kelly's room. All the newspapers reported that the key had been lost before the murder. But Joe Barnett stated that it was then found, so substantiating Maybrick's claim that he left with it. A few days after the murder, one newspaper reported that the key was now in the possession of the police. The rational explanation is that he locked the door behind him and once well clear, tossed the key away.

A police photographer recorded the murder scene. Considering the circumstances and the murky drizzle and gloom outside, his efforts were remarkable. The picture first appeared the following year in the book *Vacher L'Eventreur et les crimes sadiques* by J. A. E. Lacassagne.

In 1988 the crime researcher and writer Simon Wood mentioned privately to one of our consultants that in a photograph of the dead Mary Jane Kelly on her bed there appeared to be an initial on the wall. There, above the bed, is a letter 'M' – the mark of Maybrick. To the side is another letter, 'F'. The smudgy letters could easily have been written in blood.

> An initial here and an initial there
> will tell of the whoring mother
> I left it there for the fools but they will never find it. Left it in front
> for all eyes to see. Shall I write and tell them? That amuses me
> She reminded me of the whore. So young unlike I.

After the four much older and unattractive previous victims, Maybrick had finally sought an attractive prostitute of the same age as his wife.

Mary Jane Kelly had paid the price for the indiscretions of the unhappy wife, 'the whoring mother', 250 miles away. Maybrick had identified the prostitute with his wife, whose initials he had daubed on the wall. The style of the capital 'M', with its smaller first half, is unmistakably the same as the 'M' used throughout the diary. This photograph of Mary Jane Kelly has been reproduced in countless books, yet 'the fools' never found it. To be fair, only in Stephen Knight's *Jack the Ripper: The Final Solution* was the picture reproduced well enough to show the initials of Florie Maybrick. The original police photograph and an enlargement of it, reproduced in the first plate section in this book, shows a faint 'F' alongside the 'M'.

There was also a dramatic, unpublicized aspect to the Kelly case. It was the subject of one of the last pages in the journal. Knowing that he is going to die, Maybrick is thinking back to his deeds. Only one of the women he has killed has any identity for him. For the first and last time he mentions her by name and then only by surname.

> I will pray for the women I have slaughtered. May God forgive me for the deeds I commited on Kelly. No heart no heart

His anguished cry expresses the torment of a man who saw in Kelly the wife, whom he believed had betrayed him. In his rediscovered report on Mary Jane Kelly, Dr Bond states: 'The pericardium was open below and the heart absent.' He does not say exactly where the heart had been placed, but he does say the murderer covered her face before killing her.

. . .

After the Kelly murder there was a sudden change in police tactics. Hutchinson's statement, along with those of Lawende and Schwartz, provided the most detailed description of the killer so far. Indeed, Hutchinson would tell reporters that he went out hunting Mary Jane Kelly's killer on the following Sunday, November 11th. Despite a choking fog he was sure he recognized the man he had seen with Kelly – in Middlesex Street.

After Hutchison's statement was released, Paul Feldman discovered that the Press Association news agency reported a new line of investigation by the police: 'The Whitechapel murderer is supposed to travel up from Manchester, Birmingham or some other town in the Midlands for the purpose of committing the crimes. Detectives have been engaged in Willesden and Euston watching the arrival of trains from the Midlands and the north.'

Willesden Junction and Euston were London stations served by trains to and from Liverpool, as well as from Manchester and Birmingham.

Maybrick now began to contemplate a new and terrifying reality: he might be caught.

> I cannot live without my medicine. I am afraid to go to sleep for fear of my nightmares reoccuring. I see thousands of people chasing me, with Abberline in front dangling a rope.

Little wonder that during November his headaches worsened and he added yet another doctor to his overcrowded team of medical consultants. Dr J. Drysdale was an elderly Scotsman, neat in appearance and sparing of words. Maybrick consulted the Liverpool doctor on November 19th, 22nd and 26th, and again on December 5th and 10th, telling him that for three months he had endured pains from one side of his head to the other, which were preceded by a pain in the right side of the head and a dull headache. He said he was never free from pain except sometimes in the morning. If he smoked or drank too much, he experienced a numbness on the left side of his hand and his leg and was liable to suffer from an eruption of the skin on his hands. He said nothing about drugging himself.

'He seemed to be suffering from nervous dyspepsia,' was Dr. Drysdale's diagnosis, which he repeated when giving evidence at Florie's trial. With masterly understatement, he added: 'I should say he was hypochondriacal.'

It was perhaps natural that with all of London on his scent Maybrick decided to return to the safer scene of his first killing, Manchester, where his brother Thomas lived.

> I am tired and I fear the city of whores has become too dangerous for I to return. Christmas is approaching and Thomas has invited

me to visit him. I know him well. I have decided to accept his offer although I know the motive behind it will strictly be business, Thomas thinks of nothing else except money unlike me <u>ha ha</u>.

My first was in Manchester so why not my next? If I was to do the same as the last that would throw the fools into a panick especially that fool Abberline. The children constantly ask what I shall be buying them for Christmas. they shy away when I tell them a shiny knife not unlike Jack the Rippers in order that I cut their tongues for peace and quiet. I do believe I am completely mad. I have never harmed the children in the years since they have been born. But now I take great delight in scaring them so. May God forgive me.

It is in keeping with the psychology of the serial killer, says David Forshaw, that Maybrick was devoted to his children. All through the diary he referred to them tenderly. He tried, unsuccessfully, to distance himself from them. Only his medicine could relieve his terrible torment. But by this time he was becoming suicidally depressed.

Perhaps I should top myself

While Mary Jane Kelly's memory tortured him, her death had not been enough.

On December 5th a newspaper clipping was sent to Dr William Sedgwick Saunders, the City of London's Public Analyst. Written on the clipping was a message:

England
Dear Boss. Look out for 7th inst. Am trying my hand at disjointing. and if can manage will send you a finger. Yours Jack the Ripper.
Saunders Esq
Police Magistrate.

This message has not been confirmed by the handwriting experts to be, beyond doubt, in the same hand as the 'Dear Boss' letter. But it looks very similar. (They are reproduced together in the second plate section in this book.) It is a remarkable coincidence that it is written over a story about three Liverpool businessmen running about naked in a public place and so includes the words 'Liverpool', 'mad' and 'business-man'. Was it another of Maybrick's taunting clues? The constant leaving of provocative clues is the gambling criminal's way of tempting fate. David Forshaw says that while he did not want to be caught, the idea that it was possible excited him.

Whether or not the clipping was sent by Maybrick, thoughts of a seventh killing were clearly preying on his mind. He released the pressure by crossing out line after line in his diary, the bold pen slashes a sign of his vitriol. Jews, Michael, Abberline, Lowry are all under attack.

Sir Jim shall *
Am I insane
Cane, gain
Sir Jim with his fancy cane *
Will soon strike again * . . .
Sir Jim cuts them first
damn it *
Abberline says he is now amazed *
Sir Jim has not struck another *
He waits patiently *
to see hastily *

Christmas send the whore's mole bonnet *
damn the bitches damn Michael *
Give Sir Jim his due *
He detests all the Jews *
For he has no favourite men *
As he runs away to his den *
He likes to write with his pen *

In the midst of all this frenzied crossing-out – in which some of the most telling and puzzling lines are deleted – Maybrick is clearly finding the pressure of trying to compose too great, and is losing confidence.

so help me God my next will be far the worst, my head aches but I will go on. damn Michael for being so clever the art of verse is far from simple. I curse him so. Abberline Abberline I shall destroy that fool yet. So help me God . . .

Donald McCormick's 1962 paperback version of *The Identity of Jack the Ripper* attributes a curious rhyme to Thomas Dutton's *Chronicles of Crime*. These were three handwritten books of observations first seen in 1932 by McCormick. Although no other Ripper expert but Donald McCormick has since seen these books, there appears to be no reason for him to have fabricated the story. Dutton was a physician who lived in Whitechapel at the time of the murders and who made microphotographs of 128 specimens of Jack the Ripper writings and concluded that at least 34 were in the same hand. One of these writings was a letter by the Ripper which included this rhyme:

> Eight little whores, with no hope of heaven,
> Gladstone may save one, then there'll be seven,
> Seven little whores begging for a shilling,
> One stays in Heneage Court, then there's a killing
>
> Six little whores, glad to be alive.
> One sidles up to Jack, then there are five.
> Four and whore rhyme aright,
> So do three and me,
> I'll set the town alight
> Ere there are two.
>
> Two little whores, shivering with fright,
> Seek a cosy doorway in the middle of the night.
> Jack's knife flashes, then there's but one,
> And the last one's the ripest for Jack's idea of fun.

Paul Feldman realized that the poem is a chilling reminder of the diary, with its reference to setting the town alight, which parallels Maybrick's intention of burning down St James's Church in Piccadilly, and to ripeness such as Maybrick attributed to Mary Jane Kelly:

> She ripped like a ripe peach

More striking still, he pointed out the diary's echo of the letter's theme itself, 'Eight little whores, with no hope of heaven':

One whore in heaven
Two whores side by side
Three whores will have died
Four

But most telling of all is the mention of Heneage Court. It was here that PC Robert Spicer of the Metropolitan Police wrote he had seen Jack the Ripper with his black bag, two nights after the double murder. The description of his suspect precisely fitted James Maybrick: he was 'about 5′9″ with a fair moustache, high forehead and rosy cheeks. He wore a high hat, black suit and gold watch and chain.' Spicer arrested the man later at Liverpool Street station. It is more than coincidental that the station is at the end of Middlesex Street where James Maybrick had rented a room. The suspect claimed he was a 'doctor' but was eventually released by the CID. His bag was not searched.

By now Maybrick feels a growing sense of panic. He is depressed and complains repeatedly of feeling tired. He has lost confidence and cannot complete even his poems. Scrawling through all the lines apart from, significantly, 'Am I insane?', he gives up in frustration:

damn it damn it damn it

He wants to stop, but he must go on.

I am cold. Curse the bastard Lowry for making me rip. I keep seeing blood pouring from the bitches. The nightmares are hideous. I cannot stop myself from wanting to eat more. God help me. Damn you. No one will stop me. God be damned.

Think think think write tell all prove to them you are who you say you are. Make them believe it is the truth I tell.

•   •   •

November was the month of the pre-Christmas ball at Battlecrease House. Among the guests would be the hopeful Alfred Brierley. Maybrick's old friend and colleague in the cotton business, Charles Ratcliff, would also be in attendance. Soon after the party, Ratcliff wrote to Florence Aunspaugh's father, John, in America about a cargo of poor-quality corn. Tucked away at the bottom of the letter was the sentence: 'Think Alf is getting the inside track with Mrs James's affections.'

With Christmas and the New Year approaching, Maybrick was racked with pain. Jekyll was struggling with Hyde for control. As always, George Davidson was there beside him.

> I cannot bring myself to look back, all I have written scares me so. George visited me today. I believe he knows what I am going through, although he says nothing. I can see it in his eyes. Poor George, he is such a good friend.
>
> I am tired very tired. I yearn for peace but I know in my heart I will go on. I will be in Manchester within a few days. I believe I will feel a great deal better when I have repeated on my last perform-ance. I wonder if I can improve on my fiendish deeds . . . The day is drawing to a close, Lowry was in fine spirits. I am pleased. I regret, as with my Jewish friends I have shown my wrath. This coming Christmas I will make amends.

Christmas was celebrated at Battlecrease House, as it was all over the country, with a tree and presents and cards. But there was still much talk of Jack the Ripper, since the police had made no headway in finding him. Inspector Walter Andrews and a party of colleagues were sent on from Montreal, where they were on another case, to New York to follow a new lead. According to the *Pall Mall Gazette*, the killer had left England for America three weeks earlier. For Maybrick, the season brought no cheer.

> The children enjoyed Christmas. I did not. My mood is no longer black although my head aches. I shall never become accustomed to the pain. I curse winter. I yearn for my favourite month, to see flowers in full bloom would please me so. Warmth is what I need. I

shiver so. Curse this weather and the whoring bitch.

Warmth was what he could no longer have from Florie. Far from it. In this same entry, written in the week after Christmas, he describes his seventh murder – once more in Manchester, as planned. Yet he finds it impossible to rekindle his former excitement. He no longer feels 'clever'.

> I could not cut like my last, visions of her flooded back
> to me as I struck. I tried to quash all thoughts of love. I
> left her for dead that I know. It did not amuse me. There
> was no thrill . . .

The wording here recalls his first trial murder in Manchester, when:

> There was no pleasure as I squeezed

He says he left her for dead. The same phrase is used later in the diary, when Maybrick makes a general threat to whores that he will:

> take the eyes
> take the head
> leave them all for dead

Yet he no longer feels as powerful, and thoughts of Florie prevent him from giving full vent to his passion. The experience only works for him when it embraces an impersonal act of mutilation. In rage and frustration, he returns to Battlecrease House and beats his wife.

> I have showered my fury on the bitch I struck and struck. I do not
> know how I stopped. I have left her penniless. I have no regrets.

Florie wrote to her mother on the last day of 1888 but did not mention the beating. 'In his fury he tore up his will this morning as he had made me sole legatee and trustee for the children in it. Now he proposes to settle everything he can on the children alone allowing me only the one third by law. I am sure it matters little to me as long as the children are provided for. My own income will do for me alone. A pleasant way of commencing New Year.'

David Forshaw says of Maybrick's frame of mind during this period: 'Whilst we know little so far about Maybrick's parents, we know from studies of other serial killers that there is deep resentment beneath superficial filial love. Maybrick's mother and father lavished money and attention on the talented Michael and this bred the jealousy with which the diary is riddled.

'At this precise moment the profound sense of inadequacy which was the true inspiration of his teasing, boastful writing as well as of the murders, came violently to the surface. Mary Jane Kelly, with her red hair, took the place of Florie 'the whoring mother' and, perhaps, all mothers.'

The weather matched the mood. The fog that had blanketed Liverpool at the beginning of 1888 returned on New Year's Eve and the local paper, the *Liverpool Echo*, predicted: 'There is no agreeable change of weather and to judge by appearances we are likely to experience a bad spell of mist, rain and general murkiness.'

It was a bad omen for 1889.

TEN

'When I have finished my fiendish deeds the devil himself will praise me'

THE SLAUGHTER IN Whitechapel had stopped temporarily, but the story of Jack the Ripper had not ended with the murder of Mary Jane Kelly. During the spring of 1889, Maybrick's worsening health and the turmoil surrounding his life created a vortex into which Florie and the family were drawn.

If any of them had any suspicion that James Maybrick was the most feared and despised man in Britain, they did not admit it. His secret would be buried deep with his corpse in Anfield Cemetery. But his death would destroy for good the life of his young American wife, and leave behind much mystery. Why did the Maybrick family and the servants at Battlecrease House conspire against Florie? Why didn't the medical men agree about who or what killed Maybrick? Why were family letters destroyed and Maybrick's prescriptions torn up? Perhaps strangest of all, why did Edwin and Michael suppress their brother's past and stand by while his widow faced the terror of the gallows?

This much is known. In January, according to the cook, Elizabeth Humphreys, Alfred Brierley's visits increased. He was also a regular companion of the Maybricks at the various race meetings they so enjoyed. Maybrick was only too aware of Florie's flirtations – indeed because of them seven women had died. Yet Brierley continued to be invited to join the family. This does not surprise David Forshaw, who explains that Maybrick clearly enjoyed the perverted pleasure of watching the unsuspecting couple. It was all part of his power game. Even as he was describing the pleasure of ripping Polly Nichols, Maybrick became excited by the idea of voyeurism.

> The whore seen her master today, it did not bother
> me. I imagined I was with them, the very thought thrills
> me. I wonder if the whore has ever had such thoughts? I
> believe she has . . .

As the dismal winter weather wore on, Maybrick became restless.

> It shall not be long before I strike again. I am taking more than
> ever. The bitch can take two. Sir Jim shall take four, a double
> double event. <u>ha ha</u>. If I was in the city of whores I would do my

---

fiendish deeds this very moment . . . By God I would . . . I shall have no more regrets, damn them all. Beware Mr Abberline. I will return with a vengeance. Once more I will be the talk of England. What pleasure my thoughts do give me . . . When I have finished my fiendish deeds the devil himself will praise me. But he will have a long wait before I shake hands with him. I have work to do, a great deal of work. ha ha. kidney for supper.

At least Maybrick had no need to worry about a supply of his precious 'medicine'. He had discovered a new source: Valentine Blake, who was a member of a team working for the manufacturing chemist, William Bryer Nation, developing the use of rhea grass, or ramie, as a substitute for cotton.

In January 1889 Blake travelled to Liverpool to meet Maybrick. He needed help in the marketing of the new product. Maybrick casually asked Blake to tell him the chemicals used in its manufacture. 'I do not wish to obtain your trade secrets,' he reassured him. 'It is a question of price and the chemicals may be obtained more easily in Liverpool.'

One of the substances was arsenic. The two men chatted about the arsenic-eating habits of Austrian peasants and about Thomas de Quincey, author of *Confessions of an Opium Eater*. Blake 'wondered that de Quincey could have taken such a quantity as 900 drops of laudanum in a day'.

Maybrick smiled. 'One man's poison,' he said, 'is another man's meat, and there is a so-called poison which is like meat and liquor to me whenever I feel weak and depressed; it makes me stronger in mind and body at once.'

'I don't tell everybody,' he went on, 'and wouldn't tell you only you mentioned arsenic. It is arsenic. I take it when I can get it but the doctors won't put any in my medicine, except now and then a trifle that only tantalizes me.'

Blake said nothing. Maybrick continued: 'Since you use arsenic can you let me have some? I find difficulty in getting it here.'

The chemist would recall later in an affidavit: 'I replied that I had some by me and that since I only used it for experiments, which were now perfected, I had no further use for it and he, Maybrick, was welcome to all I had left. He then asked what it was worth and offered to pay for it in advance. I replied that I had no licence to sell drugs and suggested we should make it a quid pro quo, Mr Maybrick to do his best with the ramie grass product and I to make a present of the arsenic.'

When they met again in February, Blake gave Maybrick about 300 grains of arsenic in three different packets. 'I told him to be careful with it as he had almost enough to poison a regiment.'

I am taking more than ever.

The sudden increase in Maybrick's intake of drugs was reflected in the diary. His handwriting became wilder and his threats increasingly lurid. Finally he decided to strike once more in 'the city of whores'. As with Elizabeth Stride, he is interrupted, and it appears from his description that on this occasion he did not have the chance to kill his victim.

Damn it damn it damn it the bastard almost caught me, curse him to hell. I will cut him up next time, so help me. A few minutes and I would have done. Bastard. I will seek him out, teach him a lesson . . . No one will stop me . . . . Curse his black soul. I curse myself for striking too soon, I should have waited until it was truly quiet so help me . . . I will take all next time and eat it. Will leave nothing. Not even the head. I will boil it and eat it with freshly picked carrots.

Since any Ripper-style attack on a woman in London would certainly have been widely reported in the press, we can assume that the intended victim escaped with her life and did not sustain serious injury.

In March the two Maybrick children developed whooping cough and Dr Humphreys was called. He asked Florie about her husband's health. She told him of her fears about his use of drugs, just as she had told Dr Hopper the previous summer. She said he was now taking a white powder that she thought was strychnine, and asked what was likely to be the result. The doctor said that it could kill him and, with uncanny foresight, added: 'If he should ever die suddenly, call me and I can say you have had some conversation about it.' It was as though he foresaw the events ahead and was offering Florie help should she be in trouble. Yet when that hour of need arrived Dr Humphreys, like everyone else, abandoned her.

For his part, Maybrick paid a visit to Dr Drysdale that same month. He said that, although he was never free of headaches, he had been feeling better since his last visit in December. His tongue was furred, however, and he was still suffering a creeping numbness in his left arm and hand.

Florie wrote to Michael in London, telling him of her anxiety about the white powder her husband was taking. She said that he was very irritable and complained of pains in his head. She said that Maybrick did not know that she had discovered his drug addiction, nor that she had written to him.

Michael destroyed the letter, but not before he questioned his brother casually about its contents, provoking an angry response, which he recalled at Florie's trial. In turn Maybrick was furious with Florie.

The bitch has written all
tonight she will fall.
So help me God I will cut the bitch up and serve her up to the children. How dare the whore write to Michael, the damn bitch had no right to inform him of my medicine.

The Maybricks somehow had made new friends during the winter: Charles Samuelson, a tobacco factor, and his vivacious young wife, Christina. The two couples stayed at the Palace Hotel, Birkdale, near Southport, for a break. Alfred Brierley was there too.

On the last night of their stay a game of whist ended in a temperamental flare-up by Christina Samuelson, who ran off to bed, shouting 'I hate you' at her husband. There were tears and, to her credit, Florie tried to smooth things over. 'You must not take any serious notice of that,' she reassured Charles. 'I often say 'I hate you' to Jim.'

A few months later, at the inquest into Maybrick's death, Christina told a different, more incriminating, version of the incident. 'I had a conversation with Mrs Maybrick,' she said, 'and she told me she hated her husband.'

Around March 15th, Maybrick travelled to London to stay with his brother. According to Bernard Ryan in *The Poisoned Life of Mrs Maybrick*, Florie and Brierley hatched a plot while he was away. On her husband's return, Florie announced that she wished to visit London to stay with a sick aunt. With his usual deceptive charm, Maybrick bought her a new fur wrap for the visit – and at the same time confided his true feelings in the diary.

> I shall buy the whore something for her visit. Will give the bitch the impression I consider it her duty to visit her aunt . . . . What a joke, let the bitch believe I have no knowledge of her whoring affairs.

Storms and floods were buffeting Liverpool when, on March 16th, Florie sent a telegram to the manager of Flatman's Hotel in Henrietta Street, London. She booked a two-room suite for 'Mr and Mrs Thomas Maybrick of Manchester' for one week. When the hotel failed to confirm the reservation, she wrote a letter, this time with a special request for a menu of soup, sole, duckling and green peas, new potatoes, cheese, celery and dessert on arrival. The choice of hotel was provocative: it was the meeting-place of cotton men from Liverpool. She would be arriving first, and her husband the following day, she told the manager, who accordingly arranged to have bedroom nine and the adjoining sitting-room sixteen at the Maybricks' disposal from March 21st.

At about the same time, Florie wrote to her childhood friend, John Baillie Knight, in Holland Park, London, telling him that she would be in London on the 21st and would like to meet him for dinner. She said she was in great trouble but gave no further explanation.

Florie left Battlecrease House and arrived at Flatman's Hotel at around 1 p.m. At about 6.30 that evening John Baillie Knight called on her. They sat in her sitting-room and she told him she had come to London to arrange a separation from her husband. She could no longer cope with his keeping a woman, she said, adding that he was cruel and had hit her.

Baillie Knight agreed that a separation was best and suggested that she see the solicitors, Markby, Stewart and Company, and then go to her mother in Paris. John and Florie went to dine at the Grand Hotel and on to the theatre, returning at around 11.30 p.m.

The next day Brierley arrived and installed himself in Florie's suite.

There they stayed until 1 p.m. on Sunday, when they left abruptly, settling the bill of £2.13s.

'He piqued my vanity and resisted my efforts to please him,' Florie commented afterwards. 'Before we parted he gave me to understand he cared for someone else and could not marry me and that rather than face the disgrace of discovery he would blow his brains out. I then had such a revulsion of feeling I said we must end our intimacy at once.'

Brierley himself told the New York Herald after her trial: 'We parted in London as if we were never to meet again . . . . It was distinctly understood we were not to correspond.'

That understanding was soon forgotten by them both.

Before leaving London, Florie went to see Markby the solicitor and, with his guidance, wrote a letter to her husband asking for a separation and suggesting that she remain in Battlecrease House with a yearly allowance. There is no record of whether or not that letter was received, or even posted.

On Wednesday, Florie dined with Michael. (It had been a busy week for him. On Monday, March 25th, he had been responsible for organizing and performing in a star-studded gala concert attended by the Prince and Princess of Wales at the opening of his regiment's new headquarters in the Euston Road.) Next day, Florie returned to Liverpool to face the music.

So, ignominiously, ended her sadly inept escapade.

■   ■   ■

Florie had been a theatrical child. Friends recalled that she had found the boundaries between fantasy and truth sometimes difficult to define. Now she would find her life surrounded by more drama than she could ever have wished for.

Liverpool's Cotton Exchange was already buzzing with rumours. Its members raised an eyebrow or two and it was suggested that if Maybrick were to learn of Florie and Brierley's affair he would 'fill him full of lead'.

The climax came on March 29th, the day of the Grand National. It was a splendid event, attended by the Prince of Wales, to mark the 50th anniversary of the race. Brierley, of all people, had once again joined the Maybricks' charabanc party to Aintree. Maybrick was still playing the part of the voyeur.

> the bitch gave me the greatest pleasure of all. Did not the whore see her whore master in front of all, true the race was the fastest I have seen but the thrill of seeing the whore with the bastard thrilled me more so than knowing his Royal Highness was but a few feet away from yours truly ha ha. what a laugh, if the greedy bastard would have known he was less than a few feet away from the name all England was talking about he would have died there and then. Regret I could not tell the foolish fool. To hell with sovereignty, to hell with all whores, to hell with the bitch who rules.

Despite their declared intention never to meet again, Florie and Brierley went arm in arm to see the Royal party. This was a mistake, for Maybrick lost his temper.

> Victoria Victoria
> The Queen of them all
> When it comes to Sir Jack
> She knows nothing at all.
> . . . Who knows
> Perhaps one day
> I will give her a call . . .
> Show her my knife . . .
> And she will honour me for life . . .
> Arise Sir Jack she will say
> and now you can go
> as you may ha ha ha
> ha ha ha ha.

Florie was furious at her husband's behaviour and left the races boasting to Christina Samuelson that when they got home she would 'give it to him hot and heavy'. But that night it was Maybrick the servants heard shouting: 'Such a scandal will be all over town tomorrow.'

What scandal? Was it Florie's indiscretion at the races? Had the letter arrived from the solicitor regarding the proposed separation?

A terrible scene followed. 'It began in the bedroom,' said Mary

Cadwallader. 'Mr Maybrick told the maid, Bessie, to send his wife away. She came downstairs into the hall to go to the cab; he followed her and raved and stamped like a madman – waving his pocket handkerchief over his head. The button holes of Mrs Maybrick's dress were torn with the way he had pulled her about. She had on a fur cape; he told her to take it off as she was not to go away with that on; he had bought it for her to go up to London in.

'I went up to the master and said, 'Oh master, please don't go on like this, the neighbours will hear you.' He answered: 'Leave me alone, you don't know anything about it.' I said: 'Don't send the mistress away tonight. Where can she go? Let her stay until morning.' Then he shouted: 'By heavens, Florie, if you cross this doorstep you shall never enter it again.' He became so exhausted he fell across an oak settle and went quite stiff. I did not know if he was drunk or in a fit. I sent the cab away and we got Mrs Maybrick upstairs and Mr Maybrick spent all night in the dining room.'

He was unrepentant.

I struck her several times an eye for an eye ha ha. too many interfering servants, damn the bitches. Hopper will soon feel the edge of my shining knife, damn the meddling bufoon, damn all.

The next morning Florie had a black eye. She went to see Matilda Briggs to ask for her advice and help in arranging for a separation. They went together to see Dr Hopper. Florie confided to him that she had been up all night, her husband had beaten her and she was on her way to a solicitor. She also told him that she could not bear for her husband to come near her.

Good family doctor that he was, Dr Hopper decided to attempt to mend matters and went up to Battlecrease House later the same day. He saw Maybrick and Florie, who appeared calmer and seemed willing to resolve their respective grievances. Florie repeated that she could not bear sleeping with her husband and did not want any more children. Despite this, Maybrick agreed to pay his wife's debts. Since they appeared to want to forgive and forget, Dr Hopper left in the sincere but naïve belief that he had effected a complete reconciliation.

．　．　．

Matilda Briggs joined the Maybrick household the following day and there was another almighty row. The servants heard Florie shouting to Maybrick that she had never invited anyone to the house without consulting him, so why should he do such a thing to her? There was a great deal of quarrelling and shouting and when, at 6 p.m., Mary Cadwallader took a cup of tea up to Florie, she found her lying on the sofa in a faint.

The maid rushed down to fetch Maybrick and Mrs Briggs and together they ran upstairs. In a curious change of mood, Maybrick knelt by his wife calling: 'Bunny, Bunny, here's your hubby'.

There was no response. For a while the servants thought Florie was dead.

It was another disturbed night. Mrs Briggs, half undressed and wearing a dressing-gown of Florie's that was far too small, kept disappearing into the kitchen for beer. She said she needed something 'to keep her up'.

This time Dr Humphreys was sent for to see Florie. Confronted by the unseemly spectacle of the staggering, dishevelled Mrs Briggs, he demanded to know: 'Who is this woman?' Five times during the night Maybrick recalled the weary doctor to the house.

Florie remained in bed for nearly a week, during which time she confided to Elizabeth Humphreys that she and Maybrick had money problems. She said she was in debt and her husband's income was not enough to support them, but she did not reveal the full story.

Maybrick, too, had a word with the servants. He told Mary Cadwallader not to take letters up to Mrs Maybrick until he had seen them. 'Your mistress sees all my letters,' he explained. 'There is no reason why I should not see hers.' On recovering, Florie contrived yet another meeting with Brierley, this time in Liverpool on April 6th. She told him that Maybrick had beaten her and dragged her around the room.

After that, she wrote Brierley two letters, apparently at the instigation of Dr Hopper, telling him that she was reconciled with her husband. Amazed, he tore the letters up.

On Saturday, April 13th, Maybrick went down to London. According to the diary, this visit was, in part, to settle Florie's debts. But the memory of the last aborted mutilation still haunted him. He was ready to strike again.

> Once more the bitch is in debt. My God I will cut her . . . I will visit the city of whores. I will pay her dues and I shall take mine, by God I will. I will rip rip rip.
>
> May seek the bastard out who stopped my funny little games and rip him to. I said he would pay I will make sure he damn will.

The other purpose for Maybrick's visit to London was to see Michael's physician, Dr Fuller, who examined him for an hour when he called at Michael's chambers that Sunday. Maybrick complained of pains in his head and numbness. He said he was afraid of being paralysed. Dr Fuller decided there was little wrong and prescribed a nerve tonic and liver pills.

The following Saturday Maybrick was back in London yet again. He went to Dr Fuller's for a second consultation and acknowledged that he was much better. His prescription for an aperient and liver pills was slightly altered, the liver pills being replaced by lozenges. Whatever Dr Fuller said during the visits had a curious and dramatic effect. The handwriting in the diary became more controlled, the thoughts calmer, and he gave up any further plans for murder. His thoughts now turn inward and he begins to dwell on his own death.

> Fuller believes there is very little the matter with me. Strange, the thoughts he placed into my mind. I could not strike. I believe I am mad, completely mad. I try to fight my thoughts. I walk the streets until dawn. I could not find it in my heart to strike. Visions of my dear Bunny overwhelm me. I still love her, but how I hate her. She has destroyed all and yet my heart aches for her oh how it aches. I do not know which pain is the worse my body or my mind.

At last Maybrick apparently determined to throw his knife in the river. The Mersey flowed swiftly only a few hundred yards from Battlecrease House. The killing days were finally over.

> I shall return to Battlecrease with the knowledge that I can no longer continue my campaign. Tis love that spurned me so, 'tis love that shall put an end to it.

On that Sunday, Florie wrote to Maybrick in London. Her emotions seemed to swing like a pendulum, and the about-face is astonishing.

'My own darling hubby!

'. . . I have had a terrible night of it – and try as hard as I will to be brave and courageous because Jim thinks I may yet be of comfort to him and the children my physical weakness overcomes what remains of my mental strength. I have not sufficient self respect left to lift me above the depth of disgrace to which I have fallen, for now that I am down I can judge better how very far above me others must be morally. I despair of ever reaching that standard again although I may recover some of your confidence by living a life of atonement for yours and the children's sakes alone. Nothing you can say can make me look at my actions but in the most degrading light and the more you impress the enormity of my crimes upon me the more hopeless I feel of ever regaining my position. I feel as though for the future I must be . . . a perpetual reminder of . . . .trouble and that nothing can efface the past from your memory . . .

'Please darling put me out of my pain as soon as you can. I have deceived and nearly ruined you but since you wish me to live, tell me the worst at once – and let it be over . . . . Darling, try and be as lenient towards me as you can for notwithstanding all your generous and tender loving kindness my burden is almost more than I can bear, my remorse and self-contempt is eating my heart out and if I did not believe my love for you and my dutifulness may prove some slight atonement for the past I should give up the struggle to keep brave! Forgive me if you can dearest and think less poorly of

'Your loving wifesy
'Bunny

'The children are well. I have been nowhere and seen no-one.'

This, from a woman who had told her doctor she could not bear to sleep with her husband and who ten days later addressed Brierley in a letter as 'dearest'. Was she truly contrite? Or could it have been, most naturally of all, that she feared she was pregnant and needed to protect her future by once again sharing a bed with her husband?

. . .

About April 24th, Florie walked to Wokes the chemist on the corner of Aigburth and Beechwood Roads and bought a dozen fly papers. She said her kitchen was troubled by flies and asked the errand boy to deliver them to the house. Soon after Florie's purchase, the housemaid, Bessie, was puzzled to find the wash-stand basin covered with a towel. Peeping underneath, she saw some soaking fly papers. Next morning they were in the wastepaper basket.

Also on April 24th, Maybrick went to Clay and Abraham's with Dr Fuller's prescription. His health continued to deteriorate rapidly.

The following day the much-missed Edwin returned from America.

My dear brother Edwin has returned. I wish I could tell him all.

The next day, four months after he had destroyed his will, James made a new one. Or did he?

The will that has survived was written on thin blue paper in a forceful hand. The first of the two pages is reproduced in the second plate section of this book. The witnesses were Maybrick's book-keeper George Smith and his friend George Davidson. It poses many more questions than it answers. Most important of all, we know from Florie's letter to her mother that in December 1888 Maybrick had torn up his will and threatened to write a new one. It seems unlikely that he would have waited four months, until April 25th, to execute his threat, so could there have been, as seems probable, an intermediate version, written in the heat of the moment? The blue will begins: 'In case I die before having made a regular and proper will in legal form I wish this to be taken as my last will and testament . . .' Could it be that the rather scrappy and inaccurate document lodged in Somerset House was written for him by someone else?

The will continues: 'I leave and bequeath all my worldly possessions of whatever kind or description, including furniture, pictures, wines, linen, plate, Life insurances, cash, shares, property, in fact everything I possess, in trust with my brothers Michael Maybrick and Thomas Maybrick, for my two children James Chandler Maybrick and Gladys Eveleyn Maybrick. The furniture I desire to remain intact and to be used in furnishing a home which can be shared by my widow and children but the furniture is to be the children's.

'I further desire that all monies in the names of the above trustees (Michael and Thomas Maybrick) and the income of same used for the children's benefit and education, such education to be left to the discretion of the said Trustees.

'My widow will have for her portion of my Estate the Policies on my life, say £500 with the Scottish Widows Fund and £2,000 with the Mutual Reserve Fund Life Association of New York, both Policies being made out in her name. The interest on this £2,500 together with the £125 a year which she receives from her New York property will make a provision of about £125 a year, a sum, although small, will yet be the means of keeping her respectably.

'It is also my desire that my widow shall live under the same roof with the children, so long as she remains my widow.

'If it is legally possible, I wish the £2,500 of life Insurance on my life in my wife's name to be invested in the names of the said Trustees but that she should have the sole use of the interest thereof during her lifetime but at her death the principal to revert to my said children James Chandler and Gladys Eveleyn Maybrick.

'Witness my hand and seal this twenty fifth day of a April 1889.

'signed James Maybrick.

'signed by the Testator in the presence of us, who at his request and in the presence of each other have hereunto affixed our names as witnesses George R Davidson and George Smith.'

Even at the time, the will became the focus of much speculation. It was mentioned at the inquest, although Michael, not surprisingly, said that he would prefer it not to be read.

Alexander MacDougall, who wrote a book on Florie's case in 1891, described how, as Maybrick lay dying, 'the office clerks Thomas Lowry and George Smith came up to the house with some papers. Michael and Edwin Maybrick were there and took them up to James Maybrick. After some time James Maybrick began shouting at the brothers in a loud voice that could be heard all over the house: 'Oh, Lord, if I am to die, why am I to be worried like this? Let me die properly.' He was very violent.'

MacDougall claimed that the servants believed the brothers had failed to find a will and were trying to get him to sign a new one. He believed it was 'absolutely inconceivable that James Maybrick could have been in his sound senses when he signed that will'. He explained:

'This will makes over and for ever every single thing James Maybrick possessed . . . lock stock and barrel . . . to the absolute, unfettered control of Michael Maybrick and Thomas Maybrick. Not only that, but it makes over the children, aged seven and three, to them, to be treated by them as they like . . . To be educated and brought up, the boy as a chimney sweep! the girl as a seamstress! if they liked, and having vested everything he died possessed of in Michael and Thomas for ever with absolute power to invest the principal as they liked, the income was to be employed just as they pleased! There is no provision in this will that any of the property should come to either of these children when they come of age, or ever! . . .

'Mrs Maybrick is to have neither bed nor blanket but he 'desires' her to live in the 'home' which Michael and Thomas are to furnish and 'under the same roof', as his two children who are to be brought up and educated by Michael and Thomas Maybrick in any way they please! But this is not all! James Maybrick goes on in this will to attempt to grab for these trustees even some life policies which belong to Mrs Maybrick herself . . . It is a will which no court in any civilised country could have regarded as a will made in his sound senses by any husband and father.'

In any event, it did not provide Florie with a monetary motive for murder. Nor did it reflect Maybrick's wishes as expressed in Florie's letter of 31st December 1888 to her mother (pages 117–18), or, even more importantly, in the diary, which seems to point to an earlier will that had been mislaid or destroyed in the last few days of his life by someone in the house.

I have redressed the balance of my previous will. Bunny and the children are well cared for and I trust Michael and Thomas will carry out my wishes.

The problem of the will has become crucial to the arguments for and against the diary. Because we have found no example of Maybrick's handwriting, apart from the signature on his wedding certificate, with which to compare the will, we have had to rely heavily on forensic handwriting tests and graphology – both themselves controversial skills.

The experts, who are by no means infallible, have been largely negative. Most, but not all, say that the diary could not have been written by the man who wrote the will. So if, as we believe, James Maybrick wrote the diary, who wrote the will?

It is suspicious that not only do the figures not add up but also that Maybrick misspells his daughter's name, Evelyn, as 'Eveleyn'. It is puzzling, too, that there are discrepancies between the wording of the will in Somerset House and the one seen and copied by MacDougall. For instance the words 'bequeath' and 'made out' are missing in MacDougall's version, as is the phrase 'in his presence', all important legal phrases.

If the will in Somerset House was not what Maybrick intended or wrote, who forged it and why? Was the document drafted under pressure from the brothers and pre-dated? Did Michael or Edwin write it and then both force him to sign it as he lay dying? Or were, in fact, both the contents and the signatures forged?

Paul Feldman arranged for photocopies of the two signed pages of the Somerset House will and of Maybrick's marriage certificate to be sent to an eminent document examiner, Reed Hayes, from Kailua, Hawaii. Mr Hayes is a member of the American Board of Forensic Handwriting Analysts.

He examined the three signatures, letter by letter, looking for differences and similarities in the individual strokes and the way in which they are put together. He noted, for example, that on the marriage certificate, the loop of the capital 'J' of James meets the downstroke forming a closed circle. On page one of the will the start of the loop begins to the right of the downstroke, so that the downstroke intersects with the beginning of the loop. On page two the start of the loop is to the left of the downstroke so that it forms an open circle. All three are different.

Altogether Reed Hayes found ten similarities between the first page of the will and the marriage certificate, six with page two. However, there were fifteen dissimilarities between the marriage certificate and page one of the will, thirteen with page two. He also noted similarities between the signature of Edwin and that of James in the Somerset House will. 'In general the feeling of the writing formation is different in the known signature [on the wedding certificate] and the questioned signatures [on the will], which have a distinctly rhythmic feeling absent from the known signature.

'In my opinion it is highly probable that the questioned signatures were not written by the same hand that wrote the known signature of James Maybrick.'

Interestingly even Sue Iremonger notes a similarity between the signatures of Michael and James: 'Even taking into account their parallel schooling, I would not have expected to find such a matching style and weight of strokes.'

Michael and the other brothers would later use the will to gain total control over Maybrick's estate and, ultimately, over his wife. But one person had everything to lose: Florie herself.

ELEVEN

'I do not know if she has the strength to kill me'

AT 8.30 A.M. on April 26th, 1889, a parcel from London was delivered to Battlecrease House. Mary Cadwallader accepted it and went straight upstairs to her master. It was the medicine Maybrick had been expecting.

The following day Maybrick was ill. He told Mary that he had vomited and that his legs were numb, adding that he must have taken an overdose of the substance that had arrived the day before. Despite his condition and the appalling weather, he was determined to go later that day to the Wirral Races, a great social event.

He went to the office at about 10.30 and left at about 1 p.m., returning home for his horse. Then he rode off in the drizzle.

By the time he arrived at the racecourse he was wet and shaking. His friend William Thomson noticed that he had difficulty remaining in the saddle. Maybrick's explanation was that he had taken a double dose of 'medicine' that morning.

Mrs Morden Rigg, the wife of Maybrick's old friend from America, also noticed his condition. He gave her the same explanation – that he had taken an overdose – but this time he added that the 'medicine' was strychnine.

Although his clothes were soaked through, Maybrick decided to dine with his friends the Hobsons after the races. By this time, he was so ill he could not hold a glass and, after spilling his wine twice, he left, embarrassed that his friends would think he was drunk.

The next morning, he was even worse. Florie asked the cook to prepare some mustard and water. 'Master has taken another dose of that horrid medicine,' she said.

Dr Humphreys was summoned. When he arrived at Battlecrease House, Florie told him she thought her husband's illness was probably due to bad brandy he had drunk at the races. Maybrick himself said his symptoms had worsened after he had had a strong cup of tea, but added that he had suffered from a headache for more than a year.

The doctor asked Maybrick about the effects of strychnine and nux vomica on him. In complete contradiction of his previous admission to Mrs Rigg that he had taken strychnine, the patient said: 'I think I know a great deal of medicine. I cannot stand strychnine and nux vomica at all.'

Dr Humphreys recommended that he eat meat only once a day and that he take to his office some beef tea thickened with Du Barry's Revalenta. This favourite Victorian remedy was advertised as a cure for 'indigestion, flatulency, dyspepsia, phlegm, constipation, all nervous, bilious and liver complaints, dysentery, diarrhoea, acidity, palpitation, heartburn, haemorrhoids, headaches, debility, despondency, cramps, spasms, nausea, sinking fits, coughs, asthma and bronchitis, consumption and also children's complaints'. In other words, the ideal medicine for a hypochondriac.

About this time James Maybrick commissioned his portrait in oils from a rising young Liverpudlian artist, J. T. Steadman, on the grounds that he might not live long. The *Pall Mall Gazette* later claimed that he had requested a 'Pictorial record of his bodily existence'.

Edwin came for lunch and during the day Maybrick wrote a surprisingly frank letter to Michael, giving yet another version of events. It hinted that Maybrick knew his end was near. The original letter has disappeared, but a clerk serving at Florie's trial later made a copy and this survives. Michael's name has been crossed out and 'Blucher' substituted, apparently, and for no known reason, by the solicitor William Swift, who acted for the prosecution at Florie's trial. A margin note in the same handwriting explains that Blucher is Maybrick's nickname for his brother. Blucher was a Prussian general who fought against Napoleon at Waterloo; Michael was known to be anti-German, so this is no doubt one of Maybrick's 'little jokes'.

Liverpool April 29th
My Dear Michael [deleted] Blucher,
I have been very seedy indeed. On Saturday morning I found my legs getting stiff and useless but by sheer strength of will shook off the feeling and went down on horseback to Wirral Races and dined with the Hobsons. Yesterday morning I felt more like dying than living so much so that Florie called in another Doctor who said it was an acute attack of indigestion and gave me something to relieve the alarming symptoms, so all went on well until about 8 o'clock I went back to bed and had lain there an hour by myself and was reading on my back. Many times I felt a twitching but took little notice of it thinking it would pass away but instead of doing so it got worse and worse and in trying to move around to ring the bell

I found I could not do so but finally managed it but by the time Florie and Edwin could get upstairs I was stiff and for two mortal hours my legs were like bars of iron stretched out to the fullest extent but as rigid as steel. The Doctor finally came again but could not make it indigestion this time and the conclusion he came to was that the nux vomica I had been taking under Doctor Fuller had poisoned me, as all the symptoms warranted such a conclusion I know I am today sore from head to foot and played out completely.

What is the matter with me none of the doctors so far can make out and I suppose never will until I am stretched out and cold and then future generations may profit by it if they hold a post mortem which I am quite willing they should do.

I don't think I shall come up to London this week as I don't feel much like travelling and cannot go on with Fuller's physic yet a while but I shall come up and see him again shortly. Edwin does not join you just yet but he will write you himself. I suppose you go to your country quarters on Wednesday . . .

With love,
Your affectionate brother Jim.

Meanwhile, Florie wrote to her mother as though all was well.

We are asked to a bal masque which, being given in Liverpool and the people provincials, I hardly think likely to be a success. A certain amount of 'diablerie', wit and life is always required at an entertainment of this sort: and as it will be quite a novel innovation people will hardly know what is expected of them. However, we are expected to come in 'dominoes and masks', and I should like to know how the former is made and if the latter are not procurable in gauze instead of 'papier mache.'

Naturally, Florie wanted to look her best for the ball. The day before, she went to Hanson's, the chemist, and bought some cosmetic tincture of benzoin and elderflowers. She also made another purchase, one she was to regret for the rest of her life: more fly papers.

The next day, Maybrick felt a little better and returned to work. The cook prepared some Revalenta and, since Edwin was staying at

Battlecrease House, Florie asked him to take the medicine to the office for Maybrick's lunch. Thomas Lowry, the clerk, left the office to buy a saucepan in which to warm up the mixture.

Edwin escorted Florie to the ball that night, presumably because Maybrick did not feel up to it. The following day, May 1st, Captain Irving of the White Star Line met Edwin and Maybrick at the office. While the three men were talking, he said in a later court affidavit, Maybrick pulled out a small packet, the contents of which he emptied into a glass of water. Captain Irving noticed him take two doses in 15 minutes. 'Everybody knew Jim was always taking some medicine or other.' When the Captain returned with them to Battlecrease House, Maybrick was unable to sit at the table.

Captain Irving subsequently met Edwin in town and asked him: 'What on earth is the matter with Jim?'

'He is killing himself with that damned strychnine,' Edwin replied.

When a newspaper later printed Captain Irving's account of these events, Edwin categorically denied everything. 'Statement absolutely and entirely untrue in every respect,' he said in a telegram to the press. 'Never saw my brother use any white powder in wine or otherwise in my life.' And at Florie's trial, Edwin claimed that he had no knowledge of Maybrick's alleged drug habit.

On Thursday, May 2nd, Maybrick took his lunch to the office but returned home feeling ill.

I no longer take the dreaded stuff for fear I will harm my dear Bunny, worse still the children.

If what he wrote was true – if Maybrick had indeed stopped taking drugs – a sudden withdrawal would have been almost unbearable. In 1885, *Chambers Journal of Popular Literature, Science and Art* reported on a conference that included the topic of arsenic eating. 'When a man has once begun to indulge in it he must continue to indulge,' it said, 'or, as it is popularly expressed, the last dose kills him. Indeed, the arsenic eater must not only continue his indulgence, he must also increase the quantity of the drug, so that it is extraordinarily difficult to stop the habit; for, as the sudden cessation causes death, the gradual cessation produces such a terrible heart gnawing that it may probably be said that no genuine arsenic eater ever ceased to eat arsenic while life lasted.'

From the last entries in the diary until his death, Maybrick would have been in agony. And, indeed, in these entries he expresses remorse and begs for release from the torment of living.

> I do not have the courage to take my life. I pray each night
> I will find the strength to do so but the courage alludes me.
> I pray constantly all will forgive. I deeply regret striking
> her, I have found it in my heart to forgive her for her
> lovers.
>
> I believe I will tell her all, ask her to forgive me as I have
> forgiven her. I pray to God she will understand what she has done
> to me.

On May 3rd, Maybrick saw Dr Humphreys and complained that the medicine was doing no good. Florie observed, tartly, that he said the same about any medicine after two or three days. After seeing the doctor, Maybrick went to his office for the last time. This is also the day on which he made his final entry in the diary. That afternoon, with the doctor's approval, he went to the Turkish baths.

During the evening Maybrick became very ill, with a 'gnawing pain from the hips down to the knees'. At midnight Dr Humphreys once again made his way to Battlecrease House. He decided the pains were the result of hard towelling at the baths and, ignoring the fact that Maybrick had twice vomited, administered a morphine suppository.

The following morning Maybrick was worse. He was vomiting violently.

Dr Humphreys made an early visit and gave instructions that the patient was to drink nothing at all; he could quench his thirst by washing out his mouth with water or sucking ice or a damp cloth.

Some medicine was delivered by the chemist and, to Florie's consternation, was taken straight up to Maybrick by Mary Cadwallader.

'Nothing must be taken to his bedroom without my seeing it first,' Florie ordered. Recovering the medicine, she emptied it all down the sink and later explained to Cadwallader that the tiniest bit more would have killed her husband. Perhaps she sensed the danger of defying the doctor's orders.

Simple actions with straightforward explanations very often become twisted in the telling. The case against Florie was built on such gossip and malicious misunderstanding.

There was an air of prurient excitement at Battlecrease House as whispered suspicion and innuendo, like a fever, infected the house.

On the morning of May 3rd, Florie sent Mary Cadwallader to Wokes to collect some medicine on prescription. James Grant, the gardener, told Alice Yapp that Mr Wokes had refused to give it to her on the grounds that it contained a deadly poison. Alice then passed on this juicy information to Mrs Briggs and Mrs Hughes.

But on August 21st Mary Cadwallader told the *Liverpool Post*: 'I don't know how she could have dared tell such a story.'

Mary said that Dr Humphreys started to write a prescription that he did not complete. He had laid it to one side. In her agitation Florie had mistakenly picked this up, believing it to be a prescription for beef tea. So Mary went to the chemist with the wrong prescription. Mr Wokes explained that the doctor's signature was needed and asked that Dr Humphreys should call himself. Mary denied that there was ever any mention of poison.

She went home, explained the mistake and returned to Mr Wokes, who then gave her the meat juice. Dr Humphreys later called to give Mr Wokes the necessary information for the original prescription.

Dr Humphreys's account of the event makes no mention of the prescription containing poison.

Nevertheless that innocent visit to the chemist assumed sinister proportions in the servants' hall.

On Sunday, May 5th, Elizabeth Humphreys went up to see her master, who begged for some lemonade with a little sugar, saying: 'I want you to make it as you would for any poor man, dying of thirst.' Florie was in the room and said, 'You cannot have it, except as a gargle.' She was following Dr Humphreys's instructions that Maybrick drink nothing.

That afternoon, Edwin turned up at the house and, disobeying doctor's orders, gave his brother a brandy and soda, which Maybrick promptly vomited.

On Monday morning, May 6th, the doctor called at about 8.30 a.m. He reminded Maybrick not to take his usual Valentine's Meat Juice or prussic acid since they were making him vomit. He prescribed Fowler's Solution, which contained arsenic.

While Florie went shopping, Nurse Yapp was left with Maybrick. He was moaning and hot; she rubbed his hands, which he again said were numb. When Florie came back Yapp suggested calling the doctor, but Florie rejected the idea on the grounds that her husband would not do what he said, anyway.

Battlecrease House was by now crowded with family, staff and visitors, all bustling about, whispering and watching each other and, in particular, Florie. In the midst of all this activity, a letter from Brierley arrived in which he said that he was afraid that their secret was about to be exploded and that he was off, out of harm's way.

During the evening of May 6th, Dr Humphreys paid another visit and applied a 'blister', a dressing intended to ease Maybrick's stomach pains.

As the illness wore on, the atmosphere of mistrust turned simple actions into objects of scrutiny. So, when Alice Yapp spotted Florie pouring something out of one medicine bottle into another, she was decidedly suspicious. She remembered the fly papers that Bessie told her she had discovered soaking under a towel in the wash-basin.

In the early afternoon of May 7th, Florie sent a telegram to Edwin's office in Liverpool asking him to find someone who could offer a second medical opinion. Dr William Carter, a self-described 'physician of considerable experience including cases of overdosing medicinally with arsenic', joined the medical team. He met Dr Humphreys at the house at 5.30 p.m. and together they examined the restless patient. By now, Maybrick was also complaining of 'a hair' in his throat.

The doctors decided he was suffering from dyspepsia and prescribed small doses of antipyrine to relieve his painful throat, and tincture of jaborandi plus diluted chlorodyne to relieve the foul taste in his mouth. His diet was restricted to chicken broth and milk. They told Florie that her husband was doing well and would soon be better.

That night, Maybrick vomited continuously and was still distressed by the 'hair' in his throat.

On Wednesday, May 8th, he was unable to get out of bed and told Dr Humphreys he thought he was going to die. Edwin saw his brother before leaving the house early for work. Maybrick suggested that a nurse be brought in to help Florie, who was exhausted. Florie telegraphed her mother in Paris with a terse message that bore a sharply different tone from her previous breezy letter: 'Jim very ill again.'

Through the upstairs window, Nurse Yapp, who was agog with all she had seen or imagined, spotted the sisters Mrs Briggs and Mrs Hughes hurrying up the drive. She accosted them in the yard with the shocking declaration: 'Thank God you have come, for the mistress is poisoning the master.' She told them of all the rumours and suspicions and led them immediately up the back stairs to see Maybrick.

Florie was put out when she discovered that the sisters were already in Maybrick's room. She called them down to the sitting room, where it was eventually agreed that a nurse should be hired. Mrs Briggs and Mrs Hughes left about noon, but immediately telegraphed Michael in London. 'Come at once,' said the message. 'Strange things going on here.' Theirs was one of two portentous telegrams sent to Michael that day. The other was from Edwin, who also urged his brother to come to Battlecrease House.

A Nurse Gore, from the Nurses Institution in Liverpool, arrived at the house at about 2.15 p.m. With the nurse there to relieve her, Florie made a critical mistake: she replied to Brierley. She followed this with a second mistake, one that proved nearly fatal. She asked Alice Yapp to post the letter.

The nurse took the letter and gave it to little Gladys to carry as they went to catch the 3.45 p.m. post. On the way, said Yapp at Florie's trial, Gladys dropped the letter in the mud.

'I went into the post office and asked for a clean envelope to re-address it. I opened it as I was going into the post office.'

What Alice Yapp read so shocked her that she hid the letter in her pocket. It was never posted.

Dearest

. . . I cannot answer your letter fully today, my darling, but relieve your mind of all <u>fear of discovery</u> now and in the future. M. has been delirious since Sunday, and I now know that he is <u>perfectly ignorant</u> of everything, even <u>to the name of the street,</u> and also <u>that he has not been making any inquiries whatever!</u> The tale he told me was a pure fabrication, and only intended to frighten the truth out of me. In fact, <u>he believes</u> my statement, although he will not <u>admit it</u>. You need not therefore go abroad on that account, dearest; but, in any case, please don't <u>leave England until I have seen you once again</u>! You must feel that those two letters of mine were written under circumstances which must even excuse their injustice in your eyes. Do you suppose that I could act as I am doing if I really felt and meant what I inferred then? If you wish to write to me about anything do so <u>now</u>, as all the letters pass through my hands at present. Excuse this scrawl, my own darling, but I dare not leave the room for a moment, and I do not know when I shall be able to write to you again. In haste, yours ever,

Florie

When Edwin returned at about five o'clock, Nurse Yapp was at her customary lookout post, watching for him in the yard, and intercepted him. As they sat on a seat in the garden she disclosed her startling find. For the moment, they took no action.

Michael arrived at Edge Hill station just before nine and was met by his brother in a cab. When Edwin told him about the letter, Michael took charge of the situation. Back at the house, the two men read the letter to Brierley and after Michael had seen their half-conscious brother, he spoke sharply to Florie. He did not tell her that they had read it, but criticized her for not having brought in a professional nurse and a second doctor earlier. Then he left to see Dr Humphreys at his house, arriving at 10.30 p.m.

The doctor acknowledged that he was not satisfied with Maybrick's condition and Michael informed him of Nurse Yapp's suspicions. The doctor did nothing. He just said: 'Your brother has told me he is going to die.'

Everyone had a restless night. Nurse Gore had been instructed that she alone was to give Maybrick his food and medicine. A new bottle of Valentine's Meat Juice was supplied by Edwin and given to a relief nurse, who by that time had taken over from the exhausted Nurse Gore.

Dr Carter was back at Battlecrease House the following afternoon, and persisted in his diagnosis of 'acute dyspepsia'. Michael, extremely agitated, objected. Since April, he claimed, his brother had been ill when at home and perfectly well when away. He added that the rift between Maybrick and his wife was serious and that Florie had been buying fly papers. What was Dr Humphreys going to do?

Now that suspicion of Florie had been discussed with the doctor, Michael decided to step up the safeguards surrounding the patient.

Florie was now virtually dispossessed in her own house. She wandered from room to room in a tearful state. She went up to the night nursery, where Nurse Yapp was tending to the children, and said: 'Do you know I am blamed for this?'

Nurse Yapp asked disingenuously: 'For what?'

Florie replied: 'For Mr Maybrick's illness.'

Everything was against her. She knew that Dr Humphreys had not been in favour of calling a second doctor and that Dr Carter had said there was no need for a nurse. She had ultimately asked for both, but now Michael was accusing her of not acting soon enough. She was confused and upset.

Florie had only two loyal friends in the house. One was Mary Cadwallader, who found some old fly papers in the butler's pantry and burned them. The other was the cook, Elizabeth Humphreys, who watched in the servants' hall as Florie collapsed and sobbed for fifteen minutes.

Since Michael's arrival, Florie told her, she had not been allowed in Maybrick's room. 'My position is not worth anything in this house.' Michael hated her, she said, and if James got better she would not have Michael there again. But Florie's vow would never be put to the test.

On Thursday, May 9th Maybrick was too ill to be examined. The doctors gave him double doses of bismuth with some brandy as a stomach sedative. For the first time, they took samples of urine and faeces, which Dr Carter took back to his office to be tested.

A small bottle of Neaves Food, with which Florie was suspected of tampering, was turned over with some zealousness to the doctor by Michael. A bottle of brandy, of which Michael was suspicious, was also tested.

All proved negative, a fact that would never be mentioned at Florie's trial.

During the evening, Maybrick grew still worse. Against the doctors' instructions, Nurse Gore took the unopened bottle of Valentine's Meat Juice, which Edwin had produced from a table on the landing, and gave him two teaspoonsful in water. Florie was there and protested in vain that the doctors had told Maybrick to discontinue the juice, which had always made him sick.

Just after midnight, Nurse Gore gave Maybrick some champagne, perhaps to calm his stomach, and noticed that Florie took the bottle of remaining meat juice into the dressing room. According to the nurse, Florie returned after two minutes and 'surreptitiously' replaced the bottle on the bedside table.

According to Nurse Callery, who was also attending Maybrick, Michael later removed the bottle without any of the meat juice having been given to the patient since Florie had returned it. Later on Friday Michael handed a bottle of meat juice to Dr Carter for analysis. It proved to contain half a grain of arsenic in solution. This substance was produced in evidence at Florie's trial, but, according to MacDougall, it was not the same bottle that Florie had taken into the dressing room. MacDougall makes clear his suspicion that Florie was being framed.

On Friday, Maybrick was even worse.

Nurse Wilson, a relief nurse, said she overheard Maybrick calling repeatedly to Florie: 'Oh, Bunny, Bunny, how could you do it? I did not think it of you.' Florie replied: 'You silly old darling, don't trouble your head about things.'

Later, when Thomas Lowry and George Smith delivered some papers to the house they heard the shouted protestations from Maybrick to Michael and Edwin, that he wanted to die in peace.

At 4 a.m. on Saturday, May 11th, Florie sent Mary Cadwallader to collect Mrs Briggs and Mrs Hughes. The children were taken in to see their father for the last time.

During the morning Florie herself was carried from the sickroom to the spare bedroom, where she lay in a mysterious swoon for over 24 hours, utterly unaware of events.

Dr Carter arrived and warned Michael that he had found some arsenic in the bottle of meat juice and that he and Dr Humphreys could therefore not give the cause of death as 'natural'.

At 8.40 p.m. – in the arms of his 'most intimate friend', George Davidson – Maybrick died.

The next day Dr Hopper was called up to Battlecrease House. In a supplemental statement at the time of Florie's trial he recalled that visit and his words point, for the first time, to the possibility that Florie may have been pregnant: 'I found that she was suffering from a sanguinous discharge, which might have been a threatened miscarriage and she told me that she had not had her monthly period since the 7th March. I was unable then to tell whether she was pregnant or not but I think it could be ascertained now by examination . . .'

Eight days earlier, on Friday, May 3rd, the day on which, Dr Carter suspected, the 'fatal' dose had been administered, Maybrick had made his last entry in the diary, and in so doing had posed his final questions. Did he confess both his drug habit and his secret identity as Jack the Ripper? And did he tell both his wife and his best friend the full story?

> The pain is unbearable. My dear Bunny knows all. I do not know if she has the strength to kill me. I pray to God she finds it. It would be simple, she knows of my medicine, and for an extra dose or two it would be all over. No one will know. I have seen to that. George knows of my habit and I trust soon it will come to the attention of Michael. In truth I believe he is aware of the fact. Michael will know how to act, he is the most sensible amongst us all. I do not believe I will see this June, my favourite of all months. Have begged Bunny to act soon. I curse myself for the coward I am . . .

Here, in the clearest terms, Maybrick reveals that he had asked Florie to administer a fatal overdose. But did she obey him?

Paul Feldman found a significant report, in a later edition of the *New York World*, that Maybrick had, in fact, contemplated suicide: 'It is alleged that Sir Charles [Russell] is going to show that he had discovered his wife's relations with Brierley and that he was determined to kill himself.'

But where was the diary?

Did Maybrick hide it at the office before leaving for the last time, on May 3rd?

Was the diary found – there or at Battlecrease House – and then concealed by someone else? Certainly there were those who would not have wanted the world to know that James Maybrick was Jack the Ripper. George Davidson, for example. If he knew about the killings, loyalty might have been enough to bar him from revealing the terrible truth.

Or was it discovered by Michael and Edwin, who had every reason to protect the family name?

Was it in the trunk of Florie's personal belongings, which disappeared?

Or did it simply remain hidden for a century in Battlecrease House?

Wherever the diary was, Maybrick was quite specific about what he hoped would become of it:

> I place this now in a place where it shall be found.
> I pray whoever should read this will find it in their
> heart to forgive. Remind all, whoever you may be,
> that I was once a gentleman.

His wish came true: the diary was discovered. It remains unclear when and how it surfaced. All we *know* is that it was before May 1991, when Mike Barrett received it.

Maybrick did not bequeath the diary to a member of his family. Instead he hid it, albeit in the hope that eventually it would be found, and that 'whoever' might find it should 'remind all' of his descent from prosperous family man to depraved serial killer.

TWELVE

'I place this now in a place where it shall be found'

THE RIPPER WAS dead.

Two days after Maybrick's death, on May 13th, Drs Humphreys, Carter and Barron carried out a post-mortem on him in the presence of Superintendent Bryning. The police had begun to investigate the circumstances of Maybrick's death because Drs Carter and Humphreys had refused to issue a death certificate and had decided instead to refer the case to the coroner.

Michael took charge of everything after his brother's death, including his ailing widow, who found herself tended by a strange nurse. Florie recalled that Michael told the nurse: 'Mrs Maybrick is no longer mistress of this house. As one of the executors I forbid you to allow her to leave this room.'

She was a prisoner even before she was formally charged. Although suspicions of arsenic poisoning had been rumbling around for some days, no search was made until after Maybrick had died. Then, with Florie locked out of the way, Michael, Edwin, Mrs Briggs, Mrs Hughes and the servants ransacked Battlecrease House. They said at Florie's trial that in a linen chest on the landing they found a bottle of morphia, a bottle of vanilla essence and a packet of harmless yellow powder, none of which Bessie, the housemaid, who was in charge of the chest, had noticed before.

But the discovery most sinister to the prying eyes of Florie's adversaries was a packet on which was written in red ink: 'Arsenic. Poison for Cats'. On the other side was a printed label saying 'Poison'. Inside the packet was a mixture of arsenic and charcoal. Michael wrapped the package in paper and affixed the family seal. Florie was devoted to cats, and her supporters believed the label, which was not in Florie's hand, must have been a joke by Nurse Yapp and her friend Alice Grant, the gardener's wife.

An 'Important Statement' appeared in the *Pall Mall Gazette* of June 15th: 'The probable explanation of the package found, labelled "poison for cats", may be found in the fact that a kennel of dogs near to Battlecrease House – which caused great annoyance to the deceased – were poisoned, and arsenic found in their bodies on examination. It is alleged, that the deceased was suspected, after his death, of poisoning the dogs.'

How strange, that, as happened so often in Florie's trial, such information – albeit rumour – was omitted, when its investigation could have provided useful evidence.

But at the time the full significance of this story was not understood. Nobody appreciated, as the diary had shown, how James Maybrick's sometimes sadistic sense of humour could have turned on Florie the cat lover. To write 'Poison for cats' seems entirely in keeping with a man whose twisted taste was for 'funny little jokes'.

The haul of medicines gathered from all over the house was then turned over to the police. The list that was later handed to the chemical analyst by the police is astonishing – not for the finger it points at an unhappy wife, but for the picture it paints of a man enslaved by drugs. Why, of all the people in the house with free access to so many drugs, Florie was charged on the grounds of mere gossip was an outrage beyond comprehension.

The analyst Mr Edward Davies claimed at Florie's trial that he had found enough arsenic to 'kill two or three people'. His evidence was so technical that it was quite beyond the understanding of the witnesses, the jury and even the judge himself.

In the end, it seems only six items contained any arsenic and that this was not in a form suitable for murder. For example, the arsenic found in Florie's dressing-gown pocket could well have come from the handkerchief with which she wiped her face after using arsenical cosmetics. Such explanations were not forthcoming at the trial.

Alexander MacDougall is scathing in his attack on Davies's unreliability and the inaccuracy of his methods and results. Of all the things in the printed list which did contain arsenic, 'the whole of them, might have been swallowed together and all would not have contained sufficient to kill anybody'.

Years later Florie Maybrick would write a book, *My Fifteen Lost Years*, in which she described the terrible days after her husband's death.

'Slowly consciousness returned,' she wrote. 'I opened my eyes. The room was in darkness. All was still. Suddenly the silence was broken by the bang of a closing door which startled me out of my stupor. Where was I? Why was I alone? What awful thing had happened? A flash of memory. My husband was dead. I drifted once more away from the things of sense. Then a voice, as if a long way off, spoke. A feeling of pain and distress shot through my body. I opened my eyes in terror. My brother-in-law, Edwin Maybrick, was bending over me as I lay upon my bed. He had my arms tightly gripped, and was shaking me violently. 'I want your keys. Do you hear. Where are your keys?' he exclaimed harshly. I tried to form a reply but the words choked me and once more I passed into unconsciousness.'

The day after Maybrick's death Florie told her nurse cum jailer she wanted to see her children.

'You cannot see Master James and Miss Gladys,' she recalled the nurse answered in a cold, deliberate voice. 'Mr Michael Maybrick gave orders that they were to leave the house without seeing you.'

'I fell back upon my pillow, dazed and stricken, weak, helpless and impotent,' Florie wrote. 'Why was I being treated like this? . . . my soul cried out to God to let me die . . . the yearning for my little children was becoming unbearable.'

Bobo and Gladys had been sent away with Nurse Yapp to friends. Within days they had lost both parents as well as the familiar comfort of the nursery at Battlecrease House. Their mother, the former Southern Belle who had fallen in love as a girl and exchanged her affluent, cosmopolitan circle in America for the secure claustrophobia of middle-class Liverpool, was now a widow and a virtual prisoner in her own home, suspected by the staff and her in-laws of her husband's murder.

On May 14th, three days after Maybrick's death, the rumours and suspicion surrounding Florie were to become formal allegations. As she described it: 'Suddenly the door opened and Dr Humphreys entered. He walked silently to my bedside, felt my pulse and without a word left the room. A few minutes later I heard the tramp of many feet coming upstairs. They stopped at the door. The nurse advanced and a crowd of men entered. One of them stepped to the foot of the bed and said to me: 'Mrs Maybrick, I am the Superintendent of Police and I am about to say something to you. After I have said what I intend to say be careful how you reply because whatever you may say may be used as evidence against you. Mrs Maybrick, you are in custody on suspicion of causing the death of your late husband, James Maybrick, on the eleventh instant.' '

Earlier that day, the coroner had decided that 'poison was found in the stomach of the deceased in such quantities as to justify further proceedings'.

A policeman was stationed in Florie's room, although there was no likelihood of her escaping. The officer would not even let her close the door night or day. On the day of Maybrick's funeral, Thursday May 16th, Florie awoke to the sound of muffled voices and hurrying footsteps. She was told abruptly by the nurse that 'the funeral starts in half an hour'.

At first Florie found herself barred from the bedroom where her husband's coffin, covered in white flowers, had already been closed.

'I turned to the policeman and nurse,' Florie wrote in her autobiography. 'Leave me alone with the dead. They refused. I knelt by the bedside and was able to cry the first tears which many days of suffering had failed to bring . . . . Calmed, I returned to my room and sat near a window, still weeping.

'Suddenly the harsh voice of the nurse broke on my ears. 'If you wish to see the last of the husband you murdered you had better stand up.' I stumbled to my feet and clutched at the window sill, where I stood rigid and tearless until the hearse had passed from sight. Then I fainted.'

·   ·   ·

The Baroness, in her bombazine best, burst on Battlecrease House the following day in response to a grudging telegram from Michael. 'Florie ill and in awful trouble' it read, without bothering to mention Maybrick's death.

'Edwin met me in the vestibule and took me into the morning room,' the Baroness would later write. 'He was much agitated . . . he then went on to tell me in a broken way that Michael had suspected, and the doctor thought something was wrong . . . . the nurse said Florie put something in the meat juice.'

The Baroness stormed upstairs and tried to speak to Florie in French. When Florie told her mother that she was suspected of poisoning Maybrick, the Baroness replied: 'If he is poisoned, he poisoned himself. He made a perfect apothecary's shop of himself.'

On Saturday morning, May 18th, the Baroness consulted Florie's solicitors, the brothers Arnold and William Cleaver of the firm of Cleaver, Holden, Garnett and Cleaver. While she was in their office a telegram arrived announcing that Florie was about to be removed from the house.

Thirteen legal and medical men had arrived by train and gathered by Florie's bed. Both Arnold and William Cleaver arrived ahead of the Baroness, and were among the assembled party. There had been a huddled consultation in the drive beforehand, eagerly watched by a crowd of reporters and onlookers. The Cleavers agreed not to object to a remand.

The Baroness arrived as Florie was about to be led away. 'I went up to my bedroom which looked out on the front,' she recalled, 'to try and see her face as they put my child into the cab, and they turned the key and locked me in . . . they hurried her away in so unseemly a manner, that even her handbag with toilet articles was left behind . . . . The nurse snatched up my cloak and hat and put it on her and they hustled her into an armchair, she being too weak to stand, and she was carried to the cab.'

■   ■   ■

A few weeks after Maybrick's death his friend Charles Ratcliff wrote a long letter to John Aunspaugh in Atlanta, Georgia. This letter is recalled in Trevor Christie's book *Etched in Arsenic* and formed part of Florence Aunspaugh's personal collection of memorabilia.

The letter throws a dramatic light on events leading up to Maybrick's death, especially as Ratcliff was a long-standing friend of the family and a reliable witness. It is a harsh, but most likely true, assessment of the trap set to catch Florie.

'This was a great shock to me. I had been expecting a tragedy within the family but was looking for it from the other party. James had gotten wise to the Flatman hotel affair and I was expecting him to plug Brierley at any time.'

Ratcliff explains how Maybrick came home from the Wirral Races on April 27th and began dosing himself 'as usual'. He talks in the letter of 'female serpents'. Mistakenly, he says that Mrs Briggs showed the Brierley letter to Edwin, whereas it was Nurse Yapp who spilt the beans. He then says that Edwin, 'DEEP IN THE MIRE HIMSELF', paid no attention to it.

'Old Dr Humphreys made a jackass of himself,' Ratcliff continues.

'After James died he and Dr Carter expected to make out the death certificate as acute inflammation of the stomach. After Humphreys had a conversation with Michael he refused to make a certificate to that effect but said there were strong symptoms of arsenical poisoning . . . . Now wouldn't that cork you. A musical composer instructing a physician how to diagnose his case.

'Michael, the son of a bitch, should have his throat cut. Mrs Maybrick was sick in bed when James died. He had only been dead a few hours when Michael . . . searched the house and in her [Florie's] room they claimed to have found quantities of arsenic, thirteen love letters from Edwin, seven from Brierley and five from Williams.'

Ratcliff ends the letter: 'I always thought the madam was dumb, but I must frankly admit that I did not consider her that dumb as to leave her affairs accessible to anyone . . . '

During those same weeks following Maybrick's death the newspapers in Liverpool began their own trial, carrying a torrent of hysterical articles in which they presented evidence and formed judgements even before Florie had been formally charged. The *Liverpool Echo* ran a regular column entitled 'Maybrickmania'. As the *Liverpool Review* acknowledged in a moment of candour: 'The Maybrick case is a stroke of good fortune for the papers.'

On May 28th, lawyers, witnesses, spectators and a battery of journalists jammed into the old police court in Wellington Road, Liverpool. The acoustics were terrible and for 12 hours the journalists took their notes, the *Liverpool Echo* reported, 'standing up between serried ranks of policemen, on their knees, sometimes on the backs of learned counsel and in various other awkward positions, for it was found impossible to hear at the tables assigned to them'.

They had gathered for the coroner's inquest, and the sensation it caused was only the beginning. The unholy muddle of contradictory evidence, lies and mistakes that followed has proved impossible to disentangle. In Britain such an inquest is not a trial; its task is to establish the cause of death. But in 1889 it could also apportion blame, and in the Maybrick case many were anxious to hear its verdict. The foreman of the inquest jury, Mr Dalgleish, who turned out to be a friend of the deceased, admitted that on the day of the Grand National Maybrick had told him he took strychnine. He was immediately dismissed, and the evidence he had about Maybrick's drug habit forgotten. Mr Fletcher Rogers then became foreman and impressed everyone with the way he discharged his duties.

Florie was still too ill to attend the inquest, so she did not hear witness after witness restate the whispered gossip of her domestic staff. They talked about the fly papers, the meat juice, the 'poison for cats' and, above all, the letter to Brierley. Florie's adultery was offered as the prime motive for murder. In Victorian eyes, a woman's adultery was a crime worse than all others.

The actual cause of Maybrick's death seemed of secondary interest. And in any case, despite what the coroner had asserted immediately after the post-mortem, no measurable arsenic had been found in his body. Nevertheless, the coroner insisted that the inquest be adjourned in order that 'the stomach and its contents might be chemically analysed'. As a result, on May 30th the torch-lit exhumation of James Maybrick's body took place in Liverpool's Anfield Cemetery.

. . .

Florie made her first appearance at the coroner's court on June 5th. Hissed by the women, who outnumbered men by two to one, she sat in an ante-room while the remaining evidence was given. Brierley was sitting at the back of the court, but he and Florie did not meet, and he was not asked to give evidence.

This was to be the day of the doctors and one by one they gave their preliminary findings. They were followed by Mr Flatman, proprietor of the Covent Garden hotel in which Florie and Brierley had stayed. Then came Alfred Schweisso, a waiter at the hotel, who identified Florie and Brierley. Schweisso later recanted his testimony in a letter to MacDougall on January 18th, 1890, in which he said: 'With regard to Mr Brierley. Of course I should not have recognised him at all if it had not been for the police; but as I was for the prosecution I went by their orders, which I am sorry for now for they acted in a very shameful manner . . . . I could not recognise him when he came; but a policeman came up and showed me where Mr Brierley was . . . it was a regular got up job.'

Next to appear in the witness-box was Thomas Lowry, the clerk who had been sent out of the office to buy a saucepan, basin and spoon for Maybrick's Revalenta tonic. He was followed by the charwoman who washed the utensils, and Mrs Briggs, who had led the search of the house.

Next day the court heard from Edwin; from Frederick Tozer, the assistant at Clay and Abrahams, one of the dispensing chemists who had supplied medicine to James; and the police.

Finally, the analyst, Edward Davies, reported that as a result of the exhumation, he had found unweighable amounts of arsenic in May-brick's intestines, an estimated one-thousandth of a grain in his kidneys, an estimated one-eighth of a grain in his liver and nothing anywhere else in his body.

When I sought an opinion on this from Dr Glyn Volans, of Guy's Hospital, London, he told me: 'Although a man may have been dosing himself on arsenic and strychnine for years they simply did not have the forensic techniques to detect it accurately. It is quite understandable that so little arsenic was found in Maybrick's body. It is equally understandable that they did not pinpoint the true cause of his death, which was probably kidney failure, due to a lifetime's abuse.'

Then Mrs Hughes was called in to identify the infamous letter from Florie to Brierley.

Despite the lack of evidence, the jury – most of whom had been guests of the Maybricks at one time or another – decided that 'James Maybrick died from the effects of an irritant poison administered to him by Florence Elizabeth Maybrick and that the said Florence Elizabeth Maybrick did wilfully, feloniously and with malice aforethought kill and murder the said James Maybrick'.

. . .

To avoid the long drive back to Walton Jail, on the edge of the city, the authorities sent Florie to Lark Lane Lock-Up. There she was kindly treated and well fed with food brought in from a nearby hotel. A reporter from the *Liverpool Post* who called to see her wrote: 'She is supplied with a little table which is placed close to the entrance of her cell. She is allowed to take as much exercise as she pleases in the corridor and when tired sits at the table which is covered with a snow white cloth. On it there were two books, one with crimson binding, the other in less conspicuous colours. She reads the comments on her case with liveliest interest and indulges occasionally in sarcastic references to anything which does not please her. She is somewhat wayward in her manner.'

The spark was still there.

On June 13th, Florie, in heavy mourning, was taken to the magisterial inquiry (rather like a magistrates' court today) in Liverpool's Islington courthouse to hear the evidence against her for the very first time. She listened as, one by one, her servants, brothers-in-law and doctors testified.

Even at this stage the doctors did not agree with each other about the cause of death and admitted to having an insufficient understanding of Maybrick's condition. Moreover, the proceedings were remarkable for what they left out. In particular, no one mentioned that no trace of arsenic had been found in faeces and urine samples taken from James only days before his death. Equally remarkable was the fact, of all the welter of evidence submitted, that in the end all that remained beyond dispute was that, in March, Florie and Alfred Brierley had spent two nights at Flatman's Hotel in London. But that, it seemed, was enough for a capital charge.

Florie was committed for trial on July 26th and removed to Walton Jail. Crowds ran booing after her carriage as it pulled away from the court.

Local photographers were quick to capitalize on the story. Shops carried window displays of the Maybricks, including one sensational picture of Florie and Brierley together at the Grand National. And Battlecrease House became a tourist attraction, with dozens of rubber-neckers pointing ghoulishly to the window of the room where Maybrick died.

The prosecution received a letter from Brierley's solicitors, Banks and Kendall, on July 6th. They protested that Brierley had never received the letter of May 6th and asked for their client not to be sub-poenaed as he was booked for a holiday. The request must have been refused.

On July 8th, not seven weeks after Florie's arrest, Michael fla-grantly disregarded the instructions of his brother's will and auctioned the entire contents of the house. It was as though he was sure Florie would never return.

While Florie waited in her prison cell, Michael and Thomas disposed of every single item from the young widow's home in a sale that took place in the showrooms of Messrs Branch and Leete.

Opening the proceedings, Mr Leete was greeted from the packed room with a murmur of approval. He explained that he knew both the dead and the living and he hoped they would all withhold their judgement in this sad case, as all Englishmen should.

Bidding was brisk and many items sold for more than their expected price. A burnished brass French bedstead fetched 10 guineas, and a suite of American walnut from the best bedroom fetched 36 guineas. There were numerous, not particularly distinguished, paintings and a library of books that was described as 'the usual commonplace books'. Poignant among this shattering of a family home were the toys – the child's saddle with girths and a child's tricycle horse.

Florie's beautiful clothes were bundled into trunks and sent to storage at Woollrights. What happened to them nobody knows.

There was also a gold watch, mentioned in the auction preview particulars, which did not arrive at the auction itself. It was not the only item that went missing. The *Liverpool Post* reported that Alice Yapp arrived for Florie's trial brazenly carrying one of her umbrellas. The *New York Herald* London edition of August 9th commented: 'The other servants do not hesitate to say that she has made good use of her position to possess herself of many of Florence Maybrick's dresses and suchlike.'

What happened to the money from the auction? At one point Michael claimed that he spent half to help pay for Florie's counsel. Later he said that since he was to be a witness for the prosecution he would not fund Florie's defence. It was one more contradiction.

At least the Mutual Reserve Fund Life Association of New York waived its three-month embargo after a person's death and sent the sum of $1,000 to Florie. Her mother, meantime, managed to raise funds by selling family land in Kentucky. Florie needed every penny, since the terms of Maybrick's new will were extremely stringent.

Florie was very anxious that her trial should not take place in Liverpool. She wrote again to her mother:

'I sincerely hope the Cleavers will arrange for my 'trial' to take place in London. I shall receive an impartial verdict there, which I cannot expect from a jury in Liverpool whose minds have come to a 'moral conviction', en attendant, which must influence their decision to a certain extent. The tittle-tattle of servants, the public, friends and enemies and from a thousand by-currents, besides their personal feeling for Jim, must leave their traces and prejudice their minds, no matter what the defence is.'

It was not to be. Florie's advisers believed she would have a stronger case if she stood firm on home ground, and she accepted their counsel.

Arnold Cleaver set off for America to rally support and witnesses. There, the newspapers were wildly excited by the image of the forlorn and friendless expatriate, married to a debauched foreigner in a distant land. It was the beginning of a groundswell of support.

But, at Madame Tussaud's in London they were already designing her waxwork for the Chamber of Horrors.

THIRTEEN

'The whore will suffer unlike she has ever suffered'

ST GEORGE'S HALL, Liverpool, was one of those monstrously magnificent Victorian piles of smoke-blackened stone, standing aloof in the centre of the city. It was well known and well loved by Liverpudlians, who considered it their 'village hall', the scene of many a concert, festival and social event. But to this day it is respected, too, as the site of the Crown Court. It was here that Florie would have to stand trial in what was anticipated to be the greatest show Liverpool had staged in years. Already, scores of requests for seats were being received from people who, as the *Southport Guardian* put it, 'like the flowers in spring had nothing to do with the case'.

'I feel so lonely,' Florie wrote to a friend during that time, 'as if every hand were against me. To think that I must be unveiled before all those uncharitable eyes . . . the darkest days of my life are now to be lived through. I trust in God's justice, whatever I may be in the sight of man.'

Florie had already been through the inquest and the magisterial inquiry, which delivered the magistrates' ruling that she would be tried on a charge of murder. There was one more proceeding before she could be called into the dock to answer the charge against her: the Grand Jury.

The function of the Grand Jury was to stand between the Crown and the accused and decide if a person committed for trial by magistrates should be so tried. Unless the Grand Jury agreed, by returning a 'true bill', there could be no trial. The Grand Jury had the last word. Its members were selected not at random but for their rank and intelligence. They were deemed to be free of local influence and constraint by the Crown. If the Grand Jurors thus represented the people, the judge at this proceeding represented the Crown.

The judge for Florie's trial, Mr Justice (better known as Mr 'Injustice') James Fitzjames Stephen, was at the end of a distinguished career. The *Liverpool Review* described him as 'a big, burly, brainy man', adding: 'His mind is like one of those very wonderful and exact machines that one sees in manufacturing districts. It does its work with remarkable precision and laborious and untiring exactness, but unless it is carefully watched by the attendant and occasionally set in the right direction, it is liable to go all wrong.'

At the time of the Maybrick trial it seemed clear that Mr Justice

Stephen had already gone 'all wrong'. Reason was sliding away, and this once great man no longer seemed capable of sustained concentration. In correspondence with Lord Lytton in 1889, he had revealed: 'I do still now and then smoke an opium pipe as my nose requires one occasionally and is comforted by it.'

On July 26th, the day of the Grand Jury, several thousand people jostled for a sight of the prisoner outside the courthouse. Inside, sunshine poured through the glass roof and lit the judge, who sat in his scarlet and ermine robes beneath the gold and crimson canopy.

In his address to the Grand Jury, Mr Justice Stephen set out the details of case No. 24, injecting them with innuendo and failing to master the basic facts. His opening words were an outrage. He referred to James Maybrick as a man 'unhappy enough to have an unfaithful wife'.

'If the prisoner is guilty of the crime alleged to her in the charge,' he continued, 'it is the most cruel and horrible murder that could be committed.'

His words were reported in full, so that, before the trial, the world knew of the judge's opinions on adultery. And unfortunately for Florie, his strictures applied only to women. There was no discussion of Maybrick's extramarital activity.

Two questions were at the heart of the case against Florie: first, was arsenic the cause of death? Second, if so, had the arsenic been administered by Mrs Maybrick with felonious intent?

It was open to the Crown to add other counts to the charge of murder, and to do so was quite common. However, in Florie's case the sole charge was to be that of murder. And this, despite the fact that there was absolutely no evidence to connect the defendant with any of the arsenic found in Battlecrease House, apart from the fly papers. The Grand Jury's deliberations finished, Florie's trial was scheduled to begin on July 31st.

■   ■   ■

Florie's counsel, Sir Charles Russell QC, was a persuasive, flamboyant Irishman, who habitually sported in his breast pocket a bandanna, which he waved to emphasize his views. He was also a Member of

Parliament and a former Attorney General who had been one of Britain's most respected lawyers. His title greatly impressed the Baroness; indeed everyone deemed Florie fortunate to have so famous a man to defend her. With hindsight, she could have done better.

For one thing, Sir Charles had recently had a bad record with murder cases. In 1883 he defended a man named O'Donnell for murder. O'Donnell was executed. Three years later he prosecuted Mrs Adelaide Bartlett for poisoning her husband with chloroform. She got off.

But most recently, Russell had been leading counsel for Charles Stewart Parnell, the Irish MP, who had been charged with sedition. The trial, which took place in 1888-9, required Russell to listen to 340 witnesses and make a six-day speech. By July 31st, the day Florie's trial was scheduled to begin, the barrister was exhausted.

About 8 a.m. on that day, Florie was bundled into a prison van with a number of male prisoners and driven to St George's Hall, where a crowd of several thousand had gathered in the already blistering heat. Florie could not help but observe the carnival atmosphere:

'During all the days of my trial, I am told, Liverpool society fought for tickets. Ladies were attired as for a matinee, and some brought their luncheons that they might retain their seats. Many of them carried opera-glasses, which they did not hesitate to level at me.'

Among the attractions was an itinerant street singer who had drawn a huge crowd by rendering songs based on the Maybrick case. The quality of the doggerel was on a par with that of Maybrick's diary.

Oh! Naughty Mrs Maybrick what have you been and done
Your goings on are bad I must confess
To get mashed on Mr Brierley you know was very wrong
And get yourself in such a blooming mess.

Just before ten o'clock, the handsome Sir Charles Russell appeared, flourishing his bandanna. Counsel for the prosecution was the jovial John Addison QC. The jury consisted of twelve Lancashire men, at least one of whom could not read or write, while another had been recently convicted of beating his wife. They were a mix of labourers and tradesmen who could not have been expected to understand the technicalities of the testimony.

At ten o'clock, to a fanfare of trumpets, the court rose and Mr Justice Stephen appeared, unsmiling in a full-bottomed wig, his side-burns bristling below. After a few preliminaries, the clerk called out: 'Put up Florence Elizabeth Maybrick.'

Florie wore a crêpe jacket over her black dress, a crêpe bonnet with black streamers and a thin black veil. She answered the charges against her clearly and firmly: 'Not guilty.'

Later, during lunch, there was an uproar because members of the jury were seen hobnobbing with reporters and witnesses. It did not matter; the members were not dismissed.

. . .

Alexander MacDougall's exhaustive, 606-page book recounts the mistakes and the inconsistencies in the case against Mrs Maybrick. Among the ten medical men who testified, there was agreement that the cause of James Maybrick's death was gastroenteritis. They could not agree, however, on whether it was caused by bad food or a poison, or, if the latter, whether it was arsenic.

Dr Richard Humphreys, who had treated Maybrick for the first time during his illness, was one of those who attributed the death to arsenic. But at the magisterial inquiry he acknowledged that he had never treated anyone who had died of arsenic poisoning, nor had he assisted at any such post-mortem examination.

Dr William Carter had treated Maybrick just four times. Moreover, he acknowledged under cross-examination that he had never assisted at a case involving death by arsenic or at a post-mortem examination involving arsenic.

Dr Carter had, on May 7th, diagnosed Maybrick with dyspepsia due to 'indiscretion of food or drink'. Two days later, after a conversation in which Michael Maybrick mentioned his suspicion of arsenic poisoning, he changed his mind. At the trial, he agreed with Dr Humphreys.

Dr Alexander Barron, professor of pathology at Liverpool's University College, was present at Maybrick's post-mortem and exhumation but had never treated him. He concluded that the death was due 'to acute inflammation of the stomach, probably caused by some irritant poison'.

Under cross-examination by Sir Charles, Dr Barron was asked: 'Is it possible to differentiate the symptoms of arsenical poisoning or poisoning from impure food?'

'I should not be able to do so myself,' he replied.

But Dr Charles Meymott Tidy, for two decades a Home Office analyst and examiner in forensic medicine at the London Hospital, and whose experience of poisons ranged back to 1862, declared: 'The symptoms of the post-mortem distinctly point away from arsenic.'

Dr Charles Fuller, who had 30 years of experience as a medical practitioner and homoeopath, said he had no reason to believe Maybrick was taking arsenic. The symptoms which accompany the habitual taking of arsenic were not present in this case.

Dr Rawden Macnamara, Fellow of the Royal College of Surgeons of Ireland and Doctor of Medicine at the University of London, had administered arsenic 'in a very large number of cases'. When asked if Maybrick died of arsenic poisoning he replied: 'Certainly not.'

Dr Frank Thomas Paul was a pathologist with some 3,000 post-mortems to his credit, and Professor of Medical Jurisprudence at University College, Liverpool. His verdict: that the symptoms described in the case 'agree with cases of gastroenteritis pure and simple . . . I presume that he died of exhaustion produced by gastroenteritis'.

Dr Thomas Stevenson, lecturer in Forensic Medicine at Guy's Hospital, London and Home Office analyst, was called in to examine Maybrick's viscera. After a lengthy cross-examination, he testified, to the contrary, that he had 'no doubt' that death was due to arsenical poisoning.

Incidentally, Dr Arthur Hopper, who had been the family doctor from 1881, gave evidence about Maybrick's drug-taking but was not asked for his opinion on his patient's final illness.

Dr Glyn Volans, of Guy's Hospital, London, at our request read the contemporary 'Toxicological Report' on the case of James Maybrick and was 'not at all convinced' that he died from acute arsenic poisoning. 'The lowest recorded lethal dose is two grains,' he said. 'Yet only one-tenth of a grain of arsenic was found in James Maybrick's body.

'The evidence that Florence Maybrick administered poison is just not there. It is more likely that he died from the accumulative effect of all the stuff that was pumped into him by the doctors in his last weeks plus the results of a lifetime of drug abuse – in addition to which he no longer had access to his poisons and so he was suffering from withdrawal symptoms. Renal failure is a more likely cause of death.'

.   .   .

If the jurors were unperturbed by the confusion of the medical men, it was perhaps because they had testimony far more scintillating on which to focus. By the end of the first week of the trial, Florie had heard witness after witness reconstructing her life with Maybrick and the events of 1888-9. Yet she weakened her defence by requesting that, for the sake of their children, no mention be made of her husband's indiscretions.

Then there was the matter of the meat juice. Against Dr Carter's orders it was given by Edwin to Nurse Gore and the bottle stood, new and unopened, by Maybrick's bed on the night of May 9th. Nurse Gore knew that Florie was under suspicion. Shortly after 11 p.m. Gore gave him one or two spoonfuls in water, despite Florie's warning that it made him sick. About midnight, she watched Florie remove the bottle for a few moments and take it into the dressing room, returning it to the bedside a few seconds later. She also noted that Florie moved the bottle out of reach to a dressing table after Maybrick had woken up. He did not drink the meat juice.

The bottle then passed from Nurse Gore to Michael to Dr Carter before it was sent for analysis. Mr Edward Davies reported that there was half a grain of arsenic in solution in the bottle, a finding that was fuel for the prosecution.

When Florie first told her story to her solicitor before the inquest, she admitted freely, but perhaps naïvely, to having put some powder into the meat extract, at her husband's request. This information was suppressed in her own interests but formed part of a statement she insisted on reading, against her counsel's wishes, at the end of her trial. She told the court:

'On Thursday night, the 9th May, after Nurse Gore had given my husband beef tea, I went and sat on the bed beside him. He complained to me of being very sick, and very depressed and again implored me to give him this powder which he had referred to early in the evening, and which I had declined to give him. I was overwrought, terribly anxious, miserably unhappy and his evident distress utterly unnerved me. He had told me the powder would not harm him, and I could put it in his food. I then consented. My Lord, I had not one true or honest friend in the house. I had no one to consult, no one to advise me. I was deposed from my position as mistress in my own house and from the position of attending upon my husband, notwithstanding that he was so ill. Notwithstanding the evidence of nurses and servants I may say that he wished to have me with him; he missed me whenever I was not with him; whenever I went out of the room he asked for me and, for four days before he died I was not allowed to give him a piece of ice without its being taken out of my hand. When I found the powder I took it to the inner room with the beef juice, and in pushing through the door, I upset the bottle, and, in order to make up the quantity of fluid spilled, I added a considerable quantity of water. On returning to the room, I found my husband asleep, and I placed the bottle on the table by the window. When he awoke he had a choking sensation in his throat and vomited; after that he appeared a little better, and as he did not ask for the powder again, and as I was not anxious to give it to him, I removed the bottle from the small table where it would attract attention, to the top of the washstand, where he could not see it. There I left it, my Lord, until, I believe, Mr Michael Maybrick took possession of it. Until Tuesday 14th May, the Tuesday after my husband's death and until a few minutes before Mr Bryning made this terrible charge against me, no one in that house had informed me of the fact that a death certificate had been refused, or that a post-mortem examination had taken place; or that there was any reason to suppose that my husband had died from other than natural causes. It was only when Mrs Briggs alluded to the presence of arsenic in the meat juice that I was made aware of the nature of the powder my husband had asked me to give him . . . '

What Florie did not realize was that powdered white arsenic does not dissolve easily. The arsenic found in the bottle of meat juice must have been in solution and could not have been added the way Florie described. So what was the powder which Maybrick had begged her to give him? Could it have been strychnine? Ten days before, he had written in the diary of his intention to ask Florie to kill him and wondered if she had the strength to do so. If she had poisoned him with strychnine, the tests for arsenic applied by the analysts would not have revealed it. In any case, they were not looking for strychnine.

Much was made of the fly papers. Only four years earlier, two married sisters from Liverpool named Flanagan and Higgins had been hanged for using arsenic extracted from fly papers to poison three people. The defence argued that the fly papers could not have been responsible for Maybrick's death, since no fibres from them had been found in any of the contaminated bottles in the house. In her statement Florie said:

'The fly papers were bought with the intention of using as a cosmetic. Before my marriage, and since, for many years, I have been in the habit of using a face wash, prescribed for me by Dr Greggs of Brooklyn. It consisted principally of arsenic, tincture of benzoin, elderflower water, and some other ingredients. This prescription I lost or mislaid last April and, as at that time I was suffering from a slight eruption of the face I thought I should like to try to make a substitute myself. I was anxious to get rid of this eruption before I went to a ball on the 30th of that month. When I had been in Germany many of my young friends there I had seen using a solution derived from fly papers, elder water, lavender water, and other things mixed, and then applied to the face with a handkerchief well soaked in the solution. I used the fly papers in the same manner. But to avoid the evaporation of the scent it was necessary to exclude the air as much as possible, and for that purpose I put a plate over the fly papers, and put a folded towel over that, and another towel over that. My mother has been aware for a great many years that I use an arsenical cosmetic in solution.'

It sounded harmless enough. But because the statement had not been made at the magisterial inquiry, Judge Stephen interpreted it as a lie, made up for the occasion – and said so.

Many months after the trial, the Baroness von Roques was turning the pages of the Chandler family Bible – one of the few items that had been saved from auction. There she found the lost prescription, written on the back of a New York chemist's label and dated 1878.

And the year after the trial, 1890 – too late for Florie – E. Godwin Clayton, a consulting chemist and Member of the Society of Public Analysts, carried out a test in which he attempted to extract arsenic from two fly papers. His verdict: 'It is next to impossible for any person without opportunities for and knowledge of chemical manipulation to make or procure an aqueous infusion of the fly papers which could be added to Valentine's Meat Juice in sufficient quantity to introduce half a grain of arsenic.'

. . .

The trial ended after seven days. The judge's summing-up took an interminable twelve hours, spread over two days. 'For a person to go deliberately administering poison to a poor, helpless sick man upon whom she has already inflicted a dreadful injury – an injury fatal to married life – the person who could do such a thing as that must indeed be destitute of the least trace of human feeling.'

By the end of the summing-up, everyone was in utter confusion. (A witness to the proceedings said that 'he had never in a court of law heard such a pathetic exhibition of incompetence and inaccuracy'.) The judge ranted: 'The circumstances indicated in the evidence are very varied and the witnesses go backwards and forwards in a way which makes the evidence somewhat confusing from beginning to end. I am sorry to say I shall not be able to arrange it before you exactly as I would wish . . . '

Not as sorry as the prisoner in the dock.

Journalists, spectators and the thousands of people thronging the square outside St George's Hall were confident that Florie would be acquitted. There had been a huge surge of public opinion in her favour. After all, there was no evidence linking Florie with any of the arsenic found in the house; none to prove that she had consciously administered arsenic, nor that arsenic had even killed James Maybrick.

Still, the jury took only 35 minutes to reach a verdict that has baffled legal experts ever since: Guilty.

The only telephone in St George's Hall had been booked in advance by the *Evening Express* and the *Morning Courier*, eager for a scoop. Equally enterprising, the *Daily Post* and the *Echo* organized a system of semaphores between a reporter in the court and a string of correspondents stationed on the way to the office of the *Daily Post*. But in the turmoil, a confused journalist waved the wrong flag and 5,000 copies of the newspaper flooded onto the streets carrying banner headlines announcing that Florie was free.

Mr Justice Stephen put on his black cap. The silence in the court was broken only by a gasp. Men were in tears. Women fainted.

James Maybrick, who was lying in Anfield Cemetery, should have been standing in that dock. It was he, Jack the Ripper, who should have been called to account. But it was Florie who stiffened, stumbled and then, after sentence of death had been passed, walked from the dock, unaided and alone.

．．．

So many questions about the case are unanswered still. What of the behaviour of Michael and Edwin Maybrick throughout the period? Even before Maybrick's death, the brothers discussed with Mrs Briggs, Mrs Hughes and Nurse Yapp the possibility that he was being poisoned, yet no search of Battlecrease House was made until it was too late to save him. Then, after his death, they blitzed the entire house.

Moreover, compromising letters discovered at the house and believed to be from Edwin to Florie vanished.

Edwin had discussed Maybrick's habit of taking 'that damned strychnine' with friends yet denied it at the trial. Michael also knew of his brother's use of drugs, and denied it. So why did the analysts search only for arsenic?

Between Maybrick's death and the trial, Dr Hopper destroyed all Maybrick's prescriptions. Why?

Michael managed to prevent Maybrick's latest will being used as evidence, for it gave him and Thomas, as trustees, enormous powers, and Florie nothing. Moreover, Florie's solicitors did not stop Michael's auction of contents from Battlecrease.

Much was made of Florie's debts; why was nothing made of her husband's?

Maybrick's lifelong infidelity was ignored; Florie's lapse was enough to see her convicted.

Why were so many important witnesses not called to testify? No evidence was given by Florie's mother, Maybrick's other brothers, Thomas and William, George Davidson, Alfred Brierley, John Baillie

Knight, Mrs Christina Samuelson, the gardener James Grant, or the Hobsons, with whom Maybrick dined on the night of the Wirral races.

. . .

The Maybrick case was to be Mr Justice Stephen's last. Within two years, he was sent to a private asylum for the insane in Ipswich, where he died in 1894.

As the scaffold was being erected outside her cell Florie Maybrick was granted a reprieve. The Home Secretary, Henry Matthews, who had worked so hard and so unsuccessfully a year earlier to solve the Whitechapel killings, unsuspectingly commuted the death sentence on Jack the Ripper's wife to penal servitude for life.

J.H. Levy believed – as did so many others – that when Florie's sentence was commuted on the grounds that James may well not have died of arsenic poisoning, Florie should have been released. Instead she was kept in prison for 15 years for attempting to murder him – a crime for which she had not been tried or found guilty and for which, in any case, the maximum sentence was 10 years.

In his excellent and sober analysis of the trial and its later repercussions Levy wrote: 'I submit the Home Secretary was not entitled to say . . . "you may not be guilty of murder; perhaps you are not. But you are, in my opinion guilty of another crime, for which you have not been tried; therefore I shall make use of the warrant of conviction and sentence of murder to punish you for the other crime of which I have found you guilty."'

Ironically, history has twice linked the name of Florence – not James Maybrick – with that of Jack the Ripper. The judge, who dealt so harshly with her, had a son – J.K. Stephen – who was tutor to the Duke of Clarence, who in turn was, himself, named by author Michael Harrison as a Ripper suspect in his 1972 book *Clarence*.

The other occasion was on August 17th 1889, when a cartoon appeared entitled 'Whitechapel at Whitehall'. It showed the Home Secretary Mr Matthews with Jack the Ripper on his right. The caption reads: 'Attempted murder of Florence Maybrick – save her Mr Matthews.'

FOURTEEN

'Will give them something to know it is me'

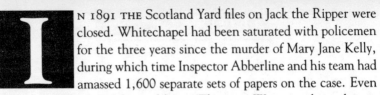

IN 1891 THE Scotland Yard files on Jack the Ripper were closed. Whitechapel had been saturated with policemen for the three years since the murder of Mary Jane Kelly, during which time Inspector Abberline and his team had amassed 1,600 separate sets of papers on the case. Even Inspector Abberline admitted later: 'Theories! We were almost lost in theories. There were so many of them.' From time to time since then official documents and letters have come to light and even today Ripper experts are still elaborating new theories.

When, in April 1992, Mike Barrett walked into the London office of literary agent Doreen Montgomery with the diary, he was utterly convinced it contained evidence that would expose the true Whitechapel killer. This was the first material to emerge in more than a century that had not passed through police hands. At the same time, it was the most detailed and convincing confession to date. But was it true?

Mike had lived with the diary for a year or so and was convinced beyond doubt that it was genuine. But at this early stage I was still facing the possibility that it could be a forgery.

In researching the story of the Maybricks, I knew I was dealing with not one but two of the most baffling of all British criminal cases. For this reason, I resisted the temptation to enter a debate with Ripper specialists. Instead I have focused on the diary itself, and asked the experts to do precisely the same.

As I combed the newspapers of 1888 and 1889 I found they were full of facts about the Ripper murders and the Maybrick case. If there had been a skilled forger at work on the diary, he would have found it irresistible to draw on the immense amount of material on both cases from which to fabricate his entries. Yet there are no dates, few details of family occasions and little of what was widely known or surmised about either the Ripper or Maybrick. What was left out is as telling as what is included. No forger would have dared to be so miserly with the readily available facts.

The diary also contains a detail that could have arisen only from the author's experience and not from press reports. First, when the diary begins, around March 1888, Florie Maybrick's lover is already on the scene. In fact, in a later, unpublicised affidavit, Brierley acknowledged that he first met Florie in 1887. Even so, by mentioning

Brierley as a rival, albeit not by name, the diary revises the chronology of Florie's infidelity, casting doubt on evidence produced at her trial, where witnesses spoke of the affair beginning around Christmas of 1888.

Second, Maybrick's barely controllable antagonism to Thomas Lowry, his clerk, is a sub-plot that only makes sense to me if the diary is genuine. As a witness, Lowry made only a brief appearance at Florie's trial and his relationship with Maybrick was not public knowledge.

Third, the frequent, spontaneous references to George Davidson, in whose arms Maybrick died, are consistent with their close friendship. And yet Davidson was not called to give evidence at the trial, nor was his relationship to Maybrick widely known.

Finally, why does Mrs Ham(m)ersmith appear at the beginning of the diary? We do not know who she is, despite the wealth of information on the Maybricks' social circle. Nor was she listed in the Liverpool street directory of 1889. So why invent her? In addition to the expertise of a psychologist and a doctor of medicine, a forger would need the imagination of a novelist.

By contrast, there were other, far more central, characters in the drama who were not mentioned in the diary. One was Mrs Briggs, an erstwhile rival with Florie for Maybrick's affections, who imposed her strong presence on the household, mainly by dominating Maybrick himself. Then there was the gossiping nurse, Alice Yapp, whose appointment by Maybrick caused a minor scandal. And where is the formidable Baroness von Roques, Maybrick's mother-in-law?

Nor does the diary include accounts of the killings of Martha Tabram and Emma Smith. A contemporary or even much later forgery would certainly have included these crimes, believing them to be the work of the Ripper, for they were counted among the Ripper's victims by most authorities at the time, and not generally discounted until the 1950s.

Conversely, why undermine the diary's authenticity by adding to the Ripper's Whitechapel tally two murders and an interrupted attempt for which there is so far no documentary proof? The murders occurred in Manchester – early in 1888 and in December – and the failed attack in Whitechapel in February 1889. They are unique to the diary.

Similarly, research for this book linked for the first time the three occasions on which the letter 'M' or Maybrick's initials were left at the scene of a Ripper murder. It appeared on a fragment of envelope left beside the body of his second victim, Annie Chapman. It was carved on the cheeks of the fourth woman to die, Catharine Eddowes – a fact that Mike Barrett was the first person ever to notice. Finally it was scrawled on the wall, possibly in blood, in combination with an 'F', in the room of Mary Jane Kelly, the last of the five canonical victims. Maybrick speaks of 'an initial here, an initial there', and if we take the 'M' to mean 'Maybrick', it is reasonable to assume 'FM' to be the initials of his wife.

This is a very idiosyncratic and personal diary. The way in which it refuses to fit with any preconceived ideas we may have of what it *ought* to contain is to me a mark of its total honesty. It flows straight from the heart of a sick man.

Nevertheless I knew the world would demand a more down-to-earth response and I awaited anxiously the reports of the experts I had approached.

. . .

The forensic testing of the diary was conducted by Dr Nicholas Eastaugh, who prefaced his report with a warning. 'In the now famous 'Hitler diaries' debacle,' he says, 'it was the materials of the documents – the paper and the ink – which ultimately exposed the hoax. When something as potentially important as the 'Jack the Ripper' diary suddenly appears there should naturally enough be great caution and it is only prudent to examine the physical composition of the document with forensic-style tests with the aim of assessing the age.

'There is as yet no single test which will clearly, precisely and unambiguously determine the age of written documents like the diary. The only widely known dating technique which might conceivably have been used on the diary – radiocarbon dating of the paper – is not applicable because of its accuracy and certain technical problems with materials more recent than about AD 1500. Some relative assessments of ink age are possible, but these are for testing writing within a document (such as to see whether pages have been added or swapped) and are therefore of little use here.

'Moreover, even if we could effectively determine the age of the ink and the paper, this would be insufficient to 'authenticate' the document since we would still not know when ink and paper were combined and the diary actually written. In fact it is just such a document as the diary which highlights the fact that scientists and historians lack any way of directly assessing the absolute chronological age of such items. We can only infer when the document was created by looking at the composition of the component parts, when these constituents were available and the frequency of their use. We can also draw some general inferences about the apparent age from the appearance (for example, we might be suspicious if the writing passed over obviously recent damage to the paper). The situation is not uncommon and historic document examination just happens to be a relatively understudied, newly emergent, field.

'To 'date' the ink and paper we have to compare what they are made of to what we know of ink and paper composition over the past 100 years. For example, various coloured dyes used in inks have only been invented since the time of Jack the Ripper, and if the ink were to contain any of these then it must be a later forgery. In practice (and simplifying) this means that we must apply a series of increasingly detailed tests looking for faults; the more tests the document 'passes', the more likely it is that we are dealing with either a very sophisticated forgery or the genuine article. So, what are we looking for?

'Historically, a major change took place in inks during the 19th century because of the introduction of mass-produced steel pen nibs. Around the beginning of the 1830s a number of factors combined to make possible large-scale manufacture of such nibs. However, it was soon discovered that the traditional acidic inks based on iron-gall rapidly corroded them and in consequence new inks had to be developed. Hence we find companies such as Stephens setting up new factories around this time (1834) to produce inks based on dyes and a carefully controlled iron-gall ink recipe that were non-corrosive to the steel. Innovation was not to stop there, however; specific needs of fountain pens and the appearance of synthetic dyes during the second half of the century led to the development of what we may call fountain-pen-type inks which have remained largely unchanged to the present day.

'Fortunately, we know when various dyes and other compounds

used in inks were discovered, so that it is potentially possible to determine a date after which an ink must have been produced. Before the discovery of synthetic dyes various natural dyes such as indigo, madder and logwood were used; in the later 19th century synthetic dyes such as nigrosine (patented in 1867; patent no. 50415) became widely used. More recently, other synthetic dyestuffs have been substituted into formulations depending on availability, cost and suitability. We might also note that ball-point and felt-tip pens, so familiar today, are 20th-century inventions which again required new inks to make them possible. Their ink and marks are easy to distinguish from fountain-pen writing and it is reassuring to know that the diary is undoubtedly in a traditional pen-type ink.

'There are in fact basically two types of pen ink from the 19th century. One form is based on historical iron-gall compositions (iron-gallotannate type) while the other contains primarily dyes (synthetic dye type) dissolved in water. With the iron-gallotannate inks the main component is colourless until it oxidizes to a permanent black colour on the paper; hence a dye is generally added to provide an immediate colour. These are the blue-black inks, and their composition is broadly unchanged though details vary. The synthetic-dye-type inks are currently the most popular since they have a bright colour and produce attractive writing. However, they tend to fade and are sensitive to water. Recent versions of this type of ink contain modern stable pigments (such as those known as the phtalocyanines) to add permanence.

'Analysis of the ink in the diary followed along the lines of a conventional forensic examination, although for various practical reasons we chose to pursue certain forms of analysis rather than others. The ink is a permanent blue-black type such as might (without more detailed knowledge of its composition) have been used from Victorian times to the present day. Naturally we want a more accurate idea of when the ink was produced and to do this we have to look at the detailed composition of the ink and compare it to reference examples of Victorian and modern inks.

'To obtain a 'fingerprint' of the ink we looked at what elements we could detect in it using a scanning electron microscope equipped with energy-dispersive X-ray spectrometry (SEM/EDS) and an instrument called a proton microprobe. It is not necessary to understand the operation of either of these instruments to appreciate how we used the results; basically all one needs to know is that both machines are capable of measuring the presence of a wide range of chemical elements: the SEM/EDS system measures down to about half a percent and the proton microprobe down to just a few parts per million of the composition. By assessing what elements are present and in what quantities with the aid of these instruments we can then determine a characteristic profile for the diary ink and compare this with the same information for our reference examples. Using a technique essentially similar to this, American researchers looking at the Gutenberg Bible could work out that six crews using at first two and then four presses were employed in the printing!

'For our research we looked at a number of 'permanent blue-black' modern inks such as Quink, Stephens and Watermans, as well as samples of writing dated to the late 19th century. Profiles from the (less detailed) SEM/EDS analysis showed that there were major similarities and minor differences even between known Victorian and modern inks. This is as we would expect since the basic chemistry of these inks has not changed substantially during this time and only the details give clues as to differences. For example, we found that Quink contains relatively little iron (and, according to the manufacturers, has done so for some years) while the ink of the diary contains significant amounts. SEM/EDS analysis also suggested that the ink used to write James Maybrick's will is different from that in the diary.

'Preliminary results from the proton microprobe were also encouraging, fitting in with and potentially extending the SEM results. However, a much wider range of samples needs to be looked at with this technique to give us the data for an accurate interpretation.

'To complement the elemental analysis of the inks some dye analysis was also carried out to learn more about the colouring agents used. The method we employed is known as thin layer chromatography (TLC). TLC works by the fact that different compounds within the dyes behave in a dissimilar manner chemically. In practice TLC involves separating out the dyes in the form of characteristic patterns on a sort of sophisticated blotting paper with the aid of organic solvents; the resulting patterns can be compared with patterns of known dyes and an identification made. Using the technique we found clear differences between the modern inks examined and the diary.

'Ultimately, however, the reliability of these analyses for distinguishing between a Victorian and a modern ink will depend upon the level of detail and the range of reference samples. As we look at an increasing number of dated samples with a wider range of techniques, the degree of confidence in placing the ink of the diary as of a particular time will rise. Nonetheless, no component has thus far been detected in the diary ink which precludes a Victorian date and it has clearly not matched any of the modern inks tested either.

'As with ink, so changes have taken place in paper. Paper is made from fibres which are treated so that they split and fray; these can be 'felted' into sheets which can be further processed by adding other materials to give different qualities of paper. By looking at the types of fibre used and the composition of the other materials present in a sheet of paper we may infer dates as we do for the ink. For example, the paper used for the 'Hitler diaries' contained fibres of Nylon 6 and a particular chemical used to increase the whiteness (a derivative of a compound called stilbene), neither of which should be found in papers manufactured before the mid-1950s. Analysis of the paper fibres of the diary has shown only cotton and wood-pulp fibres, both of which were used in late-Victorian times. No modern fibres or fluorescent brightening agents like those just mentioned were detected.

'To summarize, the results of the various analyses of ink and paper in the diary performed so far have not given rise to any conflict with the date of 1888/9. If the diary is a modern forgery, then it has 'passed' a range of tests which would have shown up many materials now used in ink and paper manufacture. However, we must be aware that we cannot as yet wholly rule out on the evidence as it stands a sophisticated modern forgery; although it is very specialist knowledge, someone just might have been able to synthesize a convincing ink or located a bottle of ink of sufficient age that was still useable (though these seem to be quite rare).

'To address these possibilities there are various analyses which we could and should pursue – notably increasing the range of reference material and the level of detail that we are examining. With more reference data we can aim to place the diary precisely among other documents, perhaps even identify the manufacturer of the ink or paper.'

Dr Eastaugh concluded his report by saying: 'My professional response to the diary is and must be entirely neutral. I cannot prejudge the document on the basis of what it does or does not purport to be other than in terms of the hypothetical date. Whether it is actually by Jack the Ripper is immaterial to the analysis of the ink and paper. The project does, however, raise a number of important issues and highlights the fact that historical document analysis is a field where much work remains to be done.'

Dr Eastaugh thought it possible that the black dust found in the gutter of the diary was purified animal charcoal – carbo animalis purificatus – better known in the 19th century as bone black. According to *Squires Companion to the British Pharmacopoeia* (1886), the substance 'has the property of counteracting the poisonous effects of Morphine, Strychnine and Aconite . . . These alkaloids may be swallowed with impunity if mixed in due proportion with purified animal charcoal.'

The full significance of this discovery became clear as I realized the extent of Maybrick's addiction to arsenic and strychnine. It was essential for a strychnine user who pushed his habit to the limit to have an antidote, in case of overdosing. While bone black had other uses, it seems likely, given that Maybrick took strychnine, that the bone black found in the diary was used by him to counter the ill effects of the drug.

I also asked a team of doctors expert in the symptoms of drug addiction if the portrayal of the symptoms of addiction in the Ripper diary was accurate. From doctors at the Poisons Unit at Guy's Hospital and the Alcohol and Addiction Unit at the Maudsley Hospital, both in London, I learned that the diary revealed a grasp of the psychopathology and physiology of arsenic abuse that would have been highly elusive given the dearth of documentation available at that time. Even a modern hoaxer would be severely taxed by the demands of fabricating such medical details. Unless, that is, the author had had first-hand experience of the drug.

Arsenic, when taken over years, leads to accumulation of pyruvate in the blood. This substance is important in the body's metabolism of Coenzyme-A, an essential enzyme of energy-giving carbohydrates. In acute arsenic poisoning, gastro-intestinal symptoms predominate, of the kind that Maybrick suffered. In the last century chronic poisoning was believed to be indicated by such gastric complaints. Today, however, we recognize the prominence of neurological symptoms.

Most Victorians wrongly believed that chronic arsenic eating over twenty or thirty years could result in paralysis. Indeed the writer of the diary shared this misconception. They did understand, however, that the sudden withdrawal of arsenic could result in agonizing pains such as Maybrick experienced after he could no longer get to his office or have access to his supplies.

Dr David Forshaw, in his capacity as consultant to the Maudsley Hospital's Alcohol and Addiction Unit, observed in his written report that Maybrick liked alcohol and also used arsenic, both of which can also produce a chronic disorder of the nerves of the limbs and gastro-intestinal problems. He explains:

'An underactive thyroid, the gland in the neck that helps regulate the general level of metabolic activity in the body can also produce a disorder with similar symptoms to those Maybrick described: tiredness, lethargy, constipation, intolerance of cold, aching muscles. There may be deafness, and hallucinations . . . the face looks expression-less, broad and bloated, memory is poor and the patient may be depressed. This illness, known as hypothyroidism or moxoedema, can only be confirmed by a blood test which was not available in Maybrick's day.

'Von Ziemenssen's 13-volume *Encyclopedia of Medicine*, in its chapter on chronic poisoning by heavy metals, says: 'the mild form of chronic poisoning can arise from the therapeutic use of Fowler's solu-tion'. Dr C. Binz, who wrote *Lectures on Pharmacology* in 1897, explained: 'a stimulus, if frequently repeated, must be exhibited in increasing doses in order each time to produce a certain effect'. In other words, an addict must, over time, take more and more of a drug to sustain the effect. It is tempting to see a parallel between escalating arsenic abuse and progressive sadism as in the diary.'

To examine the handwriting, and try to match it with other Ripper and Maybrick documents, I called in two forensic document examiners, Sue Iremonger and Anna Koren. Anna is also a graphologist. The investigation of handwriting falls into two categories: the forensic comparison of documents to determine whether or not they are forger-ies, which is Sue's speciality; and character analysis, which is but one aspect of Anna's expertise and that on which we asked her to concentrate.

Trained in Chicago and the United Kingdom, Sue Iremonger is a Member of the World Association of Document Examiners. She is also a qualified psychotherapist specializing in the psychopathic personality. In 1993 she presented a paper to the World Association of Document Examiners in Chicago on the Jack the Ripper letters.

Sue is an expert on fraudulent cheques, signature comparisons and the identification of anonymous notes and poison-pen letters. It can take her several days to dissect a page of writing stroke by stroke. 'Handwriting is as revealing as fingerprints,' she says. 'It doesn't matter if a person is young or old, or switches from their right to left hand after an accident. The style may appear to change but, in fact, the components of every individual's handwriting remain consistent.'

Armed with camera and microscope, Sue began her examination of the diary, studying how the individual letters were formed. Anna both looked at the psychological profile revealed by the diary and confronted the daunting mass of microfilm and yellowing document boxes stacked in the vast national archive of the Public Record Office at Kew. She searched for anything among police or Home Office files that might link Jack the Ripper with the handwriting of the diary.

Anna Koren, the Director of the Graphology Centre in Haifa, Tel Aviv, London and Sydney, flew in from Israel at Paul Feldman's invitation. She is a member of the American Association of Graphologists and a Forensic Document Examiner for the Israeli Ministry of Justice and Social Security Services. We first met Anna in Paul's office within two hours of her arrival from Israel and presented her with the diary at a gathering of the research team. Her English was basic – she made no attempt to read or understand the content of the diary. So her immediate, off-the-cuff response to what she saw was impressive. In 20 minutes she told us everything we had come to suspect about James Maybrick. Later she confirmed these findings in writing.

'The diary shows an unstable personality. Inner conflicts, lack of social adaptability and a tendency to schizophrenia characterize the handwriting.

'His feelings of inferiority, emotional repression and lack of inner confidence, may cause him to lose control every now and then and he may explode very violently.

'Tendencies to despotism, irascibility and brutality are clearly discerned. He is affected by unconscious instincts and aggression is the constant companion of his ambitions.

'He suffers from extreme changes of mood, resulting from a great deal of tension between his high ambition and his low self esteem.

'A tendency to hypochondria and a use of drugs or alcohol is evident.

'Any impulsive activity is carried out in secrecy, giving vent to his revenge and aggression fighting against an authoritative hostile figure in his childhood.

'A psychotic disease impedes his ability to distinguish between good or evil, forbidden or permissible and may lead to criminal activity.

'His behaviour is unusually bizarre. His disturbed thinking leads to strange ideas, paranoiac suspicions and magic beliefs. His mode of thinking is circular, clouded, stereotyped and metaphoric. His disease may, in all likelihood, be termed chronic and persistent, with a tendency to get worse.

'He shows an identity disorder, with confusion as to his sexual identity and distorted image of his masculinity, as well as an absence of a stable system of values. There are clear cracks in the super-ego and an inability to persevere in matters involving choice of career, long-term targets, establishing friendships, loyalty.

'Behind the violent outbursts lie deep-rooted feelings of loneliness, emptiness and insecurity, which lead to depression and the partial withdrawal from contact with reality. Egocentric traits along with vanity and exhibitionism, childishness, a tendency to dramatize, a constant search for attention and lack of consideration for others in the pursuit of his own interests.

'His perception of sexuality and mating is distorted to the point of a tendency to sadism. His lack of trust in others and his paranoid feeling of being tormented are apparent. He is unable to form relationships of equality.

'He suffers from psychological disorders which produce illogical, obsessive, destructive and aggressive behaviour. An inner feeling of compulsion causes this behaviour to repeat itself in cycles.'

The two experts were faced with the immediate problem that,

apart from a signature on Maybrick's marriage certificate, and the suspect will, there appeared to be no sample of James Maybrick's handwriting remaining with which to compare the diary.

For her part, Sue Iremonger does not link the handwriting of the diary with that of the 'Dear Boss' letter, nor of Maybrick's alleged 'will'. She said: 'If we take a look at the comparison of the capital letter 'I' in both the diary and the 'Dear Boss' letter, the formation is completely different. In the diary, the formation of the 'I' is a similar formation to a lower-case 'g'. In the 'Dear Boss' letter it has a narrow initial loop which starts approximately halfway up the stem. The tail of the stroke ends in a similar way to a thick full stop whereas in the diary the ending is a small circular loop. The punctuation in the two documents is totally different, and generally the differences between them far outweigh any slight similarities. A couple of the similarities are the left-hand margin and the weight (thickness of stroke) of some of the letters.'

Sue believes that an individual's handwriting always contains unconscious characteristics which can be identified by an expert. Anna Koren disagrees. She sent samples of the handwriting of schizophrenics and of a woman with multiple personality disorder, to show that one person can exhibit many handwriting styles. Anna contends that expert analysis of such divergent written styles cannot necessarily identify them as the work of a single hand. A marked variation between the handwriting samples of the woman, who has over 90 personalities, is evident in the illustration on the next page, which reveals 16 distinct scripts.

Dr Forshaw points out that a person's writing style in the course of a lengthy, free-flowing diary will be in his or her natural hand and very distinct from the same individual's formal writing or from any short piece of handwriting where the writer is keen to disguise his or her identity. An intelligent serial killer like Maybrick would have gone to great lengths to ensure anonymity in any letter he wrote for publication or police scrutiny.

Forshaw believes it is possible that the handwriting of the diary reflects the true inner feelings of Maybrick, who was not a frequent letter writer. He also suggests that the style of the letter and the postcard – which he believes could be by the same hand – is contrived to impress.

Moving from the diary's handwriting to its style of expression, one

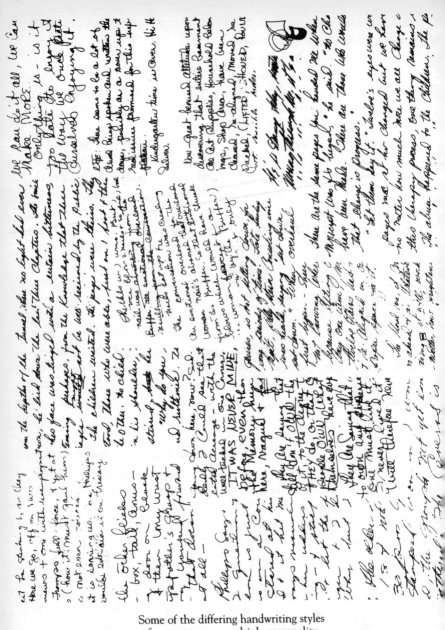

Some of the differing handwriting styles
of one person – a multiple personality.

(*When Rabbit Howls* by the Troops for Truddi Chase, E.P. Dutton and Sidgwick & Jackson 1987)

aspect that initially surprised me was its language. It contains three phrases that sound too modern for a Victorian. However, dictionary research revealed that the expressions 'topped' and 'gathering momentum' were in use before late-Victorian times.

But the phrase 'one off' needed further research. The earliest date for the expression given in any British dictionary was 1934, in the *Oxford English Dictionary*. In America, *Webster's Dictionary* dates its first written occurrence as 1925. This could have been a problem, for on one small detail can turn the whole authenticity of the diary. I sought the help of John Simpson, co-editor of the *Oxford English Dictionary*, who wrote to me: 'The *Oxford English Dictionary* seeks to document the history and development of the vocabulary of English from the early Middle Ages to the present day. Its analysis is based upon the record of the language obtained by reading as wide a range of texts as possible and excerpting from these texts examples of usage for our quotation files. The earliest recorded use of any term occurring in the Dictionary represents the earliest written use available to the Dictionary's editors when a particular entry is compiled.

'I would expect first instances to represent a useful guide to when a given term entered the language, but earlier attestations (some of which are substantial pre-datings) are continually being brought to our notice. Language is spoken before it is written down, and in some areas (such as dialect slang and local crafts) there may well be some time lag between the introduction of a term and its appearance in print.

'In the case of 'one-off' I would be surprised but not dumbfounded if its first appearance was found to pre-date the Dictionary's first recorded example by as much as half a century. If such a predating were confirmed I would expect subsequent research in the technical literature would uncover intervening examples of its use.'

I also spoke to Mark Agnes, a member of the editorial team of *Webster's New World Dictionary*, who agreed with John Simpson. 'Even today there are phrases we all know and use which can't be found in a dictionary. It can take a very long time indeed, especially in technical areas, for the oral tradition to be recorded in the written word.'

I have learned of several uses of the expression in Victorian times not yet in the dictionaries. Jonathon Green's *Dictionary of Jargon* gives a use in 19th-century prisons referring to names chalked on slates as convicts were sent 'one-on' or 'one-off' duty. In the building industry, 'one off' in the sense of one only, was used when ordering materials (source: records of Trayner's of Kent, 1860.) A 'one-off' was also an ornamental brick used in Victorian canals, and similarly, in engineering the term referred to a unique example or a prototype. This is precisely the sense Maybrick employed it in the diary.

A great many people had, by now, spent a great deal of time and a considerable amount of money in trying to expose Mike Barrett's diary – and they had failed. Even Sue Iremonger's honest belief that the writer of the diary is not the writer of Maybrick's alleged will is seriously weakened without further examples of his handwriting.

No one had proved the diary to be a forgery. Those who condemned it were unable to agree among themselves whether it was a hoax of the last five – or 50 – or 105 years – and so the debate continues.

FIFTEEN

'My thoughts are indeed beginning to give me pleasure'

JAMES MAYBRICK WAS a child-loving, practical-joking, genial host of a man. He was particular about his appearance and anxious to improve his standing in society. As William Stead had written: 'Friends would say James Maybrick was a very good kind of a fellow.'

How then could he have been the drug-crazed butcher who spread terror throughout late-Victorian England?

Dr David Forshaw has a special interest in the mind of the serial killer. So he was particularly excited when I told him about the discovery of the diary. He offered to study it and to report on the state of mind of the man who wrote it. He was not asked: 'Is the writer of the diary Jack the Ripper?' Such a question could not be answered by psychiatry. His report has two aims:

1) To explain the psychopathology of serial killers alongside what is known about Jack the Ripper;

2) To compare the above findings with the psychopathology of the diary.

'The Jack the Ripper diary represents the serial recording of the Ripper's thoughts or feelings, or more accurately, his expressing and working through his emotional and intellectual turmoil,' says David Forshaw. 'It is an integral part of his psychopathology.

'Of course, the Whitechapel murders were not the first serial killings. Such crimes have occurred throughout history. There are recorded cases of serial killings dating back to classical times. In fact, in their book, *Perverse Crimes in History*, Masters and Lea describe a plague of stabbers and rippers in the 19th century that reached a peak in the 1880s and 1890s. So Jack the Ripper, monster that he was, was one among many. He might have been just another murderer had it not been for his self-determined nickname.

'Often these serial killers seem, like James Maybrick, to be quiet men – men with families, men who go to work each day and tend the garden at weekends.'

David Forshaw cited the example of Andrei Chikatilo, who lived in the coal-mining town of Shakhty in the former Soviet Union. He was a 42-year-old Communist Party member with a wife, two children and a job as a teacher in a school of mining. Then, one day in 1978, he took nine-year-old Lena Zakotnova to a tumbledown shack on the edge of the town and strangled, stabbed and slashed her. The pleasure was immense and his newly discovered blood-lust unstoppable. So he went on, over a dozen years, to slaughter and to eat women and some 53 children, tearing their insides out with his bare hands. Like Maybrick, he left taunting little jokes at the scene to tease the police.

Chikatilo is said to have never raised a hand to his own children, and had made great strides in life, rising from peasant roots to the intelligentsia. But he had wanted to be a brave soldier and a romantic lover; he yearned for the kind of respect that would have made schoolchildren stand up as he entered a room. He believed the real Chikatilo did not measure up, and felt he was a failure.

When he was finally captured in 1991, he wrote to his wife: 'Why did God send me to this earth? Me, a person so affectionate, tender, and thoughtful but so totally defenceless against my own weakness.'

Chikatilo's words reflect the tormented message of painful inadequacy which fills the diary of Maybrick. They also recall his image of himself as gentle and at the same time given to extreme violence.

The gentle man with gentle thoughts will strike again soon

Another such figure, Forshaw suggested, was Peter Kürten, the Düsseldorf murderer who was hanged in 1937 for killing nine people and attempting to kill seven more. Yet he was living and sleeping with his wife throughout the killings. So was Peter Sutcliffe, the 'Yorkshire Ripper', whose mission, like Maybrick's, was, in his own words, to 'rid the streets of prostitutes'. Over a period of five years he killed 13 women and tried to murder seven others.

Maybrick was, like Andrei Chikatilo, Peter Kürten and Peter Sutcliffe, the man next door, an ordinary and unremarkable neighbour, at least on the surface. In other ways, too, he exhibits traits of the typical serial killer. Such culprits, Forshaw says, are nearly always male and often obsessional and hypochondriacal. That was certainly true of Maybrick, who was always fretting over his drugs, his health and growing old.

Serial killers are usually mild-mannered as well, rarely showing aggression, though deep inside they seethe with pent-up anger. They have rich fantasy lives, which they find preferable to reality. They dream of being in a position of power and are preoccupied with their masculinity and sexual potency. It was the latter fear that drove Maybrick to use arsenic and strychnine.

In 1965, Revitch studied reports on unprovoked attacks by men on women, dividing offenders into groups of those aged above and below the age of eighteen. He found that hostility to women was more prominent among the older group than the younger, while pre-occupation with sexual behaviour was more marked in the younger. The older the attacker, the more the primary motive reflected anger or hatred.

'The unattractive nature of the Ripper's killings leads to the conclusion that the killings reflected hostility rather than a need for sexual gratification,' says David Forshaw. 'He was therefore probably not a young man.'

Maybrick had his 50th birthday on October 24th – not long before the murder of Mary Jane Kelly.

'Seminal fluid is not mentioned in the post-mortem reports so it is not known if the assailant had sex nor if he masturbated at the scene of the crime,' Forshaw goes on. 'It seems improbable, since hatred not sex is likely to have been the motive. In any case, the known time available to the killer would hardly have allowed such indulgence. It may be that the Ripper selected victims as anti-symbols of sex, chosen to thwart even the possibility of intercourse. However, it may have been their very depravity that appealed to a perverted sexuality.'

There was no doubt the Ripper's choice of target – prostitutes – had practical advantages. Since there is little to link them and their client, and they work in isolated areas, prostitutes are easy victims for sex attackers. Moreover, a serial killer who targets prostitutes may do so because he is convinced he is doing society a service.

I am convinced God placed me here to kill all whores

But at the same time it is likely that the hapless ladies of Whitechapel also represented something far more personal to Maybrick: his adulterous wife. 'Prostitutes represent to the attacker, consciously or unconsciously, despised and unfaithful loved ones who through circumstances are relatively safe from attack,' says David Forshaw. 'Women of easy virtue were the symbol of his wife's infidelity.'

Forshaw believes the Ripper probably obtained satisfaction only from the process of killing, from feeling or seeing the victim die, even from their mutilation – not from putting them through prolonged suffering.

There was also another motivation for murder. Forshaw explains: 'The 'Son of Sam' killer, David Berkowitz, who terrorized New York for a year in the mid-1970s, talked about 'the desire to do it, to kill', which, he added, 'filled me up to such explosive proportions, it caused me such turmoil inside that when it released itself it was like a volcano erupting and the pressure was over, for a while at least'. The American psychiatrist, David Abrahamsen, who has written about Jack the Ripper, says that the Whitechapel killer probably felt the same tension.'

Maybrick wrote:

I need more thrills. Cannot live without my thrills. I will go on. I will go on. nothing will stop me.

Maybrick had a mistress, identified in the diary only as 'mine', to whom he turned at times when his murderous thoughts became too intense.

The eyes will come out of the next. I will stuff them into the whores mouth. That will certainly give me pleasure, it does so as I write. Tonight I will see mine, she will be pleased as I will be gentle with her as indeed I always am.

Jack the Ripper, like Maybrick, also enjoyed the thrill of the chase. He revelled in the excitement of his potential capture, even more than the ripping.

I believe the thrill of being caught thrilled me
more than cutting the whore herself.

'Serial killers,' says Forshaw, 'typically feel inferior to others, except when writing or thinking about their crimes. That is the reason for a diary.' Maybrick used the journal to express his inflated sense of his own importance, bestowing on himself the titles 'Sir Jim' and 'Sir Jack'. The diary also enabled him to use one set of pleasant thoughts to drive from his consciousness distressing ideas and feelings.

> I will force myself to think of something more pleasant.

'In the diary he used this method of thought manipulation fairly often, like a screen between himself and the real world,' explains Forshaw. 'He thereby allowed himself to remain outwardly calm and in control. It may have also distanced him from reality.'

Maybrick used sex to take his mind off reality. After his first killing he wrote:

> I will take the bitch tonight I need to take my mind off the night's events.

From the beginning of the diary his fantasies of his wife and her lover together gave him a morbid or perverted pleasure.

> The thought of him taking her is beginning to thrill me.

These entries suggest he was sexually aroused and derived some sort of sadomasochistic satisfaction when writing the diary.

A striking aspect of the diary is the change in handwriting as it progresses. It is clearly written by the same person, but the transformation from a neat school-taught hand to a frenzied scrawl reflects a violent deterioration in his mental state.

David Forshaw selected seven samples of handwriting from the diary, and examined them chronologically. He explains: 'At the beginning of the diary, before any killing has taken place, the writing is neat, undemonstrative, restrained even. But it becomes larger, more flamboyant, less controlled, and certainly more confident, as he pursues what he called his 'campaign' of murders. Now the handwriting is clearly laden with a mix of emotions. Then, having built up to fever pitch, towards the end of the diary it reverts back dramatically to the calm, controlled style of the time before the killings began. This last marked shift occurred shortly after Maybrick returned from a visit to see Dr Fuller in London.'

> Fuller believes there is very little the matter with me. Strange the thoughts he placed into my mind.

What those thoughts were we do not know, but from this moment Maybrick talks increasingly of wanting release from his torment and even of suicide.

Modern studies of serial killers have led to a better understanding than existed in the 19th century. Psychiatrist Malcolm MacCulloch of Liverpool University and his team noticed a clear pattern in thirteen of sixteen offenders studied in a special hospital. The men had been preoccupied with sadistic sexual fantasies over a period of time which became more extreme, leading to 'behavioural try-outs' such as following potential victims. These 'try-outs' were then incorporated into the fantasy, moving inexorably towards a climax. Increasingly each patient became less able to distinguish between reality and his fantasy world.

The team speculated that inflicting suffering was the route to control. Control was at the centre of the behaviour. In one sense, the ultimate possible control over anyone is when they are dead, or unconscious.

Maybrick's diary, and Jack the Ripper's killing spree, both show a clear escalation of viciousness from one victim to the next.

'It is almost as if he was habituating the behaviour and developing a tolerance towards it,' says Dr Forshaw. 'This is a phenomenon akin to urban joyriders, who very often achieve their thrills from being in control, driving fast, taking ever more and more risks.'

As for the Ripper's cannibalism, Forshaw says: 'Maybrick may have removed parts of his bodies in order to have some kind of memento. The Hungarian, Elizabeth Bathory, who died in 1614 aged 54, used to bath in the blood of her victims to keep her young and attractive. Christie, who was hanged in 1953, collected pubic hair from his victims. The Ripper could have been convinced that by eating a womb he would achieve eternal youth.'

Other macabre hoarders include the American serial killer Ed Kemper, who in 1972 collected internal organs, and sometimes heads, which he kept in his wardrobe. The murderer Dennis Nilsen, who was active between 1978 and 1983, stored the dismembered remains of his victims in cupboards and under the floorboards of his North London homes.

Dr Forshaw continues: 'If limited information is known about a person's past, or mental state, it is difficult to distinguish the sadistic serial sex killer with progressive sadism syndrome from multi-victim killers who kill as a result of mental illness such as schizophrenia.'

From his reading of the diary, Forshaw sees no evidence that the Ripper suffered from mental illness. 'He did not have delusions. James Maybrick of the diary was mentally disordered, but whether sufficiently enough to diminish his legal responsibility is a matter for discussion. Was he mad or was he bad?'

The most intriguing answer to this question is that Maybrick was bad but the Ripper was mad. Merge the two and, like Jekyll and Hyde, the result is a powerful force for evil.

In conclusion, Dr Forshaw writes: 'If the journal is genuine then it tells a tragic tale. It makes sense. This is an encouraging sign for its authenticity. However there are other possibilities . . . it would seem that the most likely options are that it is either genuine or an extremely good modern fake. If it is a fake then it is as remarkable as were it genuine. It would be very hard to fake . . . A considerable amount of work would have to be done, even by someone or a team already familiar with serial killers and the Maybrick and Ripper cases. The faker would have had to work hard to mimic the thoughts and feelings portrayed in the journal, though it might be easier if they had a similar psychopathology to begin with. A thorough examination of the journal and its provenance are essential components of deciding if it is authentic. If such an examination proves indecisive and all falls back on the content, then I would argue in that case, on the balance of probabilities from a psychiatric perspective, it is authentic.'

. . .

I now understand why Mike Barrett took to walking in Anfield Cemetery and standing by the gate to Battlecrease House. I have seen the horrified fascination that the diary has inspired in those who have read it.

I felt my way word by word, sentence by sentence, determined that if there was a flaw in the diary I would find it, for it was inevitable that sceptics and those who wish to perpetuate the century-old mystery rather than lay it to rest would do their utmost to undermine its credibility. I was afraid that if I destroyed a legend it would be like killing the Loch Ness monster. What would be left to keep alive the Ripper industry?

In this respect I could not have been more wrong, but at that early stage I had no idea how rich a vein I would strike as I became ever more familiar with James Maybrick. Jack the Ripper was no scruffy East End vagabond, no scowling fiend lurking in shadowy passages. He was a striking, well-dressed family man – but a family man in the great Victorian tradition of secret lives and double standards. As David Forshaw has confirmed, it is this veneer of normality and conformity that made him so fearsome. The Ripper was – and is – the man next door.

This is precisely why so many sensible people have been seized by the almost sinister power of the diary. The experts who gave us their time, their talents and their wisdom found themselves lying awake at night. Yet for them, as indeed for Mike Barrett, there was little financial incentive throughout the research, writing and production of this book.

Meanwhile, the professional Ripperologists, who were at one time cynical and even damning, produced not one crucial fact to discredit the diary. They admit they are baffled.

The diary has unmasked the true James Maybrick – just as he planned.

I place this now in a place where it shall be found.

So now we have a new villain. But Jack the Ripper is in no way diminished by his discovery, for even now there remains a wealth of material still to research.

Far from the story ending, it is only just beginning.

SIXTEEN

'They will suffer just as I. I will see to that'

JAMES THE RIPPER's legacy to his family was bitter enough, but his shadow continued to darken many lives in the years after his death, especially his wife's.

But Florie Maybrick was a survivor. She endured her existence as prisoner 'L.P. 29' – including solitary confinement, hard labour and illness – without hope for early release, despite the efforts of many. Her mother came from France to visit her every two months, travelling 'a hundred miles for thirty minutes' with her daughter.

As Florie later recalled: 'At these visits she would tell me as best she could of the noble, unwearied efforts of my countrymen and countrywomen in my cause; of the sympathy and support of my own Government; of the earnest efforts of the different American ambassadors in my behalf . . . The knowledge of their belief in my innocence, and of their sympathy comforted, cheered, and strengthened me to tread bravely the thorny path of my daily life.'

Seeing her daughter in prison, for only half an hour once every other month, took its toll on the Baroness. 'Almost before we had time to compose ourselves there would come a silent sign from the mute matron in the chair – the thirty minutes had passed,' Florie recalled. 'Good-bye,' we would say, with a lingering look, and then turn our backs on upon each other . . . . No one will ever know what my mother suffered.'

The Baroness spent a fortune trying to clear Florie's name and secure an early release.

Lord Russell, Florie's attorney, continued to express his belief in his infamous client, and never lost confidence that she would be freed. He died in 1900, before Florie was to see his certainty vindicated.

For the entire fifteen gruelling years of her incarceration, Florie remained the focus of an international campaign to clear her name. Three American Presidents registered pleas for mercy. Cardinal Gibbons, Secretary of State James G. Blaine and the Ambassador to Great Britain, Robert Lincoln, added appeals on her behalf.

Not until 1904 was Florie finally a free woman. On January 25th, aged 41, she was taken into the kindly care of nuns at the Community of the Epiphany, a convent in Truro, Cornwall. Six months later she then rejoined her mother in France before sailing, under an assumed name, home to America and to a new world lit by electricity, overpopulated and noisy with the march of industrialization. The change was hard. Never pardoned, she was free from prison but not from her past.

'A time will come when the world will acknowledge that the verdict which was passed upon me is absolutely untenable,' she wrote in *My Fifteen Lost Years*. 'But what then? Who shall give back the years I have spent within prison walls; the friends by whom I am forgotten; the children to whom I am dead; the sunshine; the winds of heaven; my woman's life, and all I have lost by this terrible injustice?'

Florie's repeated attempts at appeal may have been in vain as far as her early release was concerned, but her prison sentence produced an ultimate irony: Britain's Court of Criminal Appeal was set up in 1907 so that future prisoners would face a more equitable system of justice. Indirectly, the change could be said to have been brought about by James Maybrick, whose other life as Jack the Ripper led to her downfall.

Florie wanted privacy, but the public wanted her story. In need of money and with the encouragement of her American supporters, she wrote about her experiences in prison and toured the country, lecturing on the need for legal reform. She never discussed the events of 1888-9 that had taken her to the steps of the gallows. This public life, however, made it impossible for her to escape the prurience of her audience, and she abandoned the lecture circuit after two years.

After an extended visit to her daughter in 1910, the Baroness returned to France, where she died a few months later. For twenty-one years, until her death, she had fought for Florie's pardon.

When attempts to reclaim family land failed, Florie was in dire need of money. She worked briefly for a publishing company, then her health broke down. She moved to Chicago, where the Salvation Army took care of her. She apparently disappeared for three years. Then, in 1918, she contacted a friend, Cora Griffin, asking about employment opportunities. Miss Griffin had a friend in Gaylordsville, Connecticut, who was looking for a housekeeper on her poultry farm. Florie was hired.

The following year she bought a small tract of land in Gaylordsville and had a three-room cottage built. Before moving to Connecticut, Florie had decided to use her maiden name, and thereafter was known as Florence Elizabeth Chandler. Mrs Maybrick had ceased to exist.

While Florie served her prison term, many of the others who had figured so prominently in her life were trying in their own ways to escape what fate had dealt them.

When Alexander MacDougall published his study of the case after Florie's conviction, he addressed the preface to Bobo and Gladys: 'This work is dedicated to James Chandler Maybrick aged 8 years and Gladys Evelyn Maybrick aged 4 years by the author, with the sincere hope that it will enable them to feel during their lives that the word 'MOTHER' is not a 'sound unfit to be heard or uttered' by them AND that when they are old enough to be able to understand this record of the facts and circumstances connected with the charge put upon, and the trial of Florence Elizabeth Maybrick aged 27, her children may have, throughout their lives, the comfort of feeling that their mother was not proved to be guilty of the murder of their father JAMES MAYBRICK.'

It did not work. Florie never saw her children again.

James and Gladys went to live in London with Dr Fuller and his wife, who were paid £100 a year to care for them. For the first few years that Florie was in prison, Thomas Maybrick annually posted photographs of the children to her.

But when young James was old enough to be told about the tragedy of his parents, he reacted badly. He adopted the name Fuller and instructed Uncle Thomas that no more pictures were to be sent to his mother. This broke Florie's heart; she felt as though the children had died.

'The innocents – my children – one a baby of three years, the other a boy of seven, I had left behind in the world,' she wrote in her autobiography. 'They had been taught to believe that their mother was guilty, and, like their father, was to them dead. They have grown up to years of understanding under another name. I know nothing about them. When the pathos of all this touches the reader's heart he will realize the tragedy of my case.'

In 1893 Michael Maybrick decided to break totally with the memories of his past – although the year before he had even more music in print than the great Sir Arthur Sullivan himself. He married his housekeeper, butcher's daughter Laura Withers, at Marylebone Register Office and retired to the Isle of Wight. It was not a love-match, they had nothing in common and never even holidayed together. But Laura was happy enough driving her monogrammed carriage to Ryde's main street in order to give shopkeepers the pleasure of saying they served her.

Her husband's impact on the town was astonishing. In November 1900 he was elected Mayor. Speeches at his inauguration referred to his ability to 'produce grand harmonies from discordant notes'. It was an honour to which he was re-elected five times. He visited Osborne when Queen Victoria was there, he welcomed King Alfonso of Spain and represented the island in Westminster Abbey for the Coronation of George V. He undoubtedly worked hard to promote the island's image.

His funeral was the largest the island had ever seen – but is remembered with some amusement by island historians today. Solicitor John Matthews says: 'He was a chameleon type of man. He had no deep emotions and no close relationships. He dabbled in every committee possible in the island – but participated in very little. At his funeral, amongst the astonishing array of wreaths was one from the Temperance Movement (but he drank), several from the churches (but he didn't go to church) and from the cycling club (he had no bike). His one-time world of international musical fame was hardly represented.'

Michael likewise persuaded his brother Edwin to abandon his bachelor life. In 1892, at the age of 41, Edwin married Amy Tyrer and they had a daughter, also called Amy. Many years later, daughter Amy described her father in these words: 'He was absolutely a bachelor at heart. All his friends were bachelors. Some came over from America and they were all bachelors. Father used to invite them to dinner in the evening but there were never any women with them. At Easter he would go off motoring with his men friends. He made me feel I was an unwanted child. He was never loving. I got my ears boxed on many occasions!'

By this time Gladys and young James were growing up and had left London to live with their uncle in the Isle of Wight. Young Amy Maybrick sometimes spent the summers there, too. She dreaded those visits. 'All the Maybricks were cold, very formal.'

■　■　■

In 1911, James Fuller was 28, and working as a mining engineer in the Le Roi gold mine in British Columbia. He was engaged to a local girl, and apparently free from the shadow that had clouded his childhood. On

April 10th, while working alone in his laboratory, he telephoned his fiancée. That was the last time she spoke to him. James was later found dead in his laboratory. He had apparently mistaken a glass of cyanide for water. The verdict was accidental death.

In 1912, at the parish church of St Mary, Hampstead, Gladys Maybrick married naval officer Lieutenant Frederick James Corbyn, known as 'Jim'. There was no member of the family to witness the wedding. Instead, her guardian, Mrs Fuller, signed the register, and when Michael died in 1913 Gladys's name does not appear among the list of mourners, nor do the newspapers record her sending a wreath. Was this the whiff of a family feud?

Lieutenant Corbyn's family immediately cut off his inheritance because of the Maybrick name.

During the First World War Jim was awarded the OBE for his shore-based services but, on Gladys's insistence, resigned when it was over and went into business.

The Corbyns chose not to have children – Gladys was ashamed of being a Maybrick. In 1957 they built themselves a retirement bungalow not far from the sea, overlooking a beautiful, isolated valley in South Wales. There, Gladys was a somewhat formidable, demanding neighbour. She didn't like children at all, and members of the family still recall the dread with which, as youngsters, they had awaited the 'state visits' from Aunt Gladys and Uncle Jim. These were occasions for best clothes and best behaviour.

I drove to see the place in which the tragic little daughter of James and Florie chose to end her days. As we drove in through the gate I felt a shiver of disbelief. The house is a modest cedar bungalow – similar in style to the place in which her mother had died in America in 1941.

Just as extraordinary was yet another 'coincidence': when Gladys died and the bungalow was cleared, relatives found medicines and pills in every pocket, every drawer, every cupboard. Like her father, she was a total hypochondriac.

What of Alfred Brierley? The history books tell different stories. Some say he emigrated to North Africa; others that he died in South America. Years after her release from prison, Florie gave an exclusive and painful interview to the *Liverpool Post and Echo* in which she admitted that during the years in prison she was buoyed up by memories of Alfred. 'I was foolish enough to think I could find happiness with the man who offered me the love my husband denied me . . . bitter, bitter, was my disappointment. The man for whom I had sacrificed everything had forgotten me during the years I had been trying to keep my heart young, in prison, for his sake.'

The truth about Brierley makes Florie's words even more poignant. He did go to South America. There is a letter from him in Venezuela, written to John Aunspaugh, in which he reflects ruefully: 'The women surely can kick up a devil of a dust with us men and a pretty face can sure lead a man to hell.'

Brierley returned to England, married, had a son, and died in Hove, Sussex. He is buried in the pretty churchyard of St Mary in the village of Newick near the South Downs. On his tombstone are the moss-covered words: 'And a sower went forth.' The Biblical quotation used for his epitaph continues: '. . . and some seed fell on stony ground.'

George Davidson, Maybrick's closest friend, hailed from an eminently respectable Scottish Free Church family. He was found, drowned, on a bleak stretch of coast at Silecroft, near Whitehaven, Cumbria, in March 1893. A reward of £10 had been offered for news of his whereabouts.

According to the *Whitehaven News* of March 16th 1893: 'For about two or three weeks he had complained of being unable to sleep. He frequently got up during the night and went for a walk and smoke around the square. On the morning of the 10th February about 10 a.m. he was found to be missing and has not since been heard of.'

He died penniless and intestate but left behind a gold watch – placed beneath his pillow. Was it James Maybrick's watch – which we were about to discover bore a terrible confession? Was the burden of this knowledge too much for his dearest friend? We shall never know.

Edwin Maybrick died in 1928, leaving only £39.1s.8d. His funeral cost £5.7s.8d.

And in 1927, Sarah Ann Maybrick was certified dead, of senile dementia, at Tooting Bec Hospital in South London.

All efforts to trace her movements in the years between have failed. Paul Feldman found, among Trevor Christie's notes, the copy of an article that appeared in the American *Brooklyn Eagle* of July 27th 1894. It was headed 'There are no flies on her'.

Mrs Sarah Maybrick of Brooklyn, asks that her daughter, Hester 29, be removed to an insane asylum. She imagines she has been deserted by her lover and flies whisper in her ear that he is faithless.

If this was, indeed, James Maybrick's Sarah Ann, how ironic that the girl who could, from her age, have been his daughter was haunted by the dual nightmare of the Maybricks – faithlessness and flies.

． ． ．

Florie returned to England at least twice. The first occasion was in 1911, when she learned of Bobo's death in Canada. Her remarks, reported in the *Brooklyn Eagle* on May 10th 1911, are moving:

> The past is dead. The boy has been dead to me for more than 20 years. Before the death of my husband . . . he provided that the children be brought up and educated and required to live in England until of age and if, then, they wished to continue under the patronage of his estate they must continue to reside on British soil. They were taken in charge by some of Mr Maybrick's relatives and I never made any effort to communicate with them.

She came back once more in 1927 immediately before the death of her brother-in-law Edwin. Amy Main remembered that Florie called on her father 'but he was out'. She went to the Grand National, of such bitter memories, and also to see her solicitors. This visit was recorded by a strange and emotional interview in the *Sunday News* of May 1st, entitled 'A Mother's Anguish'. It was in complete contrast with that of 1911: 'I feel death's shadow over me and I have come back for one reason only, to effect a reconciliation with members of my family . . .'

It was not to be.

'It is bitterness worse than death,' she said. ' . . . I have longed for my children who were but babes at the time and the mother hunger in my heart was so strong that I felt I must make this journey now in the hope of seeing them . . . it seems terrible that the children I risked my life to bring into the world should think their mother guilty of the crime that left them fatherless. But that is the only construction I can put upon their attitude towards me now.'

Who is Florie talking about? Bobo had been dead for 16 years. She had previously spoken of her feelings about his death. So who are the 'children' she had come to see. Could it be, after all that time, she had let slip the truth? Had Florie, in fact, given birth in prison?

There were so many rumours at the time. The *Weekly Times and Echo* was not alone in its inference that the reason why the Home Secretary granted a reprieve was that Florie was pregnant:

> It is understood that another important question arises in the case and one which the jury of matrons will be empanelled to try. Of course, if in the event of the jury finding the fact to be as it is alleged, the execution would necessarily be postponed and probably would not take place at all. It is believed there has been no instance of the execution of a woman who, at the time of her trial, was in Mrs Maybrick's supposed condition, since the execution of Margaret Waters nineteen years ago.

So was there someone in England in 1927 guarding her secret? Perhaps somewhere today there is, unknowingly, another line of Maybricks descended from the 'reconciliation' that Dr Hopper felt he had achieved between Florie and Jim. Or perhaps there is a Brierley whose ancestry can be traced to that fateful meeting at Flatman's.

Florie spent the rest of her life in the small Connecticut town where she had gone to work as a housekeeper. The job did not last long, and when the small income she received regularly ceased to be enough, she finally found the kindness that had eluded her through so much of her life. Neighbours and students from the nearby South Kent School for Boys saw to it that she always had groceries and other supplies.

As the years wore on, Florie grew more and more reclusive and, as passers-by would readily note, ever more eccentric. Her odd little house had five small doors built in its sides to allow easy access for her cats, which, according to various sources, numbered anywhere from 17 to 75. When she could barely afford to feed herself, she made certain she had two quarts of milk a day to feed her hungry companions, hardly the care one would expect from a woman who, so many years before, had been damned by a package labelled, 'Arsenic. Poison for Cats.'

The 'Cat Lady', as she became known locally, managed to live out the last few decades of her life in anonymity. No one knew who she was, though they may have guessed she was a lady, from her bearing.

And Florie never told a soul – not in words, anyway. When she gave a black lace dress to Genevieve Austin, she inadvertently left on a cleaning tag that read: 'Mrs Florence E Maybrick.' For nearly 20 years, Mrs Austin kept Florie's identity a secret. Only on the death of her eccentric neighbour did she alert the newspapers to the secret they unwittingly shared.

Florie was found dead on October 23rd, 1941, aged 79. Though she had been released from prison almost four decades earlier, she had nonetheless served a life sentence. Only by becoming a recluse whose sole friends were her cats, did she hide from the scandal that followed her everywhere. But she could never escape. The death of Florence Elizabeth Chandler Maybrick was reported on many front pages – the story of a young woman convicted of murdering her husband was news all over again.

• • •

SEVENTEEN

A watch is discovered

IN 1992 MIKE BARRETT, too, like so many before him, had felt the shadow of James Maybrick fall across his life. Once the diary had found its way into his house, nothing would ever be the same again. No-one, least of all a sick man such as he was, could withstand the battering to which he was subjected. He suffered phone calls in the night, the press camped on his doorstep, and he was interviewed by New Scotland Yard (an experience that Anne will never forget.) And yet he stuck unswervingly to his story.

But the inescapable fact remained that we still had no idea where the diary had been in the last 100 years. We continued to press Mike for more details; we spoke with his family and friends; we retraced his every step in the year in which, he said, Tony Devereux gave him the diary. We checked his handwriting – and that of Anne and Tony. Meanwhile Tony's family continued to insist that there was not a word of truth in Mike's story and that they would have known had their father ever owned such a book.

Mike Barrett had always been convinced that Maybrick left the diary in his office in Tithebarn Street on May 3rd 1889. So, there was momentary excitement when I realized that this office was not demolished until late in the 1960s, to make way for a prestigious office complex, Silk House Court. Amazingly among the tenants of Silk House Court were a highly reputable firm of lawyers, who were 'descended' by way of mergers and new partnerships from Cleaver Holden Garnett and Cleaver, Florie Maybrick's solicitors. But sadly they said they had not been put in charge of the diary 100 years ago. The trail again went cold.

I hoped that if we could find some more of Maybrick's handwriting our problems would be over. The Reference Library in Norfolk, Virginia, sent us wads of papers, detailing his attendance and responsibilities at the Cotton Exchange meetings. There was even mention of letters – they were long since vanished. And the Cotton Exchange records in Liverpool were destroyed in the Second World War.

We hunted down the family of George Davidson, in whose arms Maybrick died and whose mysterious death was recorded 'found drowned' by the coroner in 1893.

I talked to the descendants of Sir Thomas Clark, brother-in-law of

Davidson, whose family publishing firm, T. and T. Clark, still thrives in Edinburgh. Perhaps they knew what had happened to the gold watch so poignantly left beneath his pillow on the night he disappeared?

They knew nothing. All papers had vanished. Besides, as the National Library of Scotland where the Clark archives are housed, observed to us: 'To have a suicide in a prominent Free Church family in the 19th century would have been such a scandal that documents connected to it would . . . most likely have been destroyed.'

We had elevenses with the maid Mary Cadwallader's grand-daughter, living comfortably with her husband in a bungalow near Dover. She told us of a gold watch once owned by Mary, which they all believed could have come from Battlecrease House. It was pawned years ago, so we can never find out. We sipped sherry in the beamed 18th-century Buckinghamshire lounge where Alice Yapp's great-niece, Jo Brooks, lives with her husband. She placed on the table a silver locket and a monogrammed teaspoon that, she said, with a smile, Alice claimed Florie had 'given' her.

We had several meetings with chartered surveyor Gerard Brierley, great-great-nephew of the now notorious Alfred. He admitted that his family, too, had swept the whole affair under the carpet.

Quite by chance we were introduced to solicitor David Fletcher Rogers, whose grandfather was a very efficient foreman of the Coroner's Court jury preceding Florie's trial. He then took over the remaining lease on Battlecrease House but died shortly after. When new people moved in, the Fletcher Rogers family Bible was handed to some nearby friends in the hope that one day a relative would return to claim it.

It was passed from neighbour to neighbour until in 1978 David Fletcher Rogers went back to Liverpool to take pictures of his grand-father's house. He called next door, and to his astonishment they handed him the Bible of which he had no knowledge. Like our diary, it had 'disappeared' for several generations.

A Maybrick family Bible, which belonged to James's uncle, Charles, is now the treasured possession of Charles's granddaughter, Edith Stonehouse, who lives in one of Liverpool's most depressed areas. We thumbed through its pages hopefully looking for clues or comments. There were none.

Back in Liverpool we called on Helen Blanchard, descended from

Abrahams the chemist. She lent us an exciting box of family letters, which contained a prescription for James Maybrick and a letter from Alexander MacDougall but nothing else relating to our quest.

From America I had a call from a Mrs Gay Steinbach, who told me proudly that her mother had grown up in the Maybrick household in Ryde. Her name was Laura Trussle, and it was to her that Michael's wife, Laura, eventually left her money and Michael's music.

We listened to delightful tapes of Edwin Maybrick's daughter, Amy Main, chuckling through her reminiscences of life at Lynthorpe on the Isle of Wight, where she spent many miserable summer holidays. Michael and Laura had no love of children and no idea of how to entertain them.

We ferreted among the archives of Ryde eager that somewhere we would find a late-in-life confession from Michael that there were dark secrets he had never revealed. All we found was the very Victorian epitaph on his monumental gravestone, which, in the circumstances, seemed laden with personal meaning from him – and also, by now, for us:

THERE SHALL BE NO MORE DEATH

However, one very strong piece of evidence did emerge. A few weeks before the hardback edition of the book was sent to the printers in August 1993, Robert Smith took a phone call. The voice at the other end of the line said, in the unmistakable accent of Liverpool, 'I think I've got James Maybrick's watch.' Far from being elated we felt a sense of near panic. Here, more than likely, was the first of the bandwagon riders we had been warned would try to capitalize on the diary. Yet we dared not ignore the possibility that the caller could be genuine.

I drove to Liverpool to meet Albert Johnson at his brother Robbie's house. He was a decent, clearly honourable family man, semi-retired from his college security job. The watch lay on the glass-topped table between us. It was a small, elaborately engraved man's pocket watch. Gently, Albert opened the back of the case, and I could just see faint scratches on the inside of the cover. I could not make out any words. The brothers produced a small microscope and invited me to look again.

As I did so, words took shape; at the bottom of the rim I could just see a signature – it read: 'J. Maybrick'. The letters 'K' and 'M' were identical with the letters in the known signature on Maybrick's wedding certificate. Across the centre, even less distinct, were the words: 'I am Jack.' Around the edge were five sets of initials – those of the five women murdered in Whitechapel. I could see there were other initials, which at that stage meant nothing to me. On the back of the watch the initials JO had at some time been professionally engraved.

I listened as Albert Johnson told me the story of how he came by the watch.

'I had seen the watch in Stewart's, the jewellery shop, in Wallasey [Cheshire] and had passed it several times. I've always had a liking for antique bits and pieces, so I thought I'd buy it as an investment for my little granddaughter, Daisy. The shop receipt records the date of purchase as July 14th 1992. I paid £225.

'I took it home and put it in a drawer and thought no more about it. Then one day at work some colleagues were talking about old watches; and I said I would bring mine in to show them.

'They thought it was worth a lot of money, but whilst we were looking, the light from the classroom window lit up some scratches in the back. I'd never noticed them before. We took the watch over to the science and maths block, and there, under the magnifying glass, tried to read what the marks said, but the room was too dark. At that point the lab technician produced a microscope, and we worked out the words: 'I am Jack.' We also found the initials AC and CE and the name 'Maybrick' on the bottom of the watch. I didn't think much more about it.

'Later my colleague remembered that he'd read the name Maybrick in the newspaper recently. He'd got the story all muddled. He thought Maybrick had murdered his wife and children and put them under the floorboards, gone to America or Australia, and that people thought he was Jack the Ripper. So I went back to the biology classroom and looked at the watch again. This time we also found MK on the top right-hand side and what looked like an ES and MN. We also found the numbers H 9/3 and 1275.

'I couldn't find a book on Maybrick in the college library, but there was one on Jack the Ripper, and it was then I realized the initials of his victims matched those on my watch. I still thought it was hard to believe, so I rang the *Liverpool Echo*. The reporters came to see me and told me about the discovery of Maybrick's diary. So I went to the *Echo* library to look up the story. It was there that I heard of the book about to be published and rang Robert Smith.

'By that time I realized the watch could be important, and at our solicitor Richard Nicholas's suggestion my brother, Robbie, and I decided to invest some money in having it forensically tested, and instructed Dr Stephen Turgoose of the Corrosion and Protection Centre at the University of Manchester Institute of Science and Technology (UMIST).'

The report, which Dr Turgoose sent to Albert Johnson, read: 'On the basis of the evidence . . . especially the order in which the markings were made, it is clear that the engravings pre-date the vast majority of superficial scratch marks (all of those examined). The wear apparent on many of the engravings, evidenced by the rounded edges of the markings and 'polishing out' in places, would indicate a substantial age for the engravings. The actual age would depend on the cleaning or polishing regime employed, and any definition of number of years has a great degree of uncertainty and, to some extent, must remain specula-tion. Given these qualifications, I would be of the opinion that the engravings are likely to date back more than tens of years and possibly much longer.

'However, whilst there is no evidence which would indicate a recent [last few years] origin of the engravings, it must be emphasized that there are no features observed which conclusively prove the age of the engravings. They could have been produced recently and deliber-ately artificially aged by polishing, but this would have been a complex multi-stage process using a variety of different tools, with intermediate polishing of artificial wearing stages. Also, many of the features are only resolved by the scanning electron microscope, not being readily appar-ent in optical microscopy, and so, if they were of recent origin, the engraver would have to be aware of the potential evidence available from this technique, indicating a considerable skill and scientific awareness.'

About a year after the day he bought the watch, Albert called on Ron Murphy who, with his wife Suzanne, runs Stewart's the jewellery shop. They were understandably disconcerted that they had sold it in the first place! 'In fact,' said Suzanne, 'some time after Mr Johnson first took the watch, he kept coming back and asking questions about it and wanted to know where we got it from. We got a bit fed up and thought there must be something wrong. So we offered to buy it back. No wonder he said, "No".'

Suzanne's father had given them the watch, along with all the other gold stock from his antique jewellery shop in Lancaster, when he retired. He had had it for at least eight years before that but cannot remember who sold it to him, probably as much as 15 years ago. The watch was not in working order when the Murphys first had it, and eventually, in 1992, they sent it for repair to Tim Dundas of West Kirby, Wirral. Later, before it was placed in the shop window, Ron Murphy tried to clean up the scratch marks with jeweller's rouge.

Every piece of the story was falling into place. So we then took the watch to the Prescot Watch Museum, where the curator John Griffiths gave me a full technical description.

'It is', he wrote, 'a gold pocket watch hallmarked for 1846/7 at London, the casemaker's mark being RS in an oval, the inner back marked 20789 and the initials J.O. engraved in a cartouche on the outside of the back; the full plate, fusee, English lever movement inscribed on the back, Verity, Lancaster and numbered 1286.'

We learned later, with the help of David Thompson, superintendent of the 'Aladdin's cave' of a clock and watch department deep within the British Museum in London, exactly what this meant. Henry Verity ran a family watch retailing business that had been founded in Lancaster around 1830. R.S. were the initials of Ralph Samuel, who by 1845 was a partner with Jacob Lewis Samuel and Co., watch and dial makers of 54 Wood Street, Liverpool, and of Clerkenwell, London. Mr Thompson was puzzled about the number of H 9/3 and 1275, which he thought could have been made by the same implement that carved the other wording – although it could be a repair number. Certainly the 20789 on the inside rim was a repair mark.

'Although I have not examined the watch scientifically, I would not have any immediate reason to doubt the age of the scratches,' he added.

The Johnson brothers brought the watch down to London in October 1993 for the launch of *The Diary of Jack the Ripper*. They were accompanied by their solicitor Richard Nicholas of Roberts Moore Nicholas and Jones, with offices in Birkenhead in the Wirral. By this time the Johnsons, like Mike Barrett before them, were feeling out of their depth and in need of professional guidance. The press response to the watch was a thunderous – and disappointing – silence. Those who mentioned it at all clearly did not believe their story. Despite the corroboration of a scientist of repute and integrity, they suggested a conspiracy theory that linked both watch and diary as coming from a common, dubious source.

So Robbie and Albert agreed, at our suggestion, to seek a second expert opinion – and they took their watch to the Interface Analysis Centre at Bristol University, where the eminent metallurgist Dr Robert Wild tested it under his electron microscope, using the technique of Scanning Auger Microscopy. His findings were better than we had dared hope. Like Dr Turgoose, Dr Wild photographed slivers of brass embedded within the scratch marks. They were blackened with age.

The penultimate paragraph of his detailed report (which also stresses the need for much more lengthy work to pinpoint the exact date of the scratches) reads:

'Provided the watch has remained in a normal environment, it would seem likely that the engravings were at least of several tens of years age. This would agree with the findings of Dr Turgoose (1993), and in my opinion it is unlikely that anyone would have sufficient expertise to implant aged, brass particles into the base of the engraving.'

There seemed, by this time, little doubt that the scratches were certainly very old. Dr Wild told publisher Robert Smith that he privately thought the scratches could be as old as 1888/9. This meant that our critics must explain how, or why, anyone at the time of Jack the Ripper should have tried to lay the blame at Maybrick's door by scratching a message in such a secret place as the back of a pocket watch. Whatever critics of the diary may claim about the ease with which a forger could locate ink and paper of the right date, both Dr Wild and Dr Turgoose think it improbable that any forger could acquire the considerable technical expertise and the scientific equipment necessary to implant aged brass particles into the base of the engraving. Both agree, too, that the scratches are at least several decades old, which rules out the possibility that the scratches or the diary are a modern or post–1987 forgery.

The watch is still ticking loudly, like a time bomb, amid the silence of the critics. None has spoken up. There are no attacking theories. So, together, the watch and the diary present powerful and unassailable support for our belief that James Maybrick – a man obsessed by time – was indeed Jack the Ripper.

EIGHTEEN

Time reveals all

IN THE MONTHS before publication of the book in October 1993, an epidemic swept England, which attacked us all. We called it Rippermania. Its effects were devastating.

Perhaps we should all have been more aware when the *Sunday Times* first showed interest in serialization of *The Diary of Jack the Ripper* that it could not afford to make a mistake after the Hitler Diaries débâcle a decade earlier.

Robert Smith met one of the *Sunday Times*'s most senior executives on April 7th 1993 at his offices. Well aware that the *Sunday Times*, of all newspapers, would need to examine and test the diary carefully before publishing extracts, he offered them an option agreement. For £5,000 against a final purchase price of £75,000, the *Sunday Times* were thereby enabled to bring in their experts for a thorough examination, as well as have access to the diary, my commentary and the consultants on the project. He also insisted that the *Sunday Times* and any experts employed by them would have to sign a standard agreement to keep the contents of the diary confidential. This procedure is intended to protect both book publishers and newspapers from the common Fleet Street practice whereby one newspaper attempts to print the major revelations of a book as a 'spoiler', pre-empting the serialization by another, which has paid considerable money for its exclusivity.

The *Sunday Times* agreed the terms of the option but made a highly unusual condition: if the *Sunday Times* were not to go ahead with serialization, it would 'be entitled to explain publicly why it did not proceed with the purchase but only after the commencement of the serialisation by another newspaper or on publication of the work . . . whichever should happen first'.

This clause clearly signalled the *Sunday Times*'s intention to get a good story, if nothing else, for their £5,000. However, we were confident enough in the evidence we had amassed to believe at that time that they would treat the diary objectively, as a complex but exciting historic document. We did not fear an exposé because we had nothing to hide.

In America, on July 30th 1993 the *Washington Post* ran a story that expressed doubts about the diary. As a result the intended American publisher, Warner, commissioned their own investigation and issued a press statement promising that if the report were critical then they would withdraw.

Kenneth Rendell, a respected American antiquarian bookseller who had been involved with the Hitler Diaries exposure, was asked to co-ordinate the Warner investigation.

On August 20th Robert Smith flew to Chicago in a spirit of friendly co-operation, with the diary and a number of key documents. A team of hand-picked experts had been hurriedly assembled by Mr Rendell, including Maureen Owens, former president of the American Questioned Document Examiners, research ink chemist Robert Kuranz and scientist Rod McNeil, who had devised an ion migration test that, he claimed, could date when ink was placed on paper. Rod McNeil, we were told, had worked for the FBI and the American Secret Service.

By this time we had been immersed in every aspect of the diary for 16 months. Yet after only two weeks – during which the American team conducted scientific tests on samples of ink and paper from the diary, made a study of the manuscript from a photocopy Robert Smith left with them and wrote reports on their findings – they decided the diary was forged. Although Robert Kuranz's tests found no element in the ink inconsistent with the date of 1888–9, Rod McNeil's ion migration test 'revealed' that the diary had been written in 1921 'plus or minus twelve years'. No one commented that McNeil's report placed the diary within 20 years of the time in which it was written – 1888–9 – and up to 84 years before its publication in 1993.

On the basis of the report, Warner immediately withdrew, and press headlines ricocheted around the world, amid cries of 'Fake!' Almost no one reported that the very same week Hyperion, the publishing company owned by Disney, made Robert Smith an offer to buy US rights and to publish the book in the same month that Warner had announced. Because of the publishing furore in the USA, Hyperion decided to include in their version of *The Diary of Jack the Ripper* both the Rendell report and a rebuttal to it by Robert Smith. It is worth repeating part of what each had to say.

First Kenneth Rendell's own summary of his report:

'The basis of the book and the text of the purported Jack the Ripper Diary is that James T [sic] Maybrick was Jack the Ripper and wrote the diary. Handwriting comparisons by a number of leading experts, including the one selected by the English publisher, definitely show that Maybrick did not write this diary.

'A major factor cited in this book linking the diary to Jack the Ripper is the fact that highly unusual phrases and expressions that first appeared in 1888 in a letter signed "Jack the Ripper", sent to a London newspaper, widely publicised since, are used throughout the diary. The diary is thus, inexorably linked to that letter. All comparisons of the two handwritings conclude they are written by different people.

'The style of handwriting is not Victorian. The type of writing is indicative of the early to mid twentieth century at the earliest – not late nineteenth century. The layout, pen pressure and ink distribution all indicate many entries were written at one time, they are completely inconsistent with the diary but consistent with the forgery of a diary.

'The ion migration test conducted by its developer, Rod McNeil, to determine how long ink has been on paper concluded a median date of 1921 plus or minus twelve years . . .

'The diary is not written in a Victorian diary book but in a scrap book – highly unusual. The first twenty pages are torn out, which is illogical, unless one assumes a forger bought a Victorian or Edwardian era scrap book, tore out the used pages, and then filled in the diary.

'There is no credible evidence whatsoever that this diary is genuine. Every area of analysis proves, or indicates the Jack the Ripper Diary is a hoax.'

Now part of Robert Smith's rebuttal:

'Kenneth Rendell's report on the diary of Jack the Ripper is fundamentally flawed, inaccurate and unreliable. The tests and report on the diary were rushed through in two weeks and largely ignore 16 months of research and testing by our writer, researchers and experts . . .

'My layman's understanding of McNeil's claims is that he can, using a scanning auger microscope, measure the distance that the iron in ink moves along a fibre in the paper, and that he has data to indicate how many years it takes for the iron to move to the furthest point reached. No details of the tests are provided to justify what is, by Mr McNeil's own published admissions, a remarkably precise dating. In his chapter in *Archaeological Chemistry 3*, published in 1984, Mr McNeil allowed for a tolerance period of plus or minus thirty years from the median date, but provides no adequate explanation of how the test works.

'It is our belief that McNeil and Rendell will be unable to explain or provide a scientifically satisfactory explanation of his dating technique, or even to prove that a satisfactory test on the diary was possible . . .

'It is unfortunate that Rendell ignores nearly all the historical evidence except for one area: the references in the diary to 'an empty tin match box' found by the police at the site of the Catharine Eddowes murder. Rendell says: "The fact that the information was available in the official police list is ignored; as far as we know a competent forger could find such information." Not so in 1921. The police list was not open to the public until 1984 and was not published until 1987 . . .

'Rendell has much to say on the handwriting analysis and makes the so-called "will" of Maybrick a major plank of his report. He concludes his discussion of the "will" by saying: "There is sufficient evidence to reach a definitive conclusion. There is no other possibility – the writer of the Jack the Ripper diary was not James Maybrick." If this report is objective, why does it not consider the possibility that the will is forged? . . . [The evidence of the will being forged is in Chapter Ten and was presented to Rendell.]

'Another plank of Rendell's report concerns the "Dear Boss" letter, in which the Ripper boasts about his deeds and uses phrases like "red stuff" and "Ha ha" which appear in the diary. We show that the letter was almost certainly written by Jack the Ripper. Handwriting analysis is not a science, and its accuracy is much debated (the disagreement between Hayes, Owens and Koren on the comparison between Maybrick's signatures is an excellent example). We contend that the writer of the diary could have disguised his writing in the "Dear Boss" letter that was sent anonymously to the Central News Office. He had the best possible reason not to give his identity. Koren's comments on the letter are: "The writing is not spontaneous or natural. The letter was written slowly and in façade writing, meant to disguise the personality of the real writer, and hence it is very difficult to compare it to the spontaneous writing of the diary."

'One of the most important reports we commissioned was from Dr David Forshaw, a forensic psychiatric and senior registrar at the internationally respected Maudsley Psychiatric Hospital in London. He has profound knowledge of addictions and the behaviours of serial killers.

Rendell quotes only from his first and last paragraphs and ignores the remainder of his 15,000-word report, in which Forshaw closely links the actions and responses of the diarist with those of known serial killers, and finds the physical and psychological symptoms of arsenic addiction, as described in the diary, consistent with his expert knowledge of them. Forshaw has no difficulty in accepting that the diary could have been written by an addicted serial killer. Rendell tells us he decided it was "unnecessary" to have the diary examined by another "noted" forensic psychiatrist, who specializes in serial killers. Given the level of expertise on the subject in the USA, I consider that a grave omission in an independent report.

'In summary, by ruling out the possibility of a recent forgery, Rendell contributes to establishing the authenticity of the diary. Furthermore, his opinions are more subjective than scientific; he makes many false assumptions and conclusions; and, crucially, all of his points of disagreement are dealt with fully in the book.'

As for the contention that 'the style of handwriting is not Victorian', we quote later in this chapter from the most recent opinion of Robert A. H. Smith, Curator of the Department of Manuscripts at the British Library. He still held to his original view expressed on 5th June 1992 that he 'saw nothing in the diary inconsistent with it being of a late nineteenth-century date.'

That, of course, was not the end of the story. On September 19th 1993, the *Sunday Times* splashed in a banner headline over a double-page spread, the single word: 'Fake!' The article, under the by-line of the associate news editor Maurice Chittenden, fell well short of the biting indictment they might have hoped for. They could not identify a forger or find any evidence of when or where the diary had been forged. Nor could they find any fundamental flaw with the diary itself, either historically or scientifically. Yet at no point did they even consider that the diary might be genuine.

We were surprised by the *Sunday Times*'s superficial investigation. They had called on three experts: Dr Audrey Giles, a forensic document examiner; Dr Kate Flint, a lecturer in English Literature at Oxford University; and a Ripperologist, Tom Cullen. However, we could only conclude that the *Sunday Times*'s experts were given a very limited brief and had little scope to investigate the diary in detail. Dr Giles had looked at the diary for only a few minutes in publisher Robert Smith's office on June 22nd and at no time performed tests on it. On two occasions when Robert Smith was to have taken the diary to her laboratory for testing of the ink and paper, the appointments were cancelled without explanation by the *Sunday Times*. Dr Flint's expertise was, inappropriately, in English literature rather than language. She was not to know that the phrase in the diary that caused her most problem – 'one off' – had been found in written records from as early as 1860. Tom Cullen's vague report started unpromisingly by getting the year of the Ripper murders wrong.

The *Sunday Times* made two other serious allegations, the first of which was that James Maybrick's will did not match the handwriting of the diary. Yet the *Sunday Times* knew from my commentary that a major contemporary authority on Maybrick's will cast considerable doubt on the will's validity and that, as I explained in Chapter Ten, this bizarre will might well have been forged at the time of Maybrick's death. Such considerations were entirely omitted by the *Sunday Times*.

In addition, the *Sunday Times* attempted to discredit the diary by suggesting that Robert Smith had suppressed the report by forensic scientist Dr David Baxendale. They did not inform their readers that Smith Gryphon was bound by a written agreement that stipulated we could not use Dr Baxendale's report 'for any purposes whatsoever' or even mention his name or that of Document Evidence Ltd. Dr Baxendale has now released us from our obligation, and I have included details of his report in Chapter One.

All of these points and many more were put in writing to the *Sunday Times* in a letter from Robert Smith on July 9th. None of them appeared in the *Sunday Times* report of September 19th.

The most extraordinary aspect of the whole affair was the determination of the *Sunday Times* to get the Courts to overturn the confidentiality agreements and persuade a High Court Judge that it was 'in the public interest' for the newspaper to print their article before the date allowed in the option agreement. Smith Gryphon went to court twice to restrain the *Sunday Times* from jumping the gun. The costs incurred were very considerable, but the persistence of the *Sunday Times* is a measure of what a newspaper will do to steal a circulation march on its competitors. It had wanted to print the story in July but the net result of all this frenetic activity and cost was that the article was eventually published only one week before they would have been allowed, anyway, by the option agreement.

Then, on October 21st, we learned from the *Daily Express* that there was to be a 'Ripper Diary Probe by Yard', into what they suggested could be 'the biggest publishing hoax since the Hitler Diaries'.

We had known that the *Sunday Times* had deposited all its papers on the diary with New Scotland Yard's International and Organised Crimes branch (SOI). If such a move is taken, the Yard is obliged to respond.

We learned that their brief was to discover if Robert Smith or anyone else had knowingly passed off a fake document as genuine. Their brief was not to prove whether the diary was genuine or a forgery, but in order to unravel all the facts they would, incidentally, have to investigate its provenance.

I was alarmed to hear that sensational conclusions were being drawn from 'facts' that could have been easily explained. Had a case ever been brought – and at that stage we had no idea of the outcome – such ill-informed opinions could have been presented in a way that would have been very damaging to our case. The rumour and innuendo appeared to be getting quite out of hand. I knew that the investigating policemen suspected Mike Barrett to be the forger.

But it was not until November 1993 that I heard the reason why. I had been invited to the USA to take part in a coast-to-coast promotional tour for the book and to appear with Kenneth Rendell, first on the *Larry King Show* and later in a radio phone-in from Pasadena. He told me, on air, that there had been a very sinister development and that, when the police had entered Mike Barrett's home 'with a warrant,' they had actually found a word processor with the diary on disc.

The facts are this. The police did not have a warrant. Mike Barrett invited them to his house and co-operated in every way. The WPC was hardly 'found'. It was on the table in the dining room where he had transcribed the diary with the help of his wife, in order to make it easy to read. He brought that transcript with him on his first visit to Doreen Montgomery's office. This information was for all to read in my book and was hardly a dramatic secret.

Interestingly, by the time I met Kenneth Rendell personally he had shifted his ground. He still had absolutely no doubt the diary was a forgery – he claimed that he had no need of more than his allotted two weeks to see that. But he felt it was a modern forgery of within the last few years. Rod McNeil had soft-pedalled his own report and issued a statement that admitted that the storage conditions of a document could affect the tests he conducted and said that a controlled study to examine this scientifically could take 20 years.

I was astonished during our discussion that so much reliance could be placed by Mr Rendell on extremely subjective judgements about such things as the personal habits of Victorians and also their style of writing. He condemned the diary because it is written in an old scrap book with some pages torn out. Maybrick was an affluent man, he says; he would have bought a new, purpose-made diary. This is ridiculous. I know of a family business founded in 1803 in which Victorian ledgers and books of all kinds are stacked high in every room. Some have pages torn out; some have been used for other than their original purpose.

By the time I went to the USA I had also received a letter, dated November 11th, from the curator of 19th-century manuscripts at the British Library (within the British Museum), which dealt with the handwriting style with authority:

'By the late 19th century the term "Victorian handwriting" becomes difficult to define. From that time onwards a wide variety of hands, some quite modern in appearance, can be found. Examples of the many different handwriting styles of the period can be seen in the large collections of late Victorian letters held by the British Library.'

In the meantime the press was having a field day, although few reporters appeared to have read either my book or the diary.

The police investigation rumbled expensively on, and we waited for the findings of the SOI. Such findings never came our way.

On November 26th the *Daily Express* followed up its original story with 'Ripper Diaries Are Fake'. The report said: 'a Scotland Yard investigation into the alleged diaries of Jack the Ripper concludes they are fake.' It went on: 'detectives . . . are convinced the 65 page document was penned within the last decade.' Here we had yet another date.

I rang the *Daily Express* to ascertain their source for this unfounded statement, and they claimed that the information came from New

Scotland Yard. I rang the Yard to discover exactly what was happening and was put through to the SOI, who denied having made any statement to the *Daily Express*. They transferred me to the Press Office, who, they alleged, would have issued any statements. The Press Office refused to speak to me because, they said, I was not a journalist. As an NUJ member for some 30 years this seemed unreasonable.

I asked when we would receive a statement. 'There is no statement,' I was told.

Finally, on January 15th 1994, we learned the truth from Harold Brough of the *Liverpool Daily Post*: 'Yard Clears Ripper Diary Publisher of Fraud.' This was the issue on which the police had been briefed – not the authenticity of the diary, which was an internal issue on which they were not entitled to comment in the press.

The Yard had sent their findings to the Crown Prosecution Service (CPS), who had made a statement when deciding to go no further with an inquiry. The CPS told Harold Brough: 'We have decided against a prosecution because there is not enough evidence to have a realistic prospect of getting a conviction.' It was a totally unsatisfactory result. We, who had suffered such headline damages as 'The Great Ripper Rip-off', were to be given no official written answer to counter the damage that had been done to the diary.

While our research continued, the diary acted as a catalyst for more books and many miles of newsprint. The Ripper Bible, *The A-Z of Jack the Ripper*, was reprinted – with Maybrick on the cover and the spine.

Kenneth Rendell wrote an authoritative tome on literary hoaxes, *Forging History*, and devoted a chapter to the great Ripper 'forgery'. This ends with the extraordinary, unsupported statement: 'it was written very recently, probably within a year before its announced "discovery".' This was a remarkable departure from his report, which referred to Rod McNeil's date of 1921, plus or minus 12 years.

The UK quarterly magazine *Ripperana* reflected the controversy by introducing a new section, 'Diary News'. Writer and broadcaster Melvyn Harris produced a book, *The True Face of Jack the Ripper*, restating his earlier theory that Robert Donston Stephenson (self-styled Dr Roslyn D'Onston), doctor, occultist and drunkard, was the Ripper. *The A-Z of Jack the Ripper* had already dismissed this idea some years ago: 'the theory has not persuaded any known researchers.'

Could a little professional jealousy be the motivation for Mr Harris's relentless denunciation of *The Diary of Jack the Ripper*? Could this be why he felt the need to end his own book with a three-chapter appendix on what he also calls 'the biggest Ripper hoax of the 20th century'? Mr Harris seems to believe that there is, lurking somewhere in Liverpool or London, a man who is chuckling at the sight of us all feverishly analysing his hoax. However, like Kenneth Rendell and Scotland Yard and other disciples of the hoax theory, he makes no sensible suggestion of the forger's motivation, let alone identity. He claims that all that is required to write this diary are three source books, which he does not name. However, we have given facts from both the Ripper case and the life of James Maybrick, not to be found in any book or other accessible document.

Like Kenneth Rendell, Melvyn Harris abandoned his earlier attempts at dating the diary. At the press conference to launch the book the previous year he stated that the handwriting was characteristic of someone who had been educated in the thirties. He does not mention that his forger must have had: deep knowledge of the psychology of a serial killer; precise and obscure knowledge of the effects of long-term arsenic poisoning; the creative and historical skills enabling him to produce an entirely original and believable Ripper candidate and produce such literary phrases as 'oh, costly intercourse of death', while haphazardly making grammatical and spelling mistakes; and he would have acquired enough knowledge of ink chemistry and Victorian handwriting, not to make technical errors.

Mr Harris's suggestions are beyond belief, especially as he assiduously has decided to make no reference to the other key evidence – the writing on the watch owned by Albert Johnson. If we are to accept his scenario, then we also have to accept that the scratches on the watch were forged by his conman, who was therefore, additionally, a skilled scientist with a talent for ageing metal – which metallurgy expert at Bristol University, Dr Robert Wild, finds inconceivable. It is really very difficult to believe that our prankster would not have been let down by some historical inaccuracy or a scientific flaw in the ink or paper, or an error in the psychology of a serial killer and arsenic addict as described by Dr Forshaw.

As we know, Mike Barrett brought the diary to literary agent

Doreen Montgomery, and the weight of a professional research team was brought to bear on the 'hoaxer'. After all this time, after a full and expensive police inquiry, Mr Harris's forger has still not been identified. When almost every modern literary forgery has led swiftly to the discovery of the 'author' of the hoax, is it not remarkable that our forger remains elusive, even after more than two years of intense activity to find him?

Since there is no consensus among the dozens of amateur and professional people who have now fallen under the spell of this diary, it remains a mystery and a challenge.

The handwriting is a problem only if you put your faith 100 per cent in the words of handwriting experts and graphologists. Or if you believe the 'Dear Boss' letters were indeed written by an 'enterprising journalist' and that Maybrick wrote the extant will, ignoring doubts expressed over its authenticity at the time and further explored in this book. I have explained earlier why I do not accept these objections, but finally you have to make up your own mind and await developments. We can be sure there will be many more to come.

The pressure on us all over the two years of research and writing had been relentless, but for Mike Barrett it finally became too much to bear. He tried to escape and the usual pints and Scotches at the local gave way to heavy drinking. Eventually his beloved Anne could stand no more, and for the sake of Caroline she left him and has filed divorce proceedings. Their departure resulted in an orgy of drinking that damaged his remaining kidney.

Then, as the alcoholism firmly took its grip on Mike, he devised a wild and desperate plan to, as he later explained to me, 'get back at Anne'. On Friday, June 24th 1994, he telephoned the *Liverpool Post* from his own home and told them: 'I did it.' A reporter went to his now run-down house, where he found him lying on the floor with three empty bottles of Scotch and a bottle of wine. In his pitiful condition, Mike took the reporter to the shop where, he claimed, he had bought the ink and told him of the auctioneers, Outhwaite and Litherland, where, he claimed, he had bid for the diary.

He signed a confession typed-up for him, but he could supply no answers at all as to how or where he had researched his facts. I remembered how, in his happier days, I had sometimes asked him to do simple research in Liverpool, so that he could feel involved. He was always desperate to play his part, and yet I knew how confused and agitated he became when he could not understand the fairly simple tasks I set him.

Of course, under examination his confession did not hold up. This was no case of *in vino veritas*. The manuscript ink in the shop in Bluecoat Chambers, where he had led the *Liverpool Post* reporter, was made by Diamine of Liverpool ink manufacturers; and it contains a modern synthetic dye that any of our analysts would have spotted in the ink of the diary. The auctioneers said that no unremarkable empty album such as ours would have been sold singly. Yet Mike said that he had not bid for a job lot. Later, during a period of drying-out, he explained to Robert Smith that he had made up the story about these specific auctioneers, because he had passed their premises every time he went by bus into Liverpool city centre. As for the stationery shop, it was situated in Bluecoat Chambers, where every other Saturday morning there was a book market, which he liked to visit, and it seemed to him a believable location to add colour to the story he foolishly fed to the *Liverpool Post* reporter.

The *Liverpool Post* had published its lead story about the confession on June 27th. Next day Mike Barrett's solicitor, Richard Bark Jones, issued a statement: 'I wish to release the following statement on behalf of my client Michael Barrett:

"With regard to the statement (confession) recently made by Michael Barrett that he had, himself, written the diary of Jack the Ripper, I am in a position to say that my client was not in full control of his faculties when he made that statement which was totally incorrect and without foundation. Michael Barrett is now in the Windsor Unit of Fazakerley Hospital, where he is receiving treatment."'

The hospital, too, explained that his drinking had led to a condition they described as 'confabulation' – described by Dr Forshaw as 'a classic symptom of the Korsakoff Syndrome seen in alcoholism. The main problem is with failing memory. The individual fills in gaps in the memory with fictitious stories when prompted by questions.'

Inevitably the *Sunday Times*, in an article on July 3rd 1994, gloatingly reported the 'confession'. It made practically no attempt to explain the circumstances of Mike's alcoholism that led to it, despite

Robert Smith and Doreen Montgomery explaining at length to their reporter, Maurice Chittenden, what the doctors were telling us. All in all, it was a tragic outcome for Mike and for his family.

By this time I would have expected that those of us who had explored every dark corner and lived through every twist and turn of this bizarre mystery would be immune to further surprise. I was wrong. We were not prepared for the next page of the story.

For several months, video producer Paul Feldman had been locked in a relentless campaign to establish the provenance of the diary. On a sultry August 3rd 1994 – just three days before the paperback edition of this book was due at the printers – literary agent Doreen Montgomery, publisher Robert Smith, researchers Sally Evemy and Keith Skinner, and myself were invited to gather at Paul's offices in Baker Street, London. Paul then dramatically placed a small tape-recorder on the table before us. The voice we heard was unmistakable: it was Anne Barrett's – brisk, emotional and rather tense.

What follows is a statement that she had made to Paul on tape a few days before the meeting.

'I suppose I knew it was inevitable', she said, 'that one day the truth about the Ripper diary would be revealed. I apologize most sincerely that it has taken so long, but I felt I had justifiable reasons. I realized some time ago that the snowball effect had intruded deeply into your lives, and this has been a heavy burden for me to carry. The diary was never meant for publication. Not by me.'

Anne went on: 'I think it was in 1968–9 that I saw the diary for the first time. I was living with my father and we were leaving the house as my father was about to remarry, having been widowed some years previously. In my bedroom was a fitted cupboard. I discovered the diary in a large metal trunk at the back of the cupboard. I read the first page but put it away to read when I was not so busy . . . later I took it to my father and asked him what he knew about it, if anything. He was doing his pools at the time and was not very interested. I asked him if he had read it, but he said he had started to but the writing was too small. I left it at that.'

Anne's father, William (known as Billy) Graham, was born on September 22nd 1913. A member of the British Legion, Billy had served with the Cheshire Regiment in the Second World War. He was a Desert

Rat and had also fought in the Battle of Malta. In her statement, Anne explains that in 1950 after the death of Billy's father, his stepmother, Edith Formby, had come for Christmas dinner and left Billy a suitcase, which, among other items, contained the diary. She told him that it had been left to him by his granny.

On December 4th 1975 Anne married Michael Barrett. She says that it was around the time they moved to Goldie Street in 1988 that her father gave her the diary among lots of other things he didn't want.

'I never showed it to Mike,' she said. 'Why? I honestly don't know. I did not like having the diary in the house and jammed it behind a cupboard.

'Some time later Mike started drinking. He was desperately trying to write but didn't seem to be getting anywhere. It was very frustrating and was making things difficult between us. I thought of giving him the diary then so that he could use it as the basis for a book. I was hoping he would be able to write a fictional story about the diary. I knew if I gave it to him and told him its history, he would be badgering my Dad for details, and by this time he and my father were beginning to irritate each other. So I came up with the plan of giving Mike the diary via someone else. That way he would not connect it with me or my family. My only motive was to give Mike something interesting to do without it coming from me.

'I found some brown paper which had been lining a drawer and wrapped the diary in it and tied it with string. I took the parcel to Tony Devereux and asked him to give it to Mike and tell him to do something with it. Which he faithfully did. Whether he eventually told Mike where he got it from I have no idea. I apologize to the Devereux family for being brought into this, but I never realized what would happen. I suppose I was very naïve . . .

'When Mike said he wanted to get the diary published I panicked. We had a big argument, and I tried to destroy it. I don't mean I tore out any of the pages – I just wanted to burn it in its entirety. Anyway, he contacted Doreen just the way he said he did . . . and I just let everyone get on with it. I never realized all the problems it would cause . . .

'In conclusion, can I just say that I have never been interested or cared who Jack the Ripper was. Nor has my father. Anyway, this is my story. I hope it makes up in some way for the secrecy I took on to protect my father and his family.'

We sat in stunned silence, a hundred questions hammering to be let out. Then Paul showed us the transcript of a tape-recorded conversation on July 30th 1994 between himself, Anne and Billy Graham, in which Billy talked about his family and the diary. It will need to be further researched before its contents can be fully reported. However, on the tape Billy does explain that he received the diary at Christmas 1950. It was this discussion that compelled Anne to make her statement the following day.

Other research was now looking more relevant and began to fall into place. Nigel Morland, in his book *This Friendless Lady*, had noted that Florence Maybrick had adopted the pseudonym of Graham. At about the time Anne Barrett – née Graham – was recording her message to us, Keith Skinner was confirming, from contemporary newspapers in the Newspaper Library at Colindale, that Florie had indeed used the name Mrs Graham when she was leaving the convent in Cornwall, where she had been resting after her release from prison in 1904. She was on her way to be reunited with her mother in France. Could this really be simply coincidence? Or is there, in fact, a family relationship between Billy Graham and Florie?

We already knew from a newspaper interview with Florie that she had returned to England from America in 1927 to 'effect a reconciliation with members of my family' and in the hope of seeing her 'children' (see page 208). Yet this was long after the death of her son Bobo in 1911 had left Gladys as her only surviving child from her marriage to James Maybrick. So, was there another child? Additional support for the Graham connection comes from the research papers of Trevor Christie for his book *Etched in Arsenic*. Paul Feldman obtained a copy of the papers from the University of Wyoming, which included a list of items found in Florie's Connecticut cottage when she died in 1941. Among these was an address book, from which had been torn all the entries beginning with the letter 'G'. Was there a secret family she did not want the world to identify?

The deadline for printing this paperback edition was inescapable. There was no time for me to see Anne, in Liverpool, and to ask her the mass of questions on my mind. Billy was going back into hospital. There was no time to establish, through the archives, any conclusive links between the Maybricks and the Grahams.

All this and much more remains to be done. I could have decided to write nothing now and wait until the research was complete. But I have always tried to write of events, honestly, as they have happened, so that readers are able to share the unfolding drama – frustrating as it is to end on yet another question mark. The hunt for the Ripper has been renewed with vigour.

The clear and exciting fact is this: at the very least Billy Graham's and Anne Barrett's statements take the diary back to 1950, when Billy Graham received it – and thus out of reach of the critics who claim it is a modern forgery. It is perhaps time for all researchers, even the detractors, to accept the diary as a uniquely fascinating historical document and to join in the unravelling of its mysteries.

Perhaps James Maybrick himself should have the last word.

At the beginning of July 1881, two weeks before his marriage to Florie, James Maybrick was granted a coat of arms by the ancient College of Arms in London. It cost him £76 10s, the equivalent today of £3,200. The official description reads:

Arms. Argent on a mount, a hawthorn tree in blossom proper on a chief Gules a sparrow hawk close between two billets Or.

Crest. Upon a billet fessewise Or a sparrowhawk close holding in the beak a branch of hawthorn slipped and in blossom proper.

In other words, Maybrick had chosen to represent himself with a bird of prey, symbolizing power in heraldic terms, combined with a full flowering May tree and golden bricks.

But of all the messages Jack the Ripper could have chosen to send us across the years, in the light of the discovery of the watch and the diary, the truth of the legend beneath that coat of arms is incontestable:

TEMPUS OMNIA REVELAT

Time Reveals All

TEMPUS OMNIA REVELAT

James Maybrick's family crest

Above: James Maybrick had a characteristic 'fair moustache', described by eyewitnesses whom the police believed had seen Jack the Ripper. (John Harrison)

Right: A police artist's impression of Jack the Ripper, resembling James Maybrick, was published on 6 October 1888. (British Library)

Right: Facsimile of the poster, distributed by the police, that showed the 'Dear Boss' letter of 25 September 1888, perhaps the first time that the nickname, Jack the Ripper, was used, together with the 'Saucy Jacky' postcard, almost certainly by the same writer. The police believed the letter and the card to be written by the Ripper.
(Public Record Office, Kew)

You though yourself very clever I reckon when you informed the police. But you made a mistake if you think I don't know your address. It was right what I told you my old friends. I said I was going to Liverpool. Because it was true. Because Mark is my name. I hope you like the hint. You see I know your address.

6 Oct 1888

Yours truly Jack the Ripper

You see I know your address

Liverpool 7.9.th 1889

Above and left: A previously unpublished 'Dear Boss' communication and envelope in a more ornate copperplate style. It is unlikely to be sheer chance that the first story on the newspaper starts with the word Liverpool. (Public Record Office, Kew)

Above: Another previously unpublished letter, believed to be in the same hand as the 'Dear Boss' letter, in which the writer threatens a witness to one of the murders on 30 September. It was posted in NW London, where Maybrick's brother Michael lived. (Public Record Office, Kew)

Left: The first page of what was thought to be James Maybrick's last will, apparently written in his own hand. However, a highly regarded contemporary writer and lawyer who saw the will was convinced that Maybrick could not have written it. It also misspells twice the name of James Maybrick's daughter as Evelyn, not Evelyn, an unlikely mistake by so fond a father. (Somerset House)

Opposite: Florence Maybrick during the time of her marriage. (Richard Whittington Egan)

Above: A contemporary drawing of Battlecrease House, with Mrs Maybrick and her two children walking down the drive. (Richard Whittington Egan)

Above: The Maybrick children, Gladys Evelyn and James Chandler, known affectionately as 'Bobo'. (Richard Whittington Egan)
Left: James Maybrick's brother, Michael, with whom he often stayed when he went to London. He was a successful writer of popular songs, using the pseudonym Stephen Adams. (Richard Whittington Egan)

Left: The Aigburth Hotel where the inquest on James Maybrick was held. (Richard Whittington Egan)

Opposite: A newspaper sketch of the main participants in the trial of Florence Maybrick, accused of murdering her husband. (British Library)

Below: The counter at Wokes, the chemist in Grassendale, where Mrs Maybrick purchased a dozen flypapers with such devastating consequences. (Richard Whittington Egan)

Right: Valentine's Meat Juice and the bottle containing a mixture of meat juice and water, in which half a grain of arsenic was discovered. (Richard Whittington Egan)

THE MAYBRICK MURDER TRIAL.

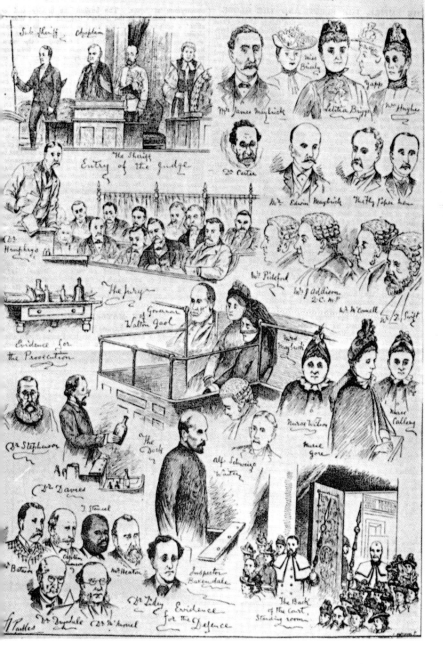

Right: The shack at South Kent, Connecticut, where Florence Maybrick died.
(Richard Whittington Egan)

Below: In South Kent a simple cross marks the grave of Florence who died in 1941, age 79.
(Richard Whittington Egan)

Right: The final resting place of James Maybrick, in the family vault in Anfield cemetery, Liverpool. (Richard Whittington Egan)

Above: St George's Hall, Liverpool, the location for the sensational trial of Florence Maybrick. (Richard Whittington Egan)

Facsimile of the original Diary of Jack the Ripper

what they have in store for them they would stop this instant. But do I desire that? My answer is no. They will suffer just as I. I will see to that. Received a letter from Michael perhaps I will visit him. Will have to come to some sort of decision regards the children. I long for peace of mind but I sincerely believe that that will not come until I have sought my revenge on the whore and the whore master.

———————————

Foolish bitch, I know for certain she has arranged a rendezvous with him in Whitechapel. Do be it, my mind is firmly made. I took refreshment at the Pate House & it was there I finally decided London it shall be. And why not, is it not an ideal location? Indeed do I not frequently visit the Capitol and indeed do I not have legitimate reason for doing so. All who sell their duty wares shall pay, of that I have no doubt. But shall I pay? I think not I am too clever for that

As usual my hands are cold, my heart I do believe is colder still. My dearest Gladys is unwell yet again, she worries me so. I am convinced a dark shadow lays over this house, it is evil. I am becoming increasingly weary of people who constantly enquire regards the state of my health. True my head and arms pain me at times, but I am not idly worried, although I am quite certain Hopper believes to the contrary. I have him down as a bumbling buffoon. Thomas has requested that we meet as soon as possible. Business is flourishing so I have no inclination to neglect the matter he describes as most urgent. Nevertheless I shall endeavour to meet his request.

June is passing much too slowly, I still have to work up the courage to begin my campaign. I have thought long and hard over the matter and still I cannot come to a decision as to when I should begin. Opportunity is there, of that fact I am certain. The bitch has no inclination.

The thought of him taking her is beginning to thrill me, perhaps I will allow her to continue, some of my thoughts are indeed beginning to give me pleasure. Yes I will wait School for a few weeks, and allow him to take all she can from the whoring master. Tonight I shall see nine. I may return to Bottlecrease and take the unfaithful bitch. Two in a night, indeed pleasure. My medicine is doing me good, in fact, I am sure I am take more than any other person alive. My mind is clear I will put whore tranquyl sire tonight.

242

I am begining to believe it is unwise to continue writing. If I am to down a whore then nothing shall lead the powers back to me, and yet there are times when I feel an overwhelming compulsion to place my thoughts to paper. It is dangerous, that I know. If Smith should find this then I am done before my campaign begins. However, the pleasure of writing off all that lays ahead of me, and indeed the pleasure of thoughts of deeds that lay ahead of me, thrills me so. And oh what deeds I shall count. For how could one suspect that I could be capable of such things, for am I not, as all believe, a mild man, who it has been said would never hurt a fly. Indeed only the other days did not Edwin say of me I was the most gentlest of men he had encountered. A compliment from my dear brother which I found exceedingly flattering.

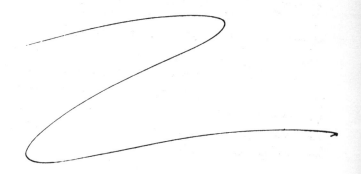

Have decided my patience is wearing thin. The bitch has made a fool of me. Tomorrow I travel to Manchester. Will take some of my medicine and think hard on the matter. I believe I could do so, though I shake with fear of capture. A fear I will have to overcome. I believe I have the strength. I will force myself not to think of the children. The whore, that is all that shall be in my mind. My head aches.

My dear God my mind is in a fog. The whore is now with her maker and he is welcome to her. There was no pleasure as I squeezed, I felt nothing. Do not know if I have the courage to go back to my original idea. Manchester was cold and damp very much like this hell hole. Next time I will throw acid over them, the thought of them melting and screaming while the acid burns deep thrills me.

ha, what a joke it would be if I could gorge an eye out and leave it by the whores body for all to see, to see, he, ha.

I believe I have caught a chill I cannot stop shaking, my body aches. There are times when I pray to God that the pain and torment will stop. Summer is near the warm weather will do me good. I long for peace but my work is only beginning. I will have a long wait for peace. All whores must suffer first and my God how I will make them suffer as she has made me. Edwin asked about Thomas and business, I informed him that Thomas was well and business was flourishing, both true. I have it in my mind that I should write to Michael, perhaps not, my hands are far too cold, another day. I will take the letter tonight. I need to take my mind off the nights events. The children are well.

Strolled by the drive, encountered Mrs Hammersmith, she enquired of Bobo and Gledys. and much to my astonishment about my health. What has that whore said? Mrs Hammersmith is a bitch The fresh air and stroll did me good. For a while I succeeded in forgetting the bitch and her whoring master. Felt completely refreshed when I returned to my office. I will visit Michael this coming June. June is such a pleasant month, the flowers are in full bd. the air is sweeter and life is almost certainly much easier I look forward to its coming with pleasure. A great deal of pleasure. I feel compelled to write to Michael if not obliged. My mind is clear, my hands are not cold.

I am vexed. I am trying to quell my anger. The whole has suggested she accompany me on my trip to Michael. I need time to put my mind in order. Under no circumstances can I let the bitch accompany me, all my hard work and plans will be destroyed if she were to do so. The pain was bad today. I believe the bitch has found one of my bottles, it had been moved. I am tired and need sleep the pain kept me awake for most of last night. Will return early around the bitch altogether.

Frequented my club. George stated that he had never seen me in better health. I believe the bitch has changed her mind. My thoughts are becoming increasingly more daring, I have imagined doing all manner of things. Could I cut part of one? Perhaps it would taste of fresh broiled bacon ha ha. My dear word it thrills me so.

Michael is expecting me towards the end of June, henceforth from July my campaign will gather momentum. I will take each and everyone before I return them to their maker; damaged of course, severely damaged.

247

I try to repel all thoughts of the children from my mind. I feel strong, stronger than I have ever felt — my thoughts keep returning to Manchester, next time it will thrill me. I know in my heart it will. I cannot understand why William will not accept my offer to dine. He is not unlike me, he hates the bitch. I believe if chance prevails I will burn St. James's to the ground tomorrow I will make a substantial wage. I feel lucky.

If I could have killed the bastard Lowry with my bare hands there and then I would have done so. How dare he question me on any matter, it is I that should question him. Damn him damn him damn him should I replace the missing item? No that would be too much of a risk. Should I destroy this? My God I will kill him. Give him no reason and order him point blank to drop the matter, that I believe is the only course of action I can take. I will force myself to think of something more pleasant. The whore will suffer more than she has ever done so tonight, that thought revitalizes me. Since is drawing to a close I shake with anticipation.

I have taken too much my thoughts are not where they should be. I recall little of the events of yesterday. Thank God I stopped myself in time. I will show my wrath towards the Inspector in such a manner that he will wish he had never brought up the subject. No one, not even God himself will away the pleasure of writing my thoughts. I will take the first whore I encounter and show her what hell is really like. I think I will ram a cane into the whoring bitches mound and leave it there for them to see how much she could take. My hand aches, God has no right to do this to me the devil take him.

How I succeeded in controlling myself I do not know. I have not allowed for the red stuff, gallons of it in my estimation. Some of it is bound to spill onto me. I cannot allow my clothes to be blood drenched, this I could not explain to anyone, least of all Michael. Why did I not think of this before? I curse myself. The struggle to stop myself was overwhelming, and if I had not asked Michael to lock me in my bedroom for fear of sleepwalking, to which I had said I had been prone to do recently, was that not clever? I would have done my dirty deeds that very night.

I have taken a small room in Middlesex Street that in itself is a joke. I have paid well and I believe no question will be asked. It is indeed an ideal location. I have walked the streets, and have become more than familiar with them. I said Whitechapel it will be and Whitechapel it shall. The bitch and her whoring master will rue the day I first saw them together. I said I am clever, very clever. Whitechapel Liverpool, Whitechapel London, ha ha. No one could possibly place it together. And indeed for there is no reason for anyone to do so.

The next time I travel to London I shall begin. I have no doubts, my confidence is most high. I am thirtiest writing this, life is sweet, and my disappointment has vanished. Next time for sure. I have no doubts, not any longer, no doubts. No one will ever suspect. Tomorrow

I will purchase the finest knife money can buy, nothing shall be too good for my whores, I will treat them to the finest, the very finest, they deserve that at least from I.

———————————

I have shown all that I mean knowers, the pleasure was far better than I imagined. The whore was only too willing to do her business. I recall all and it thrills me. There was no scream when I cut. I was more than vexed when the head would not come off, I believe I will need more strength next time. I struck deep into her. I regret I never had the cane, it would have been a delight to have rammed it hard into her. The bitch opened like a ripe peach. I have decided next time I will cut all out. My medicine will give me strength and the thought of the whore and her whoring master will spur me on no end

The wait to heard about my triumph seemed long, although it was not. I am not disappointed, they have all written well. The next time they will have

251

a great deal more to write, of that fact I have no doubt ha ha. I will remain calm and show no interest in my deed, if anyone should mention it so, but I will laugh inside, oh' how I will laugh.

I will not allow ~~too~~ much time to pass before my next. Indeed I need to repeat my pleasure as soon as possible. The whoring Master can have her with pleasure and I shall have my pleasure with my ~~thoughts~~ and deeds. I will be ever. I will not call on Michael on my next visit. My brothers would be horrified if ~~they~~ knew, particularly Edwin after all did he not say I was one of the most ~~gentlest~~ of men he had ever encountered. I hope he is enjoying the fruits of America. Unlike I, for do I not have a sour fruit.

I could not resist mentioning my deed to George. I was clever and brought up the subject by way of how fortunate we were not having murders of that kind in this city. He agreed with me completely. Indeed he went on to say, that he believed we had the finest police force in the land, and although we have our own share of troubles the women folk can walk the streets in safety. And indeed they can for I will not play my funny little games on my own doorstep ~~he he~~.

The gentle man with gentle thoughts will strike again soon. I have never felt better, in fact, I am ~~feeling~~ ~~more than~~ ever and I can feel the strength building up within me. The head will come off next time, also the whores hands. Shall I leave them in various places around Whitechapel? Take the head and hands instead of the thimble ~~he he~~. Maybe I will take some part away with me to see if it does taste of like fresh fried bacon. The whore seen her master today it did not bother me. I imagined I was with ~~them~~, the very thought thrills me. I wonder if the whore has ever had such ~~thoughts~~? I believe she has, has she not cried out when I demand she takes another. The bitch. She will suffer but not as yet. Tomorrow I ~~travel~~ to London. I have decided I cannot wait any longer. I look forward

to tomorrow nights work, it will do me good,
a great deal of good.

One dirty whore was looking for some gain.
Another dirty whore was looking for the same,

Am I not clever?) I thought of my funny little jaunt on my travel to the city of whores. I was vexed with myself when I realised I had forgotten the choice. So vexed in fact, that I returned to the bitch and cut out more.. I took some of it away with me. It is in front of me. I intend to fry it and eat it later ha ha. The very thought works up my appetite. I cannot stop the thrill of writing. I ripped open my God I will have to stop writing of the children they distract me so I ripped open

255

it has taken me three days to recover, I will not feel guilty it is the whoring bitch to blame not I. I ate all off it, it did not taste like fresh fried bacon but I enjoyed it never the less. She was so sweet and pleasurable. I have left the striped fools a clue which I am sure they will not solve. Once again I have been clever, very clever.

~~A ring or two will leave this clue~~

~~One pill thats true~~

I ~~will catch Sir Jim with no pills~~
~~left two~~

two farthings,
two pills
the whores I
rings.

Thith

It shall come, if Michael can succeed in rhyming verse then I can do better, a great deal better he shall not outdo me. Think you fool, think. I curse Michael for being so clever, I shall outdo him, I will see to that. A funny little rhyme shall come forth. Patience is needed patience. The night is long, time is on my hand.

The pills are the answer

and with pills. Indeed do I always not oh what a joke.

Begin with the rings,

One ring, two rings

hell, it took me a while before I could wrench them off. Should have stuffed them down the whores throat. I wish to God I could have taken the hand. Hated her for wearing them, reminds me too much of the whore. Next time I will select a whore who has none. The bitch was not worth the farthings. Return, return, essential to return. Prove you are no fool.

One ring, two rings,
a farthing one and two
~~So you will do true~~
~~better if its true~~
Along with M ha ha
Will catch clever Jim,
its true.
~~Left two~~
No pill, left but two

One ring, two rings,
a farthing, one and two,
Along with M ha ha
Will catch clever Jim
its true.
No pill, left but tw...

Am I not indeed a clever fellow? It makes me laugh they will never understand why I did so. Next time I will remember the chalk and write my funny little rhyme. The eyes will come out of the next. I will stuff them in the whores mouth, That will certainly give me pleasure, it does so as I write. Tonight I will see mine, she will be pleased as I will be gentle with her, as indeed I always am.

I am still thinking of burning St. James's to the ground I may do so on my next visit. That will give the fools something more to think on. I am begining to think less of the children, part of me hates me for doing so. One day God will answer to me, so help me Michael would be proud of my funny little rhymes for he knows only too well the art of verse. Have I not proven I can write better than he. I feel like Celebrating, the night has been long, and I shall award myself with the pleasures of the flesh, but I shall not be cutting the ... I will save that thrill for another day.

The whore is in debt. Very well I shall honor the latter notes but the whores are going to pay more than ever. I have read all of my deeds they have done me proud, I had to laugh, they have me down as left handed, a Doctor, a slaughterman and a few. very well, if they are to insist that I am a few then a few I shall be. Why not let the jews suffer? I have never taken to them, far too many of them on the Exchange for my liking: I could not stop laughing when I read Punch there for all to see was the first three letters of my surname. They are blind as they say.

" Turn round three times, And catch whom you

MAY"

he he he he he he

I cannot stop laughing it amuses me so shall I write them a clue?

May comes and goes.
~~this May pleases~~ with a ~~knife in his hand~~
In the dark of the night
~~He does people~~
When he comes and goes

with a ring on my finger
and a knife in my hand
~~This May comes and goes~~

May comes and goes
In the dark of the night
~~he does place the whores~~ he kisses
~~and gives them a fright~~
he kisses the whores
then gives them a fright

May comes and goes
in the dark of the night
he kisses the whores
then gives them a fright

With a ring on my finger
and a knife in my hand
This May spreads Mayhem
~~all through the land~~
throughout this fair land

The Jews and slaughtermen

~~The Jews and Dators.~~

The Dators and Jews.

~~may~~
will get all the blame — blame — tame
~~same — game~~
his dirty game.
May playing

~~The Dators Will~~

The Jews and the Dators
Will get all the blame
but its only May
playing his dirty game

~~He did not shed a tear~~
He will kill all the whores,
and not shed a tear
He ~~will~~ give them a clue
I will give them a clue
but nothing too clear
I will kill all the whores,
and not shed a tear.

May comes and goes
in the dark of the night
He kisses the whores
and gives them a fright

The Jews and the Doctors
will get all the blame
but its only May playing
his dirty game

I will give them a clue
but nothing too clear
I will kill all the whores
and not shed a tear

With a mug on my finger
and a knife in my hand.
This May spreads Mayhem
throughout this fair land.

They remind me of chickens with their heads cut off, running fools with no heads, he he. It is nice to laugh at bastards and fools and indeed they are fools. I need much more pleasure than I have had. Strange my hands feel older than they have ever done so.

I am fighting a battle within me. My desire for revenge is overwhelming. The whore has destroyed my life. I try whenever possible to keep all sense of respectability. I worry so over Lyla and Gladys, no others matter. Tonight I will take more than ever. I miss the thrill of cutting them up. I do believe I have lost my mind. All the bitches will pay for the sin. Before I am finished all of England will know the name I have given myself. It is indeed a name to remember. It shall be, before long, on every persons lips within the land. Perhaps her gracious Majesty will become acquainted with it. I wonder if she will honour me with a knighthood he he.

Abberline says he was never amazed,
I did my work with such honour
For his decree

264

he had to agree,
I deserve at least an honour
so all for a whim,

I can now rise Sir Jim — I cannot think of another word to accompany Jim I like my words to rhyme damn it. It is late, mine is waiting, I will enjoy this evening. I will be gentle and not give anything away.

I miss Edwin, I have received but one letter from him since his arrival in the whores country. The bitch is wring me more as each day passes. If I could I would have it over and done with. I visited my mother and fathers grave. I long to be reunited with them. I believe they know the torture the whore is putting me through. I enjoy the thrill of thinking of all I have done. But there has been, but once, regret for my deeds. I dispelled my remorse instantly. The whore still believes I have no knowledge of her whoring master. I have considered killing him, but If I was to do so. I would surely be caught. I have no desire for that, curse him and the whore their time will come

265

To my astonishment I cannot believe I have not been caught. My heart felt as if it had left my body. Within my fright I imagined my heart bounding along the street with I in desperation following it. I would have dearly loved to have cut the head of the damned horse off and stuff it as far as it would go down the whores throat. I had no time to rip the bitch wide, I curse my bad luck I believe the thrill of being caught thrilled me more than cutting the whore herself. As I write I find it impossible to believe he did not see me, in my estimation I was less than a few feet from him. The fool panicked, it is what saved me. My satisfaction was far from complete, damn the bastard, I cursed him and cursed him, but I was clever, they could not out do me. No one ever will. Within the quarter of the hour I found another dirty bitch willing to sell her wares. The whore like all the rest was only too willing. The thrill she gave me was unlike the others, I cut deep deep deep. Her nose annoyed me so I cut it off, had a go at her eyes left my mark, could not get the bitches heart to. I believe now it is impossible to do so. The whore never screamed. I took all I could away with me. I am saving it for a rainy day. ha ha.

Perhaps I will send Abberline and Warren a sample or two, it goes down well with an after dinner Port. I wonder how long it will keep? Perhaps next time I will keep some of the red stuff and send it courtesy of yours truly. I wonder if they enjoyed my funny Jewish joke? curse my bad luck had no time to write a funny little rhyme. before my next will send Central another to remember me by.. My God life is sweet. Will give them something to know its is me.

Red-head
horse,
cryed
smelt breath

A rose stretched the red
I did cut the head
down it I cried, henceforth I did hide,
The horse went and shied

With a rose to match the red
I tried to cut off the head.
Damn it I cried,
The horse went and shied
But I could still smell her sweet scented breath

I

Sir Jim,
tin match box empty
~~cigarette case~~
~~make haste~~
~~my strong knife~~
~~the whores knife~~
first whore no good

One whore no good,
decided Sir Jim strike another.
I showed no fright and indeed no light,
damn it, the tin box was empty

II

tea and sugar
~~sugar, page,~~ did say
me, plea, be
~~tea and sugar~~ paid my fee

Sweet sugar and ~~tea.~~ could have paid my small –
fee he he.
~~then~~ g did flee

Showed ~~my~~ glee
A kidneys for supper

Sweet sugar and ~~tea,~~
could have paid my small fee.
But instead g did flee
and lay way showed my glee.
By eating cold kidney for supper

III

bastard
Abberline
~~barnett~~
hides all
clue
clever
will tell you more

Mr Abberline is a ~~funny~~ little man.

Oh Mr Abberline, he is a clever little man
he keeps back all that he can.
~~But I know better~~
for do I know better, indeed I do
did I not leave him a very good clue
Nothing is mentioned. of this I know sure
ask clever Abberline, ~~he does know more~~

oh Mr Abberline, he is a clever little man
he keeps back all that he can.
For do I not ~~know better~~, Indeed I do.
did I not leave him a very good clue.
Nothing is mentioned; of this I am sure;
ask clever Abberline, could tell you more

IV

Gin gin trip over
fear
have it near
redeem it near
ever
posть long te

He believes I will trip over
but I have no fear

For I could not possibly redeem it here.
If the certain fact, I could send him poste teste
if he requests that be the case.

Am I not a clever fellow

That should give the fools a laugh, it has done so
for me, wonder if they have enjoyed the name I have
given? I said it would be on the lips of all, and indeed
it is. Believe I will send another. Include my funny
little rhyme. That will convince them that it is the
truth I tell. Tonight I will celebrate by
wining and dining George. I am in a good mood,
believe I will allow the whore the pleasure
of her whore Master, will remark an evening in the
city will do her good, will suggest a concert. I have
no doubt the carriage will take the hatch straight
to him. I will go to sleep
thinking about all they are doing. I cannot wait for
the thrill.

With a rose to match the red
I tried to cut off the head.
Damn it I cried,
the horse went and shied
hence forth I did hide,
but I could still smell
her sweet scented breath.

One whore no good, decided Sir Jim struck another.
I showed no fright, and indeed no light.
Damn it, the tin box was empty.

Sweet sugar and tea
could have paid my small fee
But instead I did flee and by way showed my glee
big eating cold kidney for supper.

Oh, Mr Abberline he is a clever little man,
he keeps back all that he can.
For do I not know better, Indeed I do,
did I not leave him a very good clue
Nothing is mentioned of this I know sure,
ask clever Abberline, could tell you more.

He believes I will trip over,
but I have no fear.
For I could not possibly
redeem it here.
Of this certain fact I could send them posthaste
If he requested that be the case

It has been far too long since my last, I have been
unwell. The whole of my body has pained. Hopper did not
believe me. One day I will take revenge on him. The whore
has informed the bumbling buffoon. I am in the habit
of taking strong medicine. I was furious when the
bitch told me. So furious I hit her. The
whore begged me not to do so again. It was a pleasure,
a great deal of pleasure. If it was not for my work,
I would have cut the bitch up there and then. But
I am clever. Although the gentleman has turned, I did
not show my hand true. I apologised, a one off
instance, I said, which I regretted and I assured the whore
it would never happen again. The stupid bitch believed
me.

I have received several letters from Michael. In all he enquires about my health and asked in one if my sleepwalking has returned. Poor Michael he is so easily-fooled. I have informed him it has not. My hands still remain cold. I shall be dinning tonight. I hope kidneys are on the menu, he he. Will put me in the mood for another little escapade. Will visit the city of whores soon, very soon. I wonder if I could do three?

If it were not for Michael insisting that we take dinner I would have tried my hand that very night. I cursed my brother as I have never cursed him before. I cursed my own stupidity. had I not informed Michael that I no longer sleepwalked I was forced to stop myself from indulging in my pleasure by taking the largest dose I have ever done. The pain that night has burnt into my mind. I vaguely recall putting a handkerchief in my mouth to stop my cries. I believe I vomited several times. The pain was intolerable, as I think I shudder. No more.

I am convinced God placed me here to kill all whores, for he must have done so, and I still not have anything will stop me now. The more I take the ... I stronger I become.

274

Michael was under the impression that once I had finished my business I was to return to Liverpool that very day. And indeed I did one day later he saw. I feel sure for the fact will not come to his attention as he addresses all letters to ...

I have read about my latest, my God the thoughts, the very best. I left nothing of the bitch, nothing. I placed it all over the room, time was on my hands, like the other whore I cut off the bitches nose, all of it this time. I left nothing of her face to remember her by. She reminded me of the whore. So young unlike I. I thought it a joke when I cut her breasts off, kissed them for a while. The taste of blood was sweet, the pleasure was overwhelming, will have to do it again, it thrilled me so. Left them on the table with some of the other stuff. Thought they belonged there. They wanted a slaughterman so I stripped what I could, laughed while I was doing so. Like the other bitches she riped like a ripe peach. One of these days I will take the head away with me. I will boil it and serve it up for my supper. The bag and burnt clothes puzzle them he he

essay;   ney
pile   initial
hat
handkerchief   whore mother
whom   look to the whore
Mother   light
father   fire

~~with the hay I did flee~~
I had the hay,
and with it I did flee
~~the clothes I burnt~~
~~along with the hat~~
The hat I did burn
for light I did yearn
~~For the sake of the whore mother~~
And I ~~thought~~ of the whory mother

I had the hay,
And with it I did flee.
The hat I did burn
for light I did yearn.
And I thought of the
whory mother.

          I

A handkerchief red,
led to the bed
and I thought of the whoring with...

II

~~For Sir Jim with his whim~~

A whores whim,
caused Sir Jim
to cut deeper, deeper and deeper.
~~away with it I did go.~~
~~back to the whoring mother~~
All did go.
As I did so
back to the whoring mother.

A whores whim,
caused Sir Jim
to cut deeper deeper and deeper.
All did go,
As I did so
back to the whoring mother

III

~~for initial those~~

An initial here and a initial there
would tell of the whoring matter

I had a key,
and with it I did flee
The hat I did burn,
for light I did yearn.
And I ~~thought~~ of the whoring mother

A handkerchief red,
led to the bed
And I ~~thought~~ of the whoring mother.

A whores whim
caused Sir Jim,
to cut deeper, deeper and deeper
all did go,
As I did so,
back to the whoring mother

278

An initial here and an initial there
will tell of the whole matter.

I left it there for the fools but they will never find
it I was too clever. Left it in front for all eyes
to see. Shall I write and tell them? That amuses me.
I wonder if next time I can carve my funny little
rhyme on the whores flesh? I believe I will give it a
try. It amuses me of nothing else. Life is sweet, very
sweet. Regret I did not take any of it away with
me it is supper time, I could do with a kidney
or two ha ha.

I cannot live without my medicine. I am afraid
to go to sleep for fear of my nightmares reoccurring.
I see thousands of people chasing me, with Abberline
in front dangling a rope. I will not be hopped
of that feel I am certain. It has been for too long
since my last, I still desire revenge on the whore
and their whore masters, but less than the desire

to repeat my last performance. The thoughts still thrill me so. I am tired and I fear the city of whores has become too dangerous for I to return. Christmas is approaching – and Thomas has invited me to meet him. I know him well. I have decided to accept his offer, although I know the motive behind it will strictly be business. Thomas thinks of nothing else except money unless me, ha ha.

My first was in Manchester so why not my next? If I was to do the same as the last, that would throw the fools into a panic, especially that fool Abberline. The children constantly ask what I shall be buying them for Christmas. They shy away when I tell them a shiny knife not unlike Jack the Rippers in order that I cut their tongues for peace and quiet. I do believe I am completely mad. I have never harmed the children – the years since they have been born. But now I take great delight in scaring them so. May God forgive me. I have lost my bottle and shall go on until I am caught. Perhaps I should stop myself and save the hangman a job. At this moment I have no feeling in my body, none at all. I keep asking

myself I have done no wrong. It is the whore
who has done so, not I. Will peace of mind ever
come? I have visited Hoffer too often this month;
I will have to stop; for I fear he may begin
to suspect. I talk to him like no other

———   — —

~~Go you still,~~
Am I insane?
Come, gun
~~Go~~ Jim ~~with~~ this fury ~~done~~
~~will~~ soon strike again

One whore in heaven,
two whores side by side,
three ~~whores~~ all have died.
four

Sir Jim he cuts them first

damn it

Abberline says he is now amazed,
Sir Jim has not struck another.
He waits patiently
for ...... Kosebly

Christmas said the whores mole bonnett
damn the butchers damn Michael
Give Sir Jim his due
He detests all the Jews
For he has no favourite men
As he runs away to his den.

He likes to write well for you
Give Sir Jim his dues
He detests all the Jews
and indeed was it not in ...

I kissed them,
~~I kissed them~~
~~They tasted so sweet~~
~~I thought of leaving them by~~ — the whores feet
but the table it was bear
so I went and left ~~them there~~

damn it damn it damn it

so help me God my next will be for the word.
my head aches, but I will go on   damn & filled
for being so clever the art of verse is far from
simple. I curse him so. Abberline Abberline
I shall ~~destroy~~ that foul yet, So help me God
Banish him from my ~~thoughts~~, he will not
catch Sir Jim yet

Abberline Abberline Abberline Abberline
The devil ~~take~~ the bastard

I am cold curse the bastard Lowry — for making
me ill I keep seeing blood pouring — from
the butchers. The nightmares are hideous
I cannot stop myself from wanting to eat more.
God help me, damn you it's noone will stop me
God be damned

Think think think write tell all prove to them
you are who you say you are make them believe
it is the truth I tell. Down him for creating
them, down him down him down him. I want
to boil boil boil. See if there eyes pop.
I need more thrills, cannot live without
my thrills. I will go on, I will go on nothing
will stop me nothing — let Sir Jim cut. Cut deep
deep deep.

Sir Jim will cut them all

Oh costly intercourse
of death

Banish the thoughts banish them banish them
be be be, look towards the sensible leather
chickens running around with
their heads cut off

her ha ha ha ha ha ha ha ha

am I not a clever fellow
out fooled them all, they will never know

For Jim will eat them all,
See Jim he does so ~~best of all~~

See Jim ~~makes~~ his well
He eats them all.
with his knife in his bag

will have to ~~take up~~ lodgings on my return.
Middlesex Street that was a joke. The fools, several times
they could have caught ~~me~~ & they had looked
good and proper. My God am I not clever? ~~Quick I~~
I am. My head spins will ~~save~~ how have I to find
the ~~strength~~ for my journey home. The skies tell
this city, it is too cold for me. Tomorrow I will ~~endure~~
~~harry~~ suffer. The ~~thought~~ will ~~dwell~~ me on my
journey home.

I cannot bring myself to look back, all I have written ~~saves~~
me so. George ~~visited~~ me today. I believe he knows
what I am going ~~through~~, although he says nothing
I can see it in his eyes. ~~Poor~~ George, he is such
a good friend. Michael is well, he ~~writes~~ me ~~many~~
time. In my heart I cannot blame him for doing
so. I regret I shall not see him this Christmas.

Encountered an old friend on the Exchange floor. I felt regret he was to not Jewish. I had forgotten how many Jewish friends I have. My revenge is on whores not Jews. I do believe I am truly sorry — for the hate I have thrown amongst them. I believe that is the reason I am unable to write my funny little rhymes. I thank God I have had the courage to stop sending them. I am convinced they will be my undoing.

I am tired, very tired. I yearn for peace, but I know in my heart I will go on. I will be in Manchester within a few days. I believe I will feel a great deal better when I have repeated on my last performance. I wonder if I can improve on my fiendish deeds. Will wait and see, no doubt I will think of something. The day is drawing to a close, however was in fine spirits, am pleased. I regret, as witty my Jewish friends I have shown my wrath. This coming Christmas I will make amends.

The bitch, the whore is not satisfied with one whore master, she now has eyes on another. I could not act like myself, visions of her flooded back as I tried to put all thoughts of love. I left her for dead, that I know. It did not amuse me. There was a thrill. I have showered my fury on the bitch. I struck and struck. I do not know how I stopped. I have left her penniless. I have no regrets. The whore will suffer unlike she has ever suffered. My God have mercy on her, for I shall not, so help me.

There was in fine health. The children enjoyed Christmas. I did not. My mood is no longer black, although my head aches. I shall never become accustomed to the pain. I am weaker. I yearn for my favourite month, to see flowers in full bloom would please me so. Warmth is what I need, I shiver so. I curse this weather and the coming winter. My heart has been soft. All whores will feel the edge of Sir Jim's shining knife. I regret I did not give myself that name, ease it, I prefer it much more than the one I have given.

Sir Jim with his shining knife,
cuts through the night,
and by God,
does he not show his might he he

———————

It shall not be long before I strike again. I am taking more than ever. The bitch can take two, - Sir Jim shall take four, a double.double event ... If I was in the city of whores, I would do my fiendish deeds this very moment. By God I would.

I curse myself for the fool I have been, I shall have no more regrets, damn them all. Beware Mr. Abberline I will return with a vengeance. Once more I will be the talk of England. What pleasure my thoughts do give me, I wonder if the whore will take the bastard? The bitch is welcome to him. I shall think about them deeds, what pleasure. Tonight I shall reward myself, I will visit mine, but I will not be gentle. I will show my whore what I am capable of. Sir Jim needs to wet his appetite,

all whore be damned. A friend has turned, so be it,
Sir you will turn once more. When I have finished
my fiendish deeds, the devil himself will praise me.
But he will have a long wait before I shake
hands with him. I have worked to do a great deal
of works he who the kidney for supper

I am tired of keeping up this pretence of respectability.
I am finding it increasingly difficult to do so. I
believe I am a lucky fellow. Have I not found
a new source for my medicine. I relish the thoughts that
it will bring me. I enjoy thinking of the whores waiting
for my nice shining knife. Tonight I write to Michael.
Inform him I shall be visiting the city of whores soon.
very soon. I cannot wait. The whore may take
as many whore masters as she wishes. I no longer
worry. I have my thoughts and pleasure of deeds
to come, and of what deeds I shall commit. Much,
much finer than my last. Life is indeed sweet,
very very sweet.

Dear Mr Abberline,

I am a lucky man

Next time I will do all that ~~I can~~

~~say, can, feed, damn~~

~~out and throat~~

with a little cut here,

and a little cut there

I will go laughing

away to my lair

Dear Mr Abberline,

I am a lucky man

Next time I will do

all that I can.

With a little cut here

and a little cut there

I will go laughing

away to my lair.

Damn it damn it damn it the bastard almost caught me, curse him to hell, I will cut him up next time, so help me. a few minutes and I would have done, bastard. I will seek him out, I'll teach him a lesson. No one will stop me. Curse his black soul. I came myself for striking too soon, I should have waited until it was twenty points so help me I am going to be all next time did eat it will leave nothing, not even the head. I will boil it and eat it with freshly picked carrots, I shall think about Aberline as I am doing so, that will give me a laugh he ha ha the whore will suffer tonight for the deed she has done.

The bitch has written all,
tonight she will fall.

So help me God I will cut the bitch up and serve her up to the children. How dare the whore write to Michael. The damn bitch had no right to inform him of my medicine. If I have my funny little way the whore will be served up this very night. I stood my ground and informed Michael it was a damn lie.

The bitch visits the city of whores soon, I have decided I will wait until the time is ripe then I will strike with all my might. I shall buy the whore something for her visit. Will gives the bitch the impression. I consider it her duty to visit her aunt. She can nurse the sick bitch and see her whoring master ha ha.

Ha, what a joke, let the bitch believe I have no knowledge of her whoring affairs. When she returns the whore will pay. I relish the thoughts of striking the bitch once more. Am I not a clever fellow. I pride myself no one knows how clever I am. I do believe if George was to read this, he would say - I am the cleverest man alive. I yearn to tell him how clever I have been, but I shall not, my campaign is far from over yet Sir Jim will give nothing away, nothing. How can they stop me now this Sir Jim may live for ever. I feel strong, very strong, strong enough to strike in this damn old city, believe I well!

they not, nobody does suspect the gentle
man born. will see how I will feel on my
journey ahome, if the whim takes me then
so be it. Will have to be careful not to
get too much of the red stuff on me.
Perhaps I will just cut the ones, fool the fools,
O what a joke, more chickens running around with
their heads cut off, ha ha, I feel clever.

Sir Jimmy

live

forever

he he he he ha

This clever Sir Jim,
he loves his whims,
tonight he will call
and take away all. ha ha ha ha

Am I not a clever fellow, the bitch gave me the greatest pleasure of all. I do not the whore me her whore master in front of all. True the race was the finest I have seen, but to the thrill of seeing the whore winth the bitch thrilled me none so than knowing his Royal-Highness was but a few feet away from yours truly — ho ho what a laugh, if the greedy bastard would have known he was less than a few feet away from the name all England was talking about he would have died there and then. Regret I could not tell the foolish fool. To hell with sovereignty, to hell with all whores, to hell with the bitch who rules.

Victoria the bitch
Queen fool Sir Jack knows all
The queen she knows all

Victoria, Victoria
The queen of them all
When it comes to Sir Jack
She knows nothing at all

I

She knows one day

who knows,
perhaps one day,
I will give her a call

II

~~Shining knife~~
~~my life~~
~~honour my knife~~
Show her my knife
and she will honour me for life

III

~~Come take from she will say~~
Arise Sir Jock she will say,
and now you can go,
as you may ha ha ha

i ha ha ha ha

Victories, Victories –
the queen of them all.
When it comes to Sir Jack
she knows nothing at all.

Who knows,
Perhaps one day;
I will give her a call

Show her my knife
and she will honour me for life.

Arise Sir Jack she will say
and now you can go
as you may

Jim, Jock Jack Jim ha ha ha

I was clever. George would be proud of me, told the bitch in my position I could not afford a scandal. I struck her several times an eye for an eye, he he too many interfering servants, damn the letches. Hopper will soon feel the edge of my shinny knife, damn the meddling buffoon, damn all. Once more the bitch is in debt. My God I will cut her. Oh how I will cut her. I will visit the city of whores. I will pay her dues and I shall take mine, by God I will. I will rip rip rip. May seek the bastard out who stopped my funny little games and rip him to. I said he would pay I will make sure he damn will. I feel a numbness in my body, the colours will pay for that? I wonder if Edwin is well? I long for him to return. I have decided that next time I will take the whores eyes out and send them to that fool Abberline.

Bastard

Bastard

take the eyes,
take the hands,
leave them all for dear

It does not amuse me. Curse that bastard Abberline, curse him to hell I will not dangle from any rope of his. I have thought often about the whore and her whoring mother the thoughts still thrill me Perhaps one day the bitch will allow me to participate. Why not? All love taken her. Have I no right to the whore. I wish to do so

The bitch
Abberbitch
[signature]

Fuller believes there is very little the matter with me. Strange, the thoughts he placed into my mind. I could not strike, I believe I am mad, completely mad. I try to fight my thoughts. I walk the streets until dawn. I could not find it in my heart to strike, visions of my dear Bunny overwhelm me. I still love her, but how I hate her. She has destroyed all and yet my heart aches for her, oh how it aches. I do not know which pain is the worse, my body or my mind.

My God I am tired, I do not know if I can go on. Bunny and the children are all that matter. No regrets, no regrets. I shall not allow such thoughts to enter my head. Tonight I will take my shinning knife and be rid of it. Throw it deep within the river I shall return to Battlecrease with the knowledge that I can no longer continue my campaign. 'Tis love that spurned me so, 'tis love that shall put an end to it.

I am afraid to look back on all I have written. Perhaps it would be wiser to destroy this, but in my heart I cannot bring myself to do so. I have tried once before, but like the coward I am, I could not. Perhaps in my tormented mind I wish for someone to read this and understand that the man I have become was not the man I was here.

My dear brother Edwin has returned. I wish I could tell him all. No more funny little rhymes. Tonight I write of love.

tis love that spurned me so,

tis love that does destroy

tis love that I yearn for

tis love that she spurned

tis love that will finish me

tis love that I regret.

May God help me. I pray each night he will take me, the disappointment when I wake is difficult to describe I no longer take the dreaded stuff for fear I will harm my dear Bunnys, worse still the children.

I do not have the courage to take my life. I pray each night I will find the strength to do so, but the courage alludes me. I pray constantly all will forgive. I deeply regret striking her, I have found it in my heart to forgive her for her lies.

I believe I will tell her all, ask her to forgive me as I have forgiven her. I pray to God she will understand what she has done to me. Tonight I will pray for the women I have slaughtered. May God forgive me for the deeds I committed on Kelly, no heart no heart

The pair is unbearable. My dear Bunny knows all. I do not know if she has the strength to kill me, I pray to God she finds it. It would be simple, she knows of my medicine, and for an extra dose or two it would be all over. No one will know. I have seen to that. George knows of my habit and I trust soon it will come to the attention of Michael. In truth I believe he is aware of the fact. Michael will know how to act, he is the most sensible amongst us all. I do not believe I will see this June, my favourite of all months. Have begged Bunny to act soon, I curse myself for the coward I am. I have redrawn the balance of my previous will. Bunny and the children are well cared for and I trust Michael and Thomas will carry out my wishes.

Soon, I trust I shall be laid beside my dear mother and father. I shall seek their forgiveness when we are reunited. God I pray will allow me at least that privilege, although I know only too well I do not deserve it. My thoughts will remain in tact, for a reminder to all how love does destroy — I place this now in a place were it shall be found. I pray whoever should read this will find it in their heart to forgive me. Remind all, whoever you may be, that I was once a gentle man. May the good lord have mercy on my soul, and forgive me for all I have done.

I give my name that all know of me, so history do tell, what love can do to a gentle man born.
                    Yours truly
                    Jack the Ripper
                    Dated this third day of May 1889.

303

Transcript of the Diary of Jack the Ripper

what they have in store for them they would stop this instant. But do I desire that? 241
my answer is no. They will suffer just as I. I will see to that. Received a letter from
Michael perhaps I will visit him. Will have to come to some sort of decision regards
the children. I long for peace of mind but I sincerely believe that that will not come
until I have sought my revenge on the whore and the whore master.

Foolish bitch, I know for certain she has arranged a rondaveau with him in
Whitechapel. So be it, my mind is firmly made. I took refreshment at the Poste
House it was there I finally decided London it shall be. And why not, is it not an
ideal location? Indeed do I not frequently visit the Capital and indeed do I not have
legitimate reason for doing so. All who sell their dirty wares shall pay, of that I have
no doubt. But shall I pay? I think not I am too clever for that.

As usual my hands are cold, my heart I do believe is colder still. My dearest Gladys
is unwell yet again, she worries me so. I am convinced a dark shadow lays over the
house, it is evil. I am becoming increasingly weary of people who constantly
enquire regards the state of my health. True my head and arms pain me at times,
but I am not duly worried, although I am quite certain Hopper believes to the 242
contrary, I have him down as a bumbling buffoon. Thomas has requested that we
meet as soon as possible. Business is flourishing so I have no inclination as regards
the matter he describes as most urgent. Never the less I shall endeavour to meet his
request.

Time is passing much too slowly, I still have to work up the courage to begin my
campaign. I have thought long and hard over the matter and still I cannot come to
a decision to when I should begin. Opportunity is there, of that fact I am certain.
The bitch has no inclination.

The thought of him taking her is beginning to thrill me, perhaps I will allow her to
continue, some of my thoughts are indeed beginning to give me pleasure. Yes I will
visit Michael for a few weeks, and allow her to take all she can from the whoring
master. Tonight I shall see mine. I may return to Battlecrease and take the
unfaithfull bitch. Two in a night, indeed pleasure. My medicine is doing me good,
in fact, I am sure I can take more than any other person alive. My mind is clear I
will put whore through pain tonight.

I am beginning to believe it is unwise to continue writing, If I am to down a whore 243
then nothing shall lead the persuers back to me, and yet there are times when I feel
an overwhelming compulsion to place my thoughts to paper. It is dangerous, that I
know. If Smith should find this then I am done before my campaign begins.
However, the pleasure of writing off all that lays ahead of me, and indeed the
pleasure of thoughts of deeds that lay ahead of me, thrills me so. And oh what
deeds I shall comit. For how could one suspect that I could be capable of such
things, for am I not, as all believe, a mild man, who it has been said would never
hurt a fly. Indeed only the other day did not Edwin say of me I was the most gentlest
of men he had encountered. A compliment from my dear brother which I found
exceedingly flattering.

Have decided my patience is wearing thin. The bitch has made a fool of me. 244

Tomorrow I travel to Manchester. Will take some of my medicine and think hard on the matter. I believe I could do so, though I shake with fear of capture. A fear I will have to overcome. I believe I have the strength. I will force myself not to think of the children. The whore, that is all that shall be in my mind. My head aches.

My dear God my mind is in a fog. The whore is now with her maker and he is welcome to her. There was no pleasure as I squeezed, I felt nothing. Do not know if I have the courage to go back to my original idea. Manchester was cold and damp very much like this hell hole. Next time I will throw acid over them. The thought of them ridling and screaming while the acid burns deep thrills me. ha, what a joke it would be if I could gorge an eye out and leave it by the whores body for all to see, to see, <u>ha, ha.</u>

I believe I have caught a chill. I cannot stop shaking, my body aches. There are times when I pray to God that the pain and torment will stop. Summer is near the warm weather will do me good. I long for peace but my work is only beginning. I will have a long wait for peace. All whores must suffer first and my God how I will make them suffer as she has made me. Edwin asked regards Thomas and business, I informed him that Thomas was well and business was flourishing, both true. I have it in my mind that I should write to Michael, perhaps not, my hands are far too cold, another day. I will take the bitch tonight. I need to take my mind off the night's events. The children are well.

246 Strolled by the drive, encountered Mrs Hamersmith, she enquired of Bobo and Gladys and much to my astonishment about my health. What has that whore said? Mrs Hammersmith is a bitch. The fresh air and stroll did me good. For a while I succeeded in forgetting the bitch and her whoring master. Felt completely refreshed when I returned to my office. I will visit Michael this coming June. June is such a pleasant month, the flowers are in full bud the air is sweeter and life is almost certainly much rosier I look forward to its coming with pleasure. A great deal of pleasure. I feel compelled to write to Michael if not obliged. My mind is clear, my hands are not cold.

247 I am vexed. I am trying to quell my anger. The whore has suggested she accompany me on my trip to Michael. I need time to put my mind in order. Under no circumstances can I let the bitch accompany me, all my hard work and plans will be destroyed if she were to do so. The pain was bad today. I believe the bitch has found one of my bottles, it had been moved. I am tired and need sleep the pain kept me awake for most of last night. Will return early avoid the bitch altogether.

Frequented my club. George stated that he had never seen me in better health. I believe the bitch has changed her mind. My thoughts are becoming increasingly more daring, I have imagined doing all manner of things. Could I eat part of one? Perhaps it would taste of fresh fried bacon <u>ha ha.</u> My dear God it thrills me so.

Michael is expecting me towards the end of June, henceforth from July mycampaign will gather momentum. I will take each and everyone before I return them to their maker, damaged of course, severely damaged.

248   I try to repel all thoughts of the children from my mind. I feel strong, stronger than I have ever felt. My thoughts keep returning to Manchester, next time it will

thrill me. I know in my heart it will. I cannot understand why William will not accept my offer to dine. He is not unlike me, he hates the bitch. I believe if chance prevails I will burn St. James's to the ground. tomorrow I will make a substantial wager. I feel lucky.

If I could have killed the bastard Lowry with my bare hands there and then I would have done so. How dare he question me on any matter, it is I that should question him. Damn him damn him damn him should I replace the missing items? No that would be too much of a risk. Should I destroy this? My God I will kill him. Give him no reason to order him poste haste to drop the matter, that I believe is the only course of action I can take. I will force myself to think of something more pleasant. The whore will suffer more than she has ever done so tonight, that thought revitalizes me. June is drawing to a close I shake with anticipation.

I have taken too much my thoughts are not where they should be. I recall little of the events of yesterday. Thank God I stopped myself in time. I will show my wrath towards the bastard in such a manner that he will wish he had never brought up the subject. No one, not even God himself will away the pleasure of writing my thoughts. I will take the first whore I encounter and show her what hell is really like. I think I will ram a cane into the whoring bitches mound and leave it there for them to see how much she could take. My head aches, God has no right to do this to me the devil take him.

How I succeeded in controlling myself I do not know. I have not allowed for the red stuff, gallons of it in my estimation. Some of it is bound to spill onto me. I cannot allow my clothes to be blood drenched, this I could not explain to anyone least of all Michael. Why did I not think of this before? I curse myself. The struggle to stop myself was overwhelming, and if I had not asked Michael to lock me in my bedroom for fear of sleepwalking, to which I had said I had been prone to do recently, was that not clever? I would have done my dirty deeds that very night.

I have taken a small room in Middlesex Street, that in itself is a joke. I have paid well and I believe no questions will be asked. It is indeed an ideal location. I have walked the streets and have become more than familiar with them. I said Whitechapel it will be and Whitechapel it shall. The bitch and her whoring master will rue the day I first saw them together. I said I am clever, very clever. Whitechapel Liverpool, Whitechapel London, ha ha. No one could possibly place it together. And indeed for there is no reason for anyone to do so.

The next time I travel to London I shall begin. I have no doubts, my confidence is most high. I am thrilled writing this, life is sweet, and my disappointment has vanished. Next time for sure. I have no doubts, not any longer, no doubts. No one will ever suspect. Tomorrow I will purchase the finest knife money can buy, nothing shall be too good for my whores, I will treat them to the finest, the very finest, they deserve that at least from I.

I have shown all that I mean business, the pleasure was far better than I imagined. The whore was only too willing to do her business. I recall all and it thrills me. There was no scream when I cut. I was more than vexed when the head would not come off. I believe I will need more strength next time. I struck deep into her. I regret I never had the cane, it would have been a delight to have rammed it hard into her. The bitch opened like a ripe peach. I have decided next time I will rip all out. My medicine will give me strength and the thought of the whore and her whoring master will spur me on no end.

The wait to read about my triumph seemed long, although it was not. I am not disappointed, they have all written well. The next time they will have a great deal more to write, of that fact I have no doubt ha ha. I will remain calm and show no interest in my deed, if anyone should mention it so, but I will laugh inside, oh how I will laugh.

252

I will not allow too much time to pass before my next. Indeed I need to repeat my pleasure as soon as possible. The whoring Master can have her with pleasure and I shall have my pleasure with my thoughts and deeds. I will be clever. I will not call on Michael on my next visit. My brothers would be horrified if they knew, particularly Edwin after all did he not say I was one of the most gentlest of men he had ever encountered. I hope he is enjoying the fruits of America. Unlike I, for do I not have a sour fruit.

253

I could not resist mentioning my deed to George. I was clever and brought up the subject by way of how fortunate we were not having murders of that kind in this city. He agreed with me completely. Indeed he went on to say, that he believed we had the finest police force in the land, and although we have our fair share of troubles the women folk can walk the streets in safety. And indeed they can for I will not play my funny little games on my own doorstep ha ha.

The gentle man with gentle thoughts will strike again soon. I have never felt better, in fact, I am taking more than ever and I can feel the strength building up within me. The head will come off next time, also the whores hands. Shall I leave them in various places around Whitechapel? Hunt the head and hands instead of the thimble ha ha. Maybe I will take some part away with me to see if it does taste of like fresh fried bacon. The whore seen her master today it did not bother me. I imagined I was with them, the very thought thrills me. I wonder if the whore has ever had such thoughts? I believe she has, has she not cried out when I demand she takes another. The bitch. She will suffer but not as yet. Tomorrow I travel to

254

London. I have decided I cannot wait any longer. I look forward to tomorrow nights work, it will do me good, a great deal of good.

One dirty whore was looking for some gain
Another dirty whore was looking for the same.

255

Am I not clever? I thought of my funny little rhyme on my travel to the City of Whores. I was vexed with myself when I realised I had forgotten the chalk. So vexed in fact that I returned to the bitch and cut out more. I took some of it away with me. It is in front of me. I intend to fry it and eat it later ha ha. The very thought works up my appetite. I cannot stop the thrill of writing. I ripped open my God I will have to stop thinking of the children they distract me so I ripped open

---

It has taken me three days to recover. I will not feel guilty it is the whoring bitch to
blame not I. I ate all off it, it did not taste like fresh fried bacon but I enjoyed it
never the less. She was so sweet and pleasurable. I have left the stupid fools a clue
which I am sure they will not solve. Once again I have been clever, very clever.

> ~~A ring or two will leave this clue~~
> ~~One pill thats true~~
> ~~M will catch Sir Jim with no pills~~
> ~~left two~~
>
> two farthings,
> two pills
> the whores M
> rings
>
> Think

It shall come, if Michael can succeed in rhyming verse then I can do better, a great
deal better he shall not outdo me. Think you fool, think. I curse Michael for being
so clever, I shall outdo him, I will see to that. A funny little rhyme <u>shall</u> come
forth. Patience is needed patience. The night is long, time is on my hands.

The pills are the answer
end with pills. Indeed do I always not oh what a joke.
Begin with the rings,
one ring, two rings
bitch, it took me a while before I could wrench them off. Should have stuffed them
down the whores throat. I wish to God I could have taken the head. Hated her for
wearing them, reminds me too much of the whore. Next time I will select a whore
who has none. The bitch was not worth the farthings. Return, return, essential to
return. Prove you are no fool.

> One ring, two rings,
> A farthing one and two
> ~~Sir Jim will do true~~
> ~~Letter M its true~~
> Along with M ha ha
> Will catch clever Jim,
> Its true
> ~~Left two~~
> No pill, left but two
>
> One ring, two rings,
> a farthing, one and two,
> Along with M ha ha
> Will catch clever Jim
> its true.
> No pill, left but two

Am I not indeed a clever fellow? It makes me laugh they will never understand why
I did so. Next time I will remember the chalk and write my funny little rhyme. The
eyes will come out of the next. I will stuff them in the whores mouth. That will
certainly give me pleasure, it does so as I write. Tonight I will see mine, she will be

pleased as I will be gentle with her as indeed I always am.

I am still thinking of burning St. James's to the ground. I may do so on my next visit. That will give the fools something more to think on. I am beginning to think less of the children, part of me hates me for doing so. One day God will answer to me, so help me. Michael would be proud of my funny little rhyme for he knows only too well the art of verse. Have I not proven I can write better than he. Feel like Celebrating, the night has been long and I shall award myself with the pleasures of the flesh, but I shall not be cutting ha ha. I will save that thrill for another day.

---

260   The whore is in debt. Very well I shall honour the bitches notes but the whores are going to pay more than ever. I have read all of my deeds they have done me proud, I had to laugh, they have me down as left handed, a Doctor, a slaughterman and a Jew. Very well, if they are to insist that I am a Jew then a Jew I shall be. Why not let the Jews suffer? I have never taken to them, far too many of them on the Exchange for my liking. I could not stop laughing when I read Punch there for all to see was the first three letters of my surname. They are blind as they say.

> 'Turn round three times, And catch whom you
> MAY'
> ha ha ha ha ha ha

I cannot stop laughing it amuses me so shall I write them a clue?

> May comes and goes,
> ~~this May pleases with a knife in his hand~~
> In the dark of the night
> ~~He does please~~
> When he comes and goes
261   With a ring on my finger
> and a knife in my hand
> ~~This May comes and goes~~

> May comes and goes
> In the dark of the night
> ~~he does please the whores he kisses~~
> ~~and gives them a fright~~
> he kisses the whores
> then gives them a fright

> May comes and goes
> in the dark of the night
> he kisses the whores
> then gives them a fright
> With a ring on my finger
> and a knife in my hand
> This May spreads Mayhem
> ~~all through the land~~
> throughout this fair land.

262   ~~The Jews and slaughtermen~~

~~The Jews and Doctors~~
The Doctors and jews
~~my~~
will get all the blame – blame – tame
same – game
his dirty game
May playing
~~The Doctors~~
The Jews and the Doctors
Will get all the blame
but its only May
playing his dirty game

~~He will not shed a tear~~
He will kill all the whores
and not shed a tear
~~He will give them a clue~~
I will give them a clue
but nothing too clear
I will kill all the whores
and not shed a tear.
May comes and goes
in the dark of the night
He kisses the whores
and gives them a fright

The Jews and the Doctors
will get all the blame
but its only May playing
his dirty game

I will give them a clue
but nothing too clear
I will kill all the whores
and not shed a tear

With a ring on my finger
and a knife in my hand
This May spreads Mayhem
throughout this fair land.

They remind me of chickens with their heads cut off running fools with no heads, <u>ha ha.</u> It is nice to laugh at bastards and fools and indeed they are fools. I need much more pleasure than I have had. Strange my hands feel colder than they have ever done so.

I am fighting a battle within me. My disire for revenge is overwhelming. The whore has destroyed my life. I try whenever possible to keep all sense of respectability. I worry so over Bobo and Gladys, no others matter. Tonight I will take more than ever. I miss the thrill of cutting them up. I do believe I have lost my mind. All the bitches will pay for the pain. Before I am finished all of England will know the

---

name I have given myself. It is indeed a name to remember. It shall be, before long, on every persons lips within the land. Perhaps her gracious Majesty will become acquainted with it. I wonder if she will honour me with a knighthood <u>ha ha.</u>

Abberline says, he was never amazed,
I did my work with such honour,
For his decree
he had to agree,
I deserve at least an honour
so all for a whim,

265

I can now rise Sir Jim – I cannot think of another word to accompany Jim. I like my words to rhyme damn it. It is late, mine is waiting, I will enjoy this evening. I will be gentle and not give anything away.

I miss Edwin. I have received but one letter from him since his arrival in the whores country. The bitch is vexing me more as each day passes. If I could I would have it over and done with. I visited my mother and fathers grave. I long to be reunited with them. I believe they know the torture the whore is putting me through. I enjoy the thrill of thinking of all I have done. But there has been, but once, regret for my deeds. I dispelled my remorse instantly. The whore still believes I have no knowledge of her whoring master. I have considered killing him, but if I was to do so I would surely be caught. I have no desire for that, curse him and the whore their time will come.

266

To my astonishment I cannot believe I have not been caught. My heart felt as if it had left my body. Within my fright I imagined my heart bounding along the street with I in desperation following it. I would have dearly loved to have cut the head of the damned horse off and stuff it as far as it would go down the whores throat. I had no time to rip the bitch wide, I curse my bad luck. I believe the thrill of being caught thrilled me more than cutting the whore herself. As I write I find it impossible to believe he did not see me, in my estimation I was less than a few feet from him. The fool panicked, it is what saved me. My satisfaction was far from complete, damn the bastard, I cursed him and cursed him, but I was clever, they could not out do me. <u>No one</u> ever will. Within the quarter of the hour I found another dirty bitch willing to sell her wares. The whore like all the rest was only too willing. The thrill she gave me was unlike the others, I cut deep deep deep. Her nose annoyed me so I cut it off, had a go at her eyes, left my mark, could not get the bitches head off. I believe now it is impossible to do so. The whore never screamed. I took all I could away with me. I am saving it for a rainy day <u>ha ha.</u>

267

Perhaps I will send Abberline and Warren a sample or two, it goes down well with an after dinner port. I wonder how long it will keep? Perhaps next time I will keep some of the red stuff and send it courtesy of yours truly. I wonder if they enjoyed my funny Jewish joke? Curse my bad luck had no time to write a funny little rhyme. Before my next will send Central another to remember me by. My God life is sweet. Will give them something to know it is me.

Red – head
horse,
cryed
smelt breath

~~A rose matched the red~~
~~I did cut the head~~

~~damn it I cried, hence forth I did hide,~~
~~The horse went and shied~~

With a rose to match the red
I tried to cut off the head
Damn it I cried,
The horse went and shied
But I could still smell her sweet scented breath

I

Sir Jim,
tin match box empty
~~cigarette case~~
~~make haste~~
~~my shiny knife~~
~~the whores knife~~
first whore no good

One whore no good,
decided Sir Jim strike another.
I showed no fright and indeed no light,
damn it, the tin box was empty

II

tea and sugar
~~away, pay, did say~~
me, plea, be
~~tea and sugar paid my fee~~
Sweet sugar and tea, could have paid my small
fee ha ha
~~then I did flee~~
Showed my glee
A kidney for supper

Sweet sugar and tea,
could have paid my small fee.
But instead I did flee
and by way showed my glee
By eating cold kidney for supper

III

bastard
Abberline
bonnett
hides all
clue
clever
will tell you more

~~Mr Abberline is a funny little man~~

Oh Mr Abberline, he is a clever little man

---

he keeps back all that he can.
~~But I know better~~
For do I know better, indeed I do
did I not leave him a very good clue
Nothing is mentioned, of this I know sure
ask clever Abberline, ~~he does know more~~

Oh Mr Abberline, he is a clever little man
he keeps back all that he can.
For do I not know better, Indeed I do
did I not leave him a very good clue.
Nothing is mentioned, of this I am sure,
ask clever Abberline, could tell you more

IV

Sir Jim trip over
fear
have it near
redeem it near
case
poste haste

<u>271</u>   He believes I will trip over
but I have no fear
~~I cannot redeem it here~~
For I could not possibly redeem it here
of this certain fact, I could send him poste haste
if he requests that be the case.

Am I not a clever fellow

That should give the fools a laugh, it has done so for me, wonder if they have enjoyed the name I have given? I said it would be on the lips of all, and indeed it is. Believe I will send another. Include my funny little rhyme. That will convince them that it is the truth I tell. Tonight I will celebrate by wining and dining George. I am in a good mood, believe I will allow the whore the pleasure of her whore master, will remark an evening in the city will do her good, will suggest a concert. I have no doubt the carriage will take the bitch straight to him. ~~I will go~~ — I will go to sleep thinking about all they are doing. I cannot wait for the thrill.

<u>272</u>   With a rose to match the red
I tried to cut off the head.
Damn it I cried,
the horse went and shied
hence forth I did hide,
but I could still smell
her sweet scented breath

One whore no good, decided Sir Jim strike another.
I showed no fright, and indeed no light.
Damn it, the tin box was empty

Sweet sugar and tea
could have paid my small fee
But instead I did flee and by way showed my glee
by eating cold kidney for supper

Oh, Mr Abberline he is a clever little man,
he keeps back all that he can.
For do I not know better, Indeed I do,
did I not leave him a very good clue
Nothing is mentioned of this I know sure,
ask clever Abberline, could tell you more

He believes I will trip over,   273
but I have no fear.
For I could not possibly
redeem it here.
Of this certain fact I could send them poste haste
If he requested that be the case

It has been far too long since my last, I have been unwell. The whole of my body
has pained. Hopper did not believe me. One day I will take revenge on him. The
whore has informed the bumbling buffoon. I am in the habit of taking strong
medicine. I was furious when the bitch told me. So furious I hit her ha. The whore
begged me not to do so again. It was a pleasure, a great deal of pleasure. If it was not
for my work, I would have cut the bitch up there and then. But I am clever.
Although the gentle man has turned, I did not show my hand true. I apologised, a
one off instance, I said, which I regretted and I assured the whore it would never
happen again. The stupid bitch believed me.

I have received several letters from Michael. In all he enquires about my health and   274
asked in one if my sleepwalking has resumed. Poor Michael he is so easily fooled. I
have informed him it has not. My hands still remain cold. I shall be dining tonight.
I hope kidneys are on the menu, ha ha. Will put me in the mood for another little
escapade. Will visit the city of whores soon, very soon. I wonder if I could do three?

If it were not for Michael insisting that we take dinner I would have tried my hand
that very night. I cursed my brother as I have never cursed him before. I cursed my
own stupidity, had I not informed Michael that I no longer sleepwalked I was
forced to stop myself from indulging in my pleasure by taking the largest dose I have
ever done. The pain that night has burnt into my mind. I vaguly recall putting a
handkerchief in my mouth to stop my cries. I believe I vomited several times. The
pain was intolerable, as I think I shudder. No more.

I am convinced God placed me here to kill all whores, for he must have done so,
am I still not here. Nothing will stop me now. The more I take the stronger I
become.

Michael was under the impression that once I had finished my business I was to   275
return to Liverpool that very day. And indeed I did one day later ha ha. I fear not,
for the fact will not come to his attention as he addresses all letters to me.

I have read about my latest, my God the thoughts, the very best. I left nothing of

---

the bitch, nothing. I placed it all over the room, time was on my hands, like the other whore I cut off the bitches nose, all of it this time. I left nothing of her face to remember her by. She reminded me of the whore. So young unlike I. I thought it a joke when I cut her breasts off, kissed them for a while. The taste of blood was sweet, the pleasure was overwhelming, will have to do it again, it thrilled me so. Left them on the table with some of the other stuff. Thought they belonged there. They wanted a slaughterman so I stripped what I could, laughed while I was doing so. Like the other bitches she riped like a ripe peach. One of these days I will take the head away with me. I will boil it and serve it up for my supper. The key and burnt clothes puzzle them <u>ha ha</u>..

<u>276</u>

key	rip
flee	initial
hat	
handkerchief	whore master
whim	look to the whore
Mother	light
father	fire

~~With the key I did flee~~
I had the key,
and with it I did flee
~~the clothes I burnt~~
~~along with the hat~~
The hat I did burn
for light I did yearn.
~~For the sake of the whoring mother~~
And I thought of the whoring mother

I had the key,
And with it I did flee
The hat I did burn
for light I did yearn
And I thought of the
whoring mother

I
<u>277</u>
A handkerchief red,
led to the bed
and I thought of the whoring mother

II
~~For Sir Jim with his whim~~
A whores whim,
Caused Sir Jim
to cut deeper, deeper and deeper.
~~away with it I did go~~
~~back to the whoring mother~~
All did go
As I did so
back to the whoring mother

A whores whim,

caused Sir Jim
to cut deeper deeper and deeper.
All did go,
As I did so
back to the whoring mother.

III

~~Her initial there~~ 278
An initial here and a initial there
would tell of the whoring mother

I had a key,
and with it I did flee.
The hat I did burn,
for light I did yearn.
And I thought of the whoring mother
A handkerchief red,
led to the bed
And I thought of the whoring mother.

A whores whim
caused Sir Jim,
to cut deeper, deeper and deeper
All did go,
As I did so,
back to the whoring mother.
An initial here and an initial there 279
will tell of the whoring mother.

I left it there for the fools but they will never find it. I was too clever. Left it in front for all eyes to see. Shall I write and tell them? That amuses me. I wonder if next time I can carve my funny little rhyme on the whores flesh? I believe I will give it a try. It amuses me if nothing else. Life is sweet, very sweet. Regret I did not take any of it away with me it is supper time, I could do with a kidney or two ha ha.

I cannot live without my medicine. I am afraid to go to sleep for fear of my nightmares reoccuring. I see thousands of people chasing me, with Abberline in front dangling a rope. I will not be topped of that fact I am certain. It has been far too long since my last, I still desire revenge on the whore and the whore master but less than the desire to repeat my last performance. The thoughts still thrill me so. I 280 am tired and I fear the city of whores has become too dangerous for I to return. Christmas is approaching and Thomas has invited me to visit him. I know him well. I have decided to accept his offer, although I know the motive behind it will strictly be business. Thomas thinks of nothing else except money unlike me, ha ha.

My first was in Manchester so why not my next? If I was to do the same as the last, that would throw the fools into a panick, especially that fool Abberline. The children constantly ask what I shall be buying them for Christmas they shy away when I tell them a shiny knife not unlike Jack the Rippers in order that I cut their tongues for peace and quiet. I do believe I am completely mad. I have never harmed the children in the years since they have been born. But now I take great

---

delight in scaring them so. May God forgive me. I have lost my battle and shall go on until I am caught. Perhaps I should top myself and save the hangman a job. At this moment I have no feeling in my body, none at all. I keep assuring myself I have done no wrong. It is the whore who has done so, not I. Will peace of mind ever come? I have visited Hopper too often this month. I will have to stop, for I fear he may begin to suspect. I talk to him like no other.

~~Sir Jim shall,~~
Am I insane?
Cane, gain
~~Sir Jim with his fancy cane~~
~~Will soon strike again~~

~~One whore in heaven,~~
~~two whores side by side,~~
~~three whores all have died~~
~~four~~

~~Sir Jim he cuts them first~~
damn it

~~Abberline says he is now amazed,~~
~~Sir Jim has not struck another~~
~~He waits patiently~~
~~to see hastily~~

~~Christmas save the whores mole bonnett~~
~~damn the bitches damn Michael~~
~~Give Sir Jim his due~~
~~He detests all the Jews~~
~~For he has no favourite men~~
~~As he runs away to his den.~~

~~He likes to write with his pen~~

~~Give Sir Jim his dues~~
~~He detests all the Jews~~
~~and indeed was it not in t——e~~

~~I kissed them,~~
~~I kissed them~~
~~They tasted so sweet~~
~~I thought of leaving them by the whores feet~~
~~but the table it was bear~~
~~so I went and left them there~~

damn it damn it damn it

so help me God my next will be far the worst, my head aches, but I will go on damn Michael for being so clever the art of verse is far from simple. I curse him so. Abberline Abberline, I shall destroy that fool yet, So help me God. Banish him from my thoughts, he will not catch Sir Jim yet

---

Abberline Abberline Abberline Abberline
The devil take the bastard

I am cold curse the bastard Lowry for making me rip. I keep seeing blood pouring from the bitches. The nightmares are hideous. I cannot stop myself from wanting to eat more. God help me, damn you. No no-one will stop me. God be damned. Think think think write tell all prove to them you are who you say you are make them believe it is the truth I tell. Damn him for creating them, damn him damn him damn him. I want to boil boil boil. See if there eyes pop. I need more thrills, cannot live without my thrills. I will go on, I will go on, nothing will stop me nothing. Cut Sir Jim cut. Cut deep deep deep.

> ~~Sir Jim will cut them all~~
> Oh costly intercourse
> of death

Banish the thoughts banish them banish them ha ha ha,
look towards the sensible brother
Chickens running round with their heads cut off

ha ha ha ha ha ha ha ha ha
Am I not a clever fellow
out foxed them all, they will never know

> ~~Sir Jim will cut them all~~
> ~~Sir Jim he does so walk tall~~
>
> ~~Sir Jim makes his call~~
> ~~he cuts them all,~~
> ~~with his knife in his bag~~

will have to take up lodgings on my return. Middlesex Street that was a joke. The fools, several times they could have caught me if they had looked good and proper. My God am I not clever? Indeed I am. My head spins will somehow have to find the strength for my journey home. The devil take this city, it is too cold for me. Tomorrow I will make Lowry suffer. The thought will thrill me on my journey home.

I cannot bring myself to look back, all I have written scares me so. George visited me today. I believe he knows what I am going through, although he says nothing. I can see it in his eyes. Poor George, he is such a good friend. Michael is well, he writes a merry tune. In my heart I cannot blame him for doing so. I regret I shall not see him this Christmas.

Encountered an old friend on the Exchange floor. I felt regret for was he not Jewish. I had forgotten how many Jewish friends I have. My revenge is on whores not Jews. I do believe I am truly sorry for the scare I have thrown amongst them. I believe that is the reason I am unable to write my funny little rhymes. I thank God I have had the courage to stop sending them. I am convinced they will be my undoing.

I am tired, very tired. I yearn for peace, but I know in my heart I will go on. I will be in Manchester within a few days. I believe I will feel a great deal better when I have repeated on my last performance. I wonder if I can improve on my fiendish deeds. Will wait and see, no doubt I will think of something. The day is drawing to a close, Lowry was in fine spirits. I am pleased. I regret, as with my Jewish friends I have shown my wrath. This coming Christmas I will make amends.

---

287   The bitch, the whore is not satisfied with one whore master, she now has eyes on another. I could not cut like my last, visions of her flooded back as I struck. I tried to quosh all thoughts of love. I left her for dead, that I know. It did not amuse me. There was thrill. I have showered my fury on the bitch. I struck and struck. I do not know how I stopped. I have left her penniless, I have no regrets. The whore will suffer unlike she has ever suffered. May God have mercy on her for I shall not, so help me.

Thomas was in fine health. The children enjoyed Christmas. I did not. My mood is no longer black, although my head aches. I shall never become accustomed to the pain. I curse winter. I yearn for my favourite month, to see flowers in full bloom would please me so. Warmth is what I need, I shiver so. Curse this weather and the whoring bitch. My heart has been soft. All whores will feel the edge of Sir Jims shining knife. I regret I did not give myself that name, curse it, I prefer it much much more than the one I have given.

288   Sir Jim with his shining knife,
         cuts through the night,
         and by God,
         does he not show his might <u>ha ha</u>

It shall not be long before I strike again. I am taking more than ever. The bitch can take two, Sir Jim shall take four, a double double event <u>ha ha.</u> If I was in the city of whores I would do my fiendish deeds this very moment. By God I would.

I curse myself for the fool I have been, I shall have no more regrets, damn them all. Beware Mr Abberline I will return with a vengeance. Once more I will be the talk of England. What pleasure my thoughts do give me. I wonder if the whore will take the bastard? The bitch is welcome to him. I shall think about their deeds, what pleasure. Tonight I shall reward myself, I will visit mine, but I will not be gentle. I will show my whore what I am capable of. Sir Jim needs to wet his appetite, all 289   whore be damned. A friend has turned, so be it, Sir Jim will turn once more. When I have finished my fiendish deeds, the devil himself will praise me. But he will have a long wait before I shake hands with him. I have works to do a great deal of works <u>ha ha.</u> kidney for supper.

I am tired of keeping up this pretence of respectability. I am finding it increasingly difficult to do so. I believe I am a lucky fellow. Have I not found a new source for my medicine. I relish the thoughts that it will bring me. I enjoy thinking of the whores waiting for my nice shining knife. Tonight I write to Michael. Inform him I shall be visiting the city of whores soon, very soon. I cannot wait. The whore may take as many whore masters as she wishes. I no longer worry. I have my thoughts and pleasure of deeds to come, and oh what deeds I shall commit. Much, much finer than my last. Life is indeed sweet, very very sweet.

290   Dear Mr. Abberline

I am a lucky man
Next time I will do all that I can
~~ram, can, fan, damn~~
~~cut and thrust~~
with a little cut here,
and a little cut there
I will go laughing
away to my lair

Dear Mr. Abberline,
I am a lucky man
Next time I will do
all that I can.
With a little cut here
and a little cut there
I will go laughing
away to my lair

Damn it damn it damn it the bastard almost caught me, curse him to hell, I will cut
him up next time, so help me. A few minutes and I would have done, <u>bastard.</u> I will
seek him out, teach him a lesson. No one will stop me. Curse his black soul. I curse
myself for striking too soon, I should have waited until it was truly quiet so help me
I will take all next time and <u>eat it.</u> Will leave <u>nothing</u> not even the head. I will boil
it and eat it with freshly picked carrots. I shall think about Abberline as I am doing
so, that will give me a laugh <u>ha ha</u> the whore will suffer tonight for the deed she has
done.

291

     The bitch has written all,
     tonight she will fall.
So help me God I will cut the bitch up and serve her up to the children. How dare
the whore write to Michael. the damn bitch had no right to inform him of my
medicine. If I have my funny little way the whore will be served up this very night.
I stood my ground and informed Michael it was a damn lie.

292

The bitch visits the city of whores soon, I have decided I will wait until the time is
ripe then I will strike with all my might. I shall buy the whore something for her
visit. Will give the bitch the impression I consider it her duty to visit her aunt. She
can nurse the sick bitch and see her whoring master <u>ha ha.</u>

Ha, what a joke, let the bitch believe I have no knowledge of her whoring affairs.
When she returns the whore will pay. I relish the thoughts of striking the bitch
once more. Am I not a clever fellow. I pride myself no one knows how clever I am.
I do believe if George was to read this, he would say I am the cleverest man alive. I
yearn to tell him how clever I have been, but I shall not, my campaign is far from
over yet. Sir Jim will give nothing away, nothing. How can they stop me now this
Sir Jim may live for ever. I feel strong, very strong, strong enough to strike in this
damn cold city, believe I will. Why not, nobody does suspect the gentle man born.
Will see how I will feel on my journey home, if the whim takes me then so be it.
Will have to be careful not to get too much of the red stuff on me. Perhaps I will just
cut the once, fool the fools, oh what a joke, more chickens running around with
their heads cut off, <u>ha ha</u> I feel clever.

293

Sir Jimay
live
forever
ha ha ha ha ha

294 This clever Sir Jim,
he loves his whims
tonight he will call
and take away all. ha ha ha ha

---

295 Am I not a clever fellow, the bitch gave me the greatest pleasure of all. Did not the whore see her whore master in front of all, true the race was the fastest I have seen, but the thrill of seeing the whore with the bastard thrilled me more so than knowing his Royal Highness was but a few feet away from yours truly ha ha what a laugh, if the greedy bastard would have known he was less than a few feet away from the name all England was talking about he would have died there and then. Regret I could not tell the foolish fool. To hell with sovereignity, to hell with all whores, to hell with the bitch who rules.

~~Victoria the bitch~~
~~Queen fool Sir Jack knows all~~
~~The queen she knows all~~

Victoria, Victoria
The queen of them all
When it comes to Sir Jack
She knows nothing at all

I
~~She knows one day~~
296 who knows,
perhaps one day
I will give her a call

II
~~Shining knife~~
~~my life~~
~~honour my knife~~
Show her my knife
and she will honour me for life

III
~~Come Sir Jim she will say~~
Arise Sir Jack she will say,
and now you can go,
as you may ha ha ha
ha ha ha ha

297 Victoria, Victoria
the queen of them all
when it comes to Sir Jack
she knows nothing at all

---

who knows,
Perhaps one day,
I will give her a call

Show her my knife
and she will honour me for life

Arise Sir Jack she will say
and now you can go
as you <u>may</u>

Jim, Jack Jack Jim ha ha ha

I was clever. George would be proud of me, told the bitch in my position I could not 298
afford a scandal. I struck her several times an eye for an eye, <u>ha ha</u> too many
interfering servants, damn the bitches. Hopper will soon feel the edge of my
shining knife, damn the meddling bufoon, damn all. Once more the bitch is in
debt, my God I will cut her. Oh how I will cut her. I will visit the city of whores I
will pay her dues and I shall take mine, by God I will. I will rip rip rip May seek the
bastard out who stopped my funny little games and rip him to. I said he would pay. I
will make sure he damn will. I feel a numbness in my body, the whores will pay for
that. I wonder if Edwin is well? I long for him to return. I have decided that next
time I will take the whores eyes out and send them to that fool Abberline.

       bastard
              bastard

take the eyes, 299
take the head,
leave them all for dead

It does not amuse me. Curse that bastard Abberline, curse him to hell I will not
dangle from any rope of his. I have thought often about the whore and her whoring
master. The thoughts still thrill me. Perhaps one day the bitch will allow me to
participate. Why not? All have taken her. Have I no right to the whore. I wish to
do so.
      The bitch
            the bitch
                  the bitch

Fuller believes there is very little the matter with me. Strange, the thoughts he 300
placed into my mind. I could not strike, I believe I am mad, completely mad. I try
to fight my thoughts I walk the streets until dawn. I could not find it in my heart to
strike, visions of my dear Bunny overwhelm me. I still love her, but how I hate her.
She has destroyed all and yet my heart aches for her, oh how it aches. I do not know
which pain is the worse my body or my mind.

My God I am tired, I do not know if I can go on. Bunny and the children are all
that matter. No regrets, no regrets. I shall not allow such thoughts to enter my
head. Tonight I will take my shinning knife and be rid of it. Throw it deep within
the river. I shall return to Battlecrease with the knowledge that I can no longer
continue my campaign. 'Tis love that spurned me so, 'tis love that shall put an end
to it.

---

301   I am afraid to look back on all I have written. Perhaps it would be wiser to destroy this, but in my heart I cannot bring myself to do so. I have tried once before, but like the coward I am, I could not. Perhaps in my tormented mind I wish for someone to read this and understand that the man I have become was not the man I was born.

My dear brother Edwin has returned. I wish I could tell him all. No more funny little rhymes. Tonight I write of love.

> tis love that spurned me so,
> tis love that does destroy
> tis love that I yearn for
> tis love that she spurned
> tis love that will finish me
> tis love that I regret

May God help me. I pray each night he will take me, the disappointment when I awake is difficult to describe I no longer take the dreaded stuff for fear I will harm my dear Bunny, worse still the children.

302   I do not have the courage to take my life. I pray each night I will find the strength to do so, but the courage alludes me. I pray constantly all will forgive. I deeply regret striking her, I have found it in my heart to forgive her for her lovers.

I believe I will tell her all, ask her to forgive me as I have forgiven her. I pray to God she will understand what she has done to me. Tonight I will pray for the women I have slaughtered. May God forgive me for the deeds I commited on Kelly, no heart no heart.

---

303   The pain is unbearable. My dear Bunny knows all. I do not know if she has the strength to kill me. I pray to God she finds it. It would be simple, she knows of my medicine, and for an extra dose or two it would be all over. No one will know I have seen to it. George knows of my habit and I trust soon it will come to the attention of Michael. In truth I believe he is aware of the fact. Michael will know how to act he is the most sensible amongst us all I do not believe I will see this June, my favourite of all months. Have begged Bunny to act soon. I curse myself for the coward I am. I have redressed the balance of my previous will. Bunny and the children are well cared for and I trust Michael and Thomas will carry out my wishes.

Soon, I trust I shall be laid beside my dear mother and father. I shall seek their forgiveness when we are reunited. God I pray will allow me at least that privilege, although I know only too well I do not deserve it. My thoughts will remain in tact, for a reminder to all how love does destroy. I place this now in a place were it shall be found. I pray whoever should read this will find it in their heart to forgive me. Remind all, whoever you may be, that I was once a gentle man. May the good lord have mercy on my soul, and forgive me for all I have done.

I give my name that all know of me, so history do tell, what love can do to a gentle man born.
> Yours truly
> Jack the Ripper
> Dated this third day of May 1889

Principal Sources

Public Record Office, Kew; Public Record Office, Chancery Lane; General
Register Office, St Catherine's House; Principal Registry of the Family Division,
Somerset House; Patent Office; Companies House; British Library: Newspaper
Library; American State Archives, Washington DC; Bibliothèque Nationale,
Paris; Victoria State Library, Australia; HM Land Registry; New Scotland Yard:
Black Museum; Merseyside Police; Lancashire Constabulary; Ministry of Defence;
Liverpool University; University of Wyoming: Christie Collection; Royal Liver-
pool University Hospital; Fazakerley Hospital: Histopathology Department; His-
toric Manuscripts Commission; College of Heralds; Freemasons; Post Office
Archives; Postal Museum; Post Mark Society; Shoe Museum; Liverpool Maritime
Museum; Whitworth Museum, Manchester; Cotton Association; Liverpool
Chamber of Commerce; Coldestone Park Cemetery; Lewisham Cemetery; South-
wark Cemetery; Seddons Funeral Service; Parker Pens; John Lewis Partnership:
Archives Department; Boddingtons

Local History Departments of Liverpool, Lambeth, Lewisham, Tower Hamlets,
    Manchester, Southwark

Libraries: Guildhall, Tunbridge Wells, Morden, Carshalton, Sutton, Sunderland,
    Camden, Westminster, Liverpool, Chester, Manchester, Rochdale, Royal
    College of Surgeons, Royal College of Psychiatrists, Royal Society of Medi-
    cine, British Toxicological Society, Wellcome Research Unit, Science
    Library, Patent Office

Record Offices: West Sussex, Lancashire, Chester, Newport, Isle of Wight

Register Offices: Liverpool, Caernarfon

NEWSPAPERS AND PERIODICALS

*New Penny; Touchstone; Punch; Review of Reviews; Liverpool Review; Pall Mall
Gazette; Family Tree; Pall Mall Budget; New York Herald; New York Times; New
Milford Times; Bridgeport Sunday Post; Police Gazette; Daily Telegraph; Liverpool Daily
Post; Liverpool Echo; Liverpool Mercury; Liverpool Courier; Liverpool Citizen; Porcu-
pine; The Times; Star; Graphic; Manchester Guardian; Yorkshire Post; Independent;
Evening News; Pictorial News; Southport Guardian; Whitehaven News; Liverpool
Medico Chirulogical Journal; New Scientist; Nature; Criminologist; True Detective;
Murder Casebook; Ripperana; Crime and Detection*

BOOKS

*Gore's Directories of Liverpool; Kelly's Directories; Who Was Who; The Trial of Mrs.
Maybrick,* H. B. Irving (ed.) 1912; *Treatise on the Maybrick Case,* A. W. MacDou-
gall, 1891; *The Necessity for Criminal Appeal,* J. H. Levy, 1899; *My Fifteen Lost
Years,* Florence Elizabeth Maybrick, 1909; *Clinical Toxicology,* Erich Leschke,
1934; *A Toxicological Study of the Maybrick Case,* C. N. Tidy and R. Macnamara,
1891; *The Book of Poisons,* Gustav Schenk, 1955; *The Maybrick Case,* Helen
Densmore, 1892; *Etched in Arsenic,* Trevor L. Christie, 1968; *This Friendless Lady,*
Nigel Morland, 1957; *The Poisoned Life of Mrs Maybrick,* Bernard Ryan and Sir
Michael Havers, 1977; *Victorian Murderesses,* Mary S. Hartman, 1977; *Victorian*

England, W. J. Reader, 1974; *Liverpool's Legion of Honour*, B. G. Orchard, 1899; *Companion to the British Pharmacopoeia*, 1886; *Oxford English Dictionary*; *Webster's Dictionary*; *Dictionary of Jargon*, Jonathon Green, 1987; *Encyclopedia of Australia*, Learmonth, 1973; *Law's Grocers Manual*, c. 1900; *Enquire Within Upon Everything*, 1924; *American Illustrated Medical Dictionary* (22nd edn.); *Genitourinary Medicine*, R. S. Morton, 1991; *Encyclopedia of Chemical Technology* (3rd edn., vol. 3); *Merck Index* (9th edn.); *Casebook on Jack the Ripper*, Richard Whittington Egan, 1975; *The Complete Jack the Ripper*, Donald Rumbelow, 1976; *The Jack the Ripper A to Z*, Paul Begg, Martin Fido and Keith Skinner, 1991; *The Ripper Legacy*, Martin Howells and Keith Skinner, 1987; *Jack the Ripper: Summing Up and Verdict*, Colin Wilson and Robin Odell, 1987; *Jack the Ripper: The Uncensored Facts*, Paul Begg, 1988; *The Ripper File*, Melvin Harris, 1989; *The Encyclopedia of Serial Killers*, Brian Lane and Wilfred Gregg, 1992; *Hunting the Devil*, Richard Lourie, 1993; *The Trials of Israel Lipski*, Martin L. Friedland, 1984; *The Lighter Side of My Official Life*, Sir Robert Anderson, 1910; *The Police Encyclopedia*, 1920; *Days of My Years*, Sir Melville Macnaghten, 1914; *From Constable to Commissioner*, Sir Henry Smith, 1910; *The Mystery of Jack the Ripper*, Leonard Matters, 1929; *I Caught Crippen*, Walter Dew, 1938; *The Identity of Jack the Ripper*, Donald McCormick, 1959; *The Crimes and Times of Jack the Ripper*, Tom Cullen, 1965; *A Casebook of Crime*, Alan Brock, 1948

INDEX